THE CULTURALLY
SAVVY CHRISTIAN

Other Books by Dick Staub

Too Christian, Too Pagan:
How to Love the World Without Falling for It

Christian Wisdom of the Jedi Masters

JB JOSSEY-BASS

The Culturally Savvy Christian

A MANIFESTO FOR DEEPENING FAITH AND ENRICHING POPULAR CULTURE IN AN AGE OF CHRISTIANITY-LITE

DICK STAUB

John Wiley & Sons, Inc.

Published by Jossey-Bass
A Wiley Imprint
989 Market Street, San Francisco, CA 94103-1741   www.josseybass.com

Jossey-Bass books and products are available through most bookstores. To contact Jossey-Bass directly call our Customer Care Department within the U.S. at 800-956-7739, outside the U.S. at 317-572-3986, or fax 317-572-4002.

Jossey-Bass also publishes its books in a variety of electronic formats. Some content that appears in print may not be available in electronic books.

Unless otherwise noted, Scripture is taken from The Holy Bible *English Standard Version* (Wheaton: Crossway Bibles, a division of Good News Publishers, 2001). Used by permission. All rights reserved.

Excerpt from *"To Juan at the Winter Solstice"* from *Complete Poems* by Robert Graves (Manchester, U.K.: Carcanet, 1995, 1996, 1997). All rights reserved. Used by permission.

Library of Congress Cataloging-in-Publication Data

Staub, Dick, date.
  The culturally savvy Christian : a manifesto for deepening faith and enriching popular culture in an age of Christianity-lite / Dick Staub. –
1st ed.
    p. cm.
  Includes bibliographical references and index.
  ISBN-13: 978-0-7879-7893-8 (alk. paper)
  ISBN-10: 0-7879-7893-0 (alk. paper)
  ISBN-13: 978-0-4703-4403-3 (paperback)
  ISBN-10: 0-4703-4403-2 (paperback)
1. Christianity and culture. 2. Popular culture—Religious aspects—Christianity. I. Title.
  BR115.C8S73   2007
  261–dc22   2006036090

Printed in the United States of America

FIRST EDITION
HB Printing   10 9 8 7 6 5 4 3 2 1
PB Printing   10 9 8 7 6 5 4 3 2 1

CONTENTS

DEDICATION

To Rev. John Stott & Rev. Earl Palmer
for shaping my vision of
culturally savvy Christians as
serious about faith
savvy about faith and culture
skilled in relating the two

To Nigel Goodwin & Dwight Ozard
for embodying
deeply spiritual, fully human
culturally savvy Christianity

ACKNOWLEDGMENTS

I wish to acknowledge my appreciation for the whole Jossey-Bass team, but especially Julianna Gustafson for her tireless efforts on *Christian Wisdom of the Jedi Masters* and *The Culturally Savvy Christian*. She believed in these projects, championed them and made them better. She did so energetically, optimistically, intelligently, and cheerfully—seldom was heard a discouraging word and the skies were not cloudy all day (except in Seattle—even JG couldn't change that).

Thanks to my many friends who have supported me and my work, especially Joe and Judy for the Cle Elum getaway. Thanks most of all to my wife Kathy, my children, and grandchildren for keeping my ideas rooted in reality. And thanks to God whose sustaining mercies are new every morning.

INTRODUCTION

In this intellectually and aesthetically impoverished age of Christianity-Lite, it is heartening to remember that for centuries, Christians were known for their intellectual, artistic, and spiritual contributions to society. Bach, Mendelssohn, Dante, Dostoevsky, Newton, Pascal, and Rembrandt are but a few who personified the rich tradition of faith, producing the highest and best work, motivated by a desire to glorify God and offered in service of others for the enrichment of our common environment: culture. These were culturally savvy Christians—serious about the centrality of faith in their lives, savvy about both faith and culture, and skilled in relating the two. Their calling was to follow in the footsteps of Jesus, who came into the world as a loving, transforming presence. They transformed culture by fulfilling their roles as creators of culture, as communicators in culture, and, at times, as countercultural influencers who operated like aliens in a foreign land.

Just sixty years ago, during World War II, a culturally savvy Christian, C. S. Lewis, calmed and comforted a frazzled British population by delivering a rousing set of radio talks that aimed to explain Christianity to a so-called Christian nation. Fifty years ago, that series of talks was published as *Mere Christianity*, taking its place alongside Lewis's sixty other published works in genres as diverse as children's fiction (*The Chronicles of Narnia*), science fiction (*Perelandra*), satire (*The Screwtape Letters*), autobiography (*Surprised by Joy*), and Christian apologetics (*Miracles, The Problem of Pain*). Lewis's friend J.R.R. Tolkien, another culturally savvy Christian, labored over his crowning achievement *The Lord of the*

Rings, which he unapologetically described as a "fundamentally religious and Catholic work"[1] and which was named the most influential book of the twentieth century in four separate polls.

Lewis, who died in 1963, and Tolkien, who died in 1973, passed from the scene when they were needed most—during an era of global cultural devolution characterized by the rising influence of popular culture and the declining influence of Christianity. Their generation of thoughtful creatives, whose work was built on a solid foundation of spiritual depth, intellectual rigor, and creative excellence and was therefore influential in the broader culture, was succeeded by a generation of Christians who were content to withdraw from culture, do combat with it, or, worse yet, build an imitative, intellectually and aesthetically vacuous parallel culture.

This book was born as Lewis and Tolkien were exiting the stage. In 1966, I was sitting at San Francisco's Fillmore West concert venue, sandwiched between two guys on an overstuffed couch, both of them smoking marijuana, all of us listening to Jefferson Airplane, with me asking how the Jesus I had recently rediscovered related to the adventurous, unorthodox spiritual quest of my generation. In retrospect, that was my life's defining moment. Since then, I have spent my life at this intersection, understanding faith and culture and interpreting each to the other. In this book, I share the conclusions I've reached after observing faith and popular culture since the 1960s. It is my hope that it will serve as both provocateur and peacemaker in a vigorous discussion about the causal relationship between the depth of spiritual life and the richness of cultural life.

I have concluded that both popular culture and Christian faith are mired in intellectual superficiality and artistic mediocrity, the result of seeds sown in the 1960s that are now deeply rooted and in full bloom. The hopeful new spiritual era promised by the pervasive, powerful popular culture created by my generation in the 1960s has produced, for the most part, an unsatisfying, mindless, soulless, and spiritually delusional popular culture today.

The same may also be said of American Christianity. Since the 1960s, many conservative Christians have sought comfort in a protective cocoon, circling the wagons to keep the "good people" inside and the "bad people" out, only occasionally venturing out of the cocoon to do combat with the wider culture. They view popular culture as a threat because it conveys beliefs, values, and behaviors antithetical to faith, and they wish not to enrich culture by actively participating in it but rather to isolate themselves from culture or to prevail in culture through the political process.

Furthermore, it is my position that the evangelical movement, which from its earliest days chose not to withdraw from culture but rather to influence it, has instead been more influenced by the culture than influential in it. To their credit, the founders of the evangelical movement recognized that popular culture was becoming a common language, which once learned, would allow them access to a spiritual conversation already taking place in culture. Their instincts were right, but over time, they paid a price in their quest for relevance and influence. Today, evangelicalism is the fastest-growing and, arguably, the most influential Christian movement in America. The press describes evangelicals as a large and powerful voting bloc; a marketing niche that purchases billions of dollars' worth of books, music, and other commercial products; and a burgeoning distribution network of megachurches, colleges, publishers, and broadcasters. But when did you last hear evangelicals described as an intellectual and artistic force in the broader culture? Sadly, I have concluded that the early intellectual and cultural aspirations of evangelicals have, with some exceptions, largely given way to a pop Christianity that mirrors and sometimes exceeds the superficiality of popular culture.

We've arrived at a crossroads in faith and culture. The Christian community has degenerated into an intellectually and artistically anemic subculture, and the general population is consuming an unsatisfying blend of mindless, soulless, spiritually delusional entertainment. We are caught between a popular culture attempting to build art without God and a religious culture that believes in a God disinterested in art.

Every human is created in God's image, with spiritual, intellectual, creative, relational, and moral capacities, and therefore cannot be satisfied with today's superficiality, whether in faith or in culture. This explains our universal spiritual longing. Today, religious and irreligious alike face the lose-lose proposition of both a superficial culture and a superficial faith. I'm reminded of an old rabbinic story of three men who were rowing a boat together when one began to drill a hole in the bottom. As his panicked friends urged him to stop, he replied that he was only drilling a hole under his part of the boat, to which the other two replied, "But we're all in the same boat!"

Thoughtful humans, both religious and irreligious, recognize the symptoms of cultural and spiritual banality described by culture's thoughtful creatives. In *Fight Club*, writer Chuck Palahniuk gives voice to a lost generation: "We are the middle children of history—no purpose or place. There is no great war for us to fight, no great depression. Our great war is a spiritual war. Our great depression is our lives. We've all been raised on television to believe that one day we'll be millionaires, and movie gods, and rock stars. But we won't. We're slowly learning that fact. And we're very, very pissed off."[2] Michael Stipe, lead singer of REM, adds, "We are floundering more—culturally, politically, spiritually—than I can imagine anyone has been in several centuries. It's hard to imagine that so many people are confused about who they are, what their dreams, hopes and aspirations and desires are—and who's pulling the strings."[3] The late writer Walker Percy observed, "You live in a deranged age, more deranged than usual, because in spite of great scientific and technological advances, man has not the faintest idea of who he is or what he is doing."[4]

All humans share a common need and desire for a creative, spiritual, intellectual, moral, and relational renaissance, and yet, in today's polarized culture war, we are not talking to each other. Our stalemate is like the one reached by John Adams and Thomas Jefferson, who, while forging their fledgling democracy, found their disagreements so severe that they broke off what was once a close friendship. After years of silence, a mutual friend persuaded them to write to each other. Adams's letter began with these touching words: "You and I ought not to die before we have explained ourselves to each other."[5]

Before you and I die, I'd like us to examine together the cause-and-effect relationship between the quality and depth of our spiritual life and the richness of our cultural life. I'd like to explain my conclusion that today's superficial spirituality is incapable of producing a deep, rich culture. I'd also like to explore how a new generation of culturally savvy Christians—the old kind of Christian in the mold of Lewis and Tolkien, who, today, will look like a new kind of Christian—can be the catalysts for transforming culture.

Unfortunately the absence of a robust, rich Christian presence in today's culture means that the very idea of a culturally savvy Christian has become oxymoronic, in a league with other conceptual contradictions like a fine mess, all-natural artificial flavor, a literal interpretation, or deafening silence. It can be argued that the health of the church, measured by the potency of its art and ideas, is at a low point, despite our high rate of church attendance. Cultural renewal requires personal renewal, and personal renewal will require the rediscovery of the essence of our faith, which leads me to the ivory-billed woodpecker and the dodo bird.

The sad saga of the dodo bird begins in 1598 with Portuguese sailors, who discovered the dodo when they landed on the island of Mauritius. They named the bird *dodo*, which means "simpleton" in Portuguese, because, having been isolated from humans and having faced no predators, the flightless birds seemed stupid, displaying a childlike innocence when greeting the invaders. The sailors killed most of the birds, and the rest were wiped out after the introduction of predatory dogs and pigs. Within twenty years, the dodo was extinct.

Not long ago, the British Broadcasting Corporation (BBC) aired a happier story, reporting on possible evidence for the existence, in Arkansas, of an ivory-billed woodpecker long thought to be extinct.[6] Among the world's largest woodpeckers, the ivory-billed woodpecker is one of six North American bird species suspected or known to have gone extinct since 1880. Ornithologists were stunned at its rediscovery, comparing it to finding the long-extinct dodo. Frank Gill of the National Audubon Society in the United States exclaimed, "This is huge, just huge. It is kind of like finding Elvis." "Just to think this bird made it into the 21st century gives me chills," said Tim Gallagher, editor of *Living Bird* magazine, adding, "It's like a funeral shroud has been pulled back, giving us a glimpse of a living bird, rising Lazarus-like from the grave." John Fitzpatrick of Cornell University headed the search party and explained the significance of the finding. "Amazingly, America may have another chance to protect the future of this spectacular bird and the awesome forests in which it lives," Fitzpatrick said. "It is the most beautiful bird we could imagine rediscovering. It is a magical bird. For those of us who tenaciously cling to the idea that man can live alongside fellow species, this is the most incredible ray of hope."

What do the dodo and the ivory-billed woodpecker have to do with culturally savvy Christians? Absolutely everything. First, Christians who enter culture naively risk perishing like the dodo bird, consumed by predators. Second, a remnant of culturally savvy Christians survives, but they have already faced harsh conditions and are nearly extinct, like the ivory-billed woodpecker. Third, unlike the ivory-billed woodpecker whose disappearance is sad but not fatal for the environment, with the disappearance of individuals aglow with God's presence, we are witnessing a rapid deterioration of our spiritual, intellectual, and aesthetic cultural environment. Fourth, as a result, like spiritual environmentalists, we need to find culturally savvy Christians, nurture them back to health, help them to multiply, and carefully reintroduce them into society.

In this book, you'll discover why I have concluded that the hope of the human race lies in the rediscovery of our common lineage as humans created in the image of God and made to glow with God's presence. You'll see why I believe that, as Hans Rookmaaker said, "Jesus did not come to make us Christian; Jesus came to make us fully human."[7] We'll explore why recent evangelistic efforts are producing Christians who are unaware of God's intention to make them fully human. You'll see how evidence of God's presence and transforming work in an individual's life is revealed in the culture produced by that person. Evaluated by that standard, both today's culture and the Christian subculture operating within it reflect a spiritual, intellectual, artistic, relational, and moral impoverishment.

I am not a hand-wringing doomsayer. Critics have always issued alarming worst-case scenarios based on contemporary trends. For goodness's sake, eight centuries before Jesus, the Greek poet Hesiod opined, "I see no hope for the future of our people if they depend on the frivolous youth of today, for certainly all youth are reckless beyond words. When I was a boy we were taught to be discreet and respectful of elders, but the present youth are exceedingly wild and impatient of restraint!"[8] Let me assure you, I do believe that there is hope, and I believe that the next generation is poised to embrace a deeper faith and create a richer culture.

In the first three chapters of this book, I'll identify the dangers in our current situation. We'll then turn the corner to six chapters brimming with hope. Ultimately, I will show how God offers a new, richer, deeper life that can transform us and, through us, civilization. For we are called to be culturally savvy Christians, who are *serious* about faith, *savvy* about faith and culture, and *skilled* at fulfilling our calling to be a loving, transforming presence in the world. Such radically fully human people, aglow with God's presence, will create culture, counter culture, and communicate a better way of life in culture.

To return to the ornithologist's quotes and the woodpecker metaphor, finding this culturally savvy Christian, who was previously thought to be extinct, is huge, just huge. It's kind of like finding Elvis. Just to think that these Christians made it into the twenty-first century should give us the chills. The reemergence of this new kind of Christian should be as if a funeral shroud has been pulled back, giving us a glimpse of a living person, the most beautiful person we could imagine rediscovering, a magical person rising Lazarus-like from the grave. And for those who tenaciously cling to the idea that culturally savvy Christians can survive alongside their fellow humans, the reemergence of culturally savvy Christians will be the most incredible ray of hope.

THE CULTURALLY
SAVVY CHRISTIAN

SAVVY

The culturally savvy Christian is

serious about faith,

savvy about faith and culture,

and skilled in relating the two.

1

THE POPULAR CULTURE
WE ARE IN

Whoever marries the spirit of this age will
find himself a widower in the next.
WILLIAM R. INGE

In 1966, sitting in San Francisco's Fillmore West between two guys who were smoking marijuana on the overstuffed couch, listening to Jefferson Airplane, way before the trendy bracelet told me to, I asked myself, "What would Jesus do?" I was drawn to this question by what I observed around me. It was an age of spiritual yearning and an influential popular culture. It was an age of inauthentic churches and disillusioned youth. I could not have known then what I know now—that San Francisco, famous for its earthquakes, was in fact the epicenter of a cultural quake whose aftershocks are still felt to this day. The culturally seismic sixties gave rise to a powerful, pervasive popular culture offering both what Joni Mitchell described as "a song and a celebration"[1] and a hopeful new path to spiritual enlightenment while dialogue about the divine morphed beyond the religious arena and into movies and music suddenly brimming with sacred lyrics.

The Doobie Brothers belted out "Jesus Is Just Alright"; Norman Greenbaum declared, "You gotta have a friend in Jesus, so you know that when you die, he's gonna recommend you to the spirit in the sky."[2] The Beatles embodied the leap to the East, a widespread interest in Hinduism and Japanese Buddhism. George Harrison, the only Beatle for whom Eastern religion actually stuck, sang his tribute to Krishna, "My Sweet Lord." Joni Mitchell's "Ladies of the

Canyon" weighed in with all the fury and insight of an Old Testament prophet, denouncing consumerism, fame, and apathy about the environment. Spiritual optimism reigned, as exemplified in "Aquarius," which promised "harmony and understanding, sympathy and trust abounding!"[3] The locus of spiritual dialogue was migrating out of the church and into popular culture. The convergence of these contemporary forces would crack the foundations of organized religion, erode its authority and confidence, and, in many ways, displace it as the center of spiritual influence. In a lightning-rod moment, John Lennon quipped that the Beatles were more popular than Jesus. In a subsequent press conference, Lennon explained that he was actually deploring the rising influence of everything popular and the diminishment of religion: "I could have said TV or cinema or anything else that's popular. Or motorcars are bigger than Jesus. . . . I'm not knocking Christianity or saying it's bad, I'm just saying it seems to be shrinking and losing contact. . . . We [the Beatles] all deplored the fact that it is, you know. And nothing better seems to be replacing it."[4]

But something *was* replacing it. Media consultant Michael Wolfe said recently in *The New Yorker*, "I really believe entertainment in a lot of ways has become a way for people to come together. It has, in fact, become—I'm convinced of this, it's become a replacement for religion; in the same way people used to quote scripture, they're now quoting Seinfeld."[5]

Catholic sociologist Andrew Greeley goes even further, arguing that popular culture is not just a source of dialogue about the ideas conveyed by popular culture's stories and characters but a place where God chooses to encounter people. He concludes, "My thesis is simple enough: Popular culture is a 'locus theologicus,' a theological place, the locale in which one may encounter God. Popular culture provides an opportunity to experience God and to tell stories of God, to put the matter more abstractly, to learn about God and to teach about God."[6]

In *Reel Spirituality*, Fuller Seminary's Robert Johnston observes a progression in how even religious people relate to film, charting a continuum of theological approaches to movies, beginning with avoidance, moving to caution, dialogue, appropriation, and, ultimately, to an understanding of film as a place for "divine encounter." It is a place where "God shows up."[7] This significant shift from identifying popular culture as a place "about God" to thinking of it as a "God place" means spiritual seekers, whether irreligious or religious, consider movies and music as places to encounter the transcendent, to meet God and to "do theology."

With Gallup polls consistently showing 82 percent of Americans saying that they are spiritual seekers and 52 percent saying that they've talked about spiritual issues in the previous twenty-four hours,[8] it is important to understand how popular culture influences our spiritual journeys and quests for truth and meaning in our lives. If to be savvy means "to get it," the four dynamics of today's popular culture that we need to "get" are its general superficiality, its soullessness, its powerful influence, and its spiritual delusions.

The Superficiality of Popular Culture

In light of the influence and power we've given popular culture, which extends even to shaping our spiritual journeys, one might think that it is thoughtful and substantial, but in fact, it suffers from an almost unbearable lightness. Though popular culture holds tremendous potential for good, unfortunately, today's trend is toward a diversionary, mindless, celebrity-driven superficiality. Sadly, this reflects our general societal condition, for popular culture can only rise to the spiritual, intellectual, and artistic heights of its average citizenry. As music critic and sociologist Simon Frith says, "popular" and "culture" combine to produce a culture "*for* the people, *of* the people, and *by* the people."[9]

Popular culture need not be mindless and superficial; as a matter of fact, at one time, America boasted a significant middlebrow culture, a population interested in ideas and issues, equally turned off by the pretensions and elitism of highbrow culture and by lowbrow mindlessness. But in the 1960s, the emerging youth culture valued feelings and experience over ideas, and the continual introduction of new technologies provided immediate and regular access rather than occasional availability. In a few brief decades technology has advanced from vacuum tubes to transistors and transistors to digital chips, allowing a progression in portability from the immobile Philco console radio in the living room to the hand-held transistor radio to the pocket-sized MP3 player. At the same time computers got faster while shrinking from room-sized mainframes to the laptop, and the World Wide Web and cellular phones allowed connectivity to anyone, anywhere and anytime—24/7!

Overnight, there was a demand for more culturally accessible, less demanding, youth-oriented entertainment. British artist Richard Hamilton, credited with creating the first work of pop art, was also the first to define its ethic: "mass-produced, low-cost, young, sexy, witty, transient, glamorous, gimmicky, expendable and popular."[10]

Today's popular culture generally reveals that humans, despite our magnificent spiritual, intellectual, and imaginative capacities, have chosen to wade in the shallow but spiritually toxic waters of superficiality.

Popular Culture Is Diversionary Entertainment

The word *entertainment* means diversionary, something that draws our attention from one thing to another. Diversion is not necessarily a pejorative term—a person can be diverted from the frivolous to the serious through entertainment. Film director Sydney Pollack tells the story of two Oxford dons and playwrights who were sitting at the Boarshead, grousing because neither one of them could get produced and neither one could get performed. One turned to the other and said, "Oh, the hell with it. Let's just do what Shakespeare did—give them entertainment."[11] We recognize, of course, that Shakespeare was using diversionary entertainment to draw attention to important issues of his time.

However, we ought to be wary of entertainment when it occupies a disproportionate amount of our time or consistently diverts

our attention away from issues that matter and toward the inconsequential. That is the situation today. As we increasingly morph real
life into entertainment and vice versa, entertainment is becoming
our central reality, and real life is becoming subsumed in our entertainments. In *Life the Movie,* Neil Gabler says, "It is not any 'ism'
but entertainment that is arguably the most pervasive, powerful,
and ineluctable force of our time—a force so overwhelming that it
has finally metastasized into life."[12]

The reality TV fad exemplifies this merging of entertainment
and real life. News organizations once provided citizens with information and thoughtful commentary so they could make informed
choices, but today, real-life tragedies and the mundane failures and
heartaches of ordinary people are hyped like new movie releases,
complete with special effects. The normal human response to a person in need is to help, but that is not the case in an entertainment
culture. Actor George Clooney observes, "People's misery becoming entertainment, that's what's dangerous. And that seems to be
the place we're going."[13] Humans sit in front of television sets, passively watching human misery unfold, while just outside their door,
down the street, or in an apartment next door, a real person faces
the same problem and there is no one to help them because we're
all preoccupied with our favorite characters on reality TV.

When diversion becomes a way of life, we avoid the very issues
to which we should be most attentive. We are diverted from the
grim, unpleasant truth that our lives lack meaning without God,
that consumption does not satisfy, that the differential between
wealth and poverty is unjust, that our neighbor is in need, and that
the appropriate human response to people in need is sleeves-rolled-
up service, not simply watching.

Popular Culture Is Mindless Amusement

The word *amusement* means "to entertain or occupy in a pleasant
manner; to stir with pleasing or mirthful emotions," but if you read
the word *amuse* as *a* ("not") and *muse* "to think," you could define

it as "to be absent in mind." Today's electronic amusement appeals to senses and emotions rather than to the mind. Such appeals produce what sociologist Pitirim Sorokin called a "sensate" culture, one that values what can be grasped through the senses rather than what is grasped through the thoughtful consideration of ideas.[14]

Appealing to the senses is not unimportant or bad. In addition to giving us mental capacities, God created us with physical, emotional, and spiritual capacities. The senses can work in harmony with the mind, as Flannery O'Connor explains: "The beginning of human knowledge is through the senses, and the fiction writer begins where human perception begins. He appeals through the senses, and you cannot appeal to the sense with abstractions. The first and most obvious characteristic of fiction is that it deals with reality through what can be seen, heard, smelt, tasted and touched."[15]

However, with the advent of television, E. B. White warned that the visual might replace words: "TV has taken a big bite out of the written word. But words still count with me."[16] Why are words so important? Words convey ideas, and ideas engage the mind. White's prediction is proving true; today's popular culture often depreciates words, ideas, and, consequently, the mind. In his classic book *Amusing Ourselves to Death*, Neil Postman developed this thought: "To engage the written word means to follow a line of thought, which requires considerable powers of classifying, inference making, and reasoning." He goes on to say, "An image-based society, on the other hand, dispenses with all these because images do not demand them. How much logical discipline does one need to recognize a picture?"[17] Postman's worst fears about the emergence of the nonlinear sensate over the rational are confirmed by MTV's founding chairman Bob Pittman: "What we've introduced is nonnarrative form; we rely on mood and emotion. We make you feel a certain way as opposed to you walking away with any particular knowledge."[18]

When feelings and sensory inputs replace words and ideas, will the daily consumption of such media diminish our reasoning abilities? Media researcher David Harvey's work shows how exposure to a regular, repeated collage of unrelated images and apparently equal events affects television viewers: "As a result of the dominance of television, one idea seems as good as another. Entertainment, gratification and sensory stimulation displace reason, morality and truth."[19]

Amusement culture can be addictive; its very superficiality and weightlessness is what makes it so consumable. Orson Welles confessed, "I hate television. I hate it as much as peanuts. But I can't stop eating peanuts."[20] Because sensory repetition can desensitize the audience to a particular sensation, producers have learned that to retain an audience and avoid boredom requires a constant escalation of new and more sensational experiences.

The thoughtful person knows that superficial pop culture is the cultural equivalent of junk food; it looks, feels, and tastes good but is often utterly lacking in nutrients. Sorokin argued that sensate cultures eventually collapse because humans are designed for intellectual stimulation, not just sensory manipulation. What are the implications of being commanded to love God with our mind in a mindless entertainment age?

Popular Culture Is Celebrity-Driven

After years of studying the inner workings of Hollywood and its effect on American culture, movie critic Richard Schickel concluded, "Celebrity is possibly the most vital shaping force in our society."[21] The late Peter Jennings concurred: "No country in the world is so driven by personality, has such a hunger to identify with personalities, larger-than-life personalities especially . . . as this one."[22]

An adoring public turns to their icons for advice on what to believe and how to live. *Vanity Fair* said, "Oprah Winfrey arguably has more influence on the culture than any university president, politician or religious leader except the Pope,"[23] and *Christianity Today* lamented, "To her audience of more than 22 million mostly female viewers, [Oprah] has become a post-modern priestess—an icon of church-free spirituality."[24] As one young woman said, "Those of us who are fans, we use these celebrity lives in ways that transform our own. I sometimes think that these are our gods and goddesses, these are our icons, and their stories become kind of parables for how to lead our lives."[25]

Today, celebrities are often known for their "known-ness" rather than substantial accomplishments, personal character, or virtues; Paris Hilton is an obvious example. A bemused scholarly librarian of Congress, Daniel Boorstein, notes, "Shakespeare divided great men into three classes: those born great, those who achieved greatness, those who had greatness thrust upon them. It never occurred to him to mention those who hired public relations experts and press secretaries to make themselves look great."[26] Human greatness is diminished by this devolution from accomplishment as the basis for being known to "being known for being known." Certainly, Mother Teresa's lifetime of service is of greater value than the accomplishments of today's revolving-door celebrities who achieve notoriety in a transitory fifteen minutes of fame.

A thoughtful person might ask, What are the implications of allowing our lives to be influenced by people whom we do not know and will never meet and whose beliefs and values are often antithetical to our own? What need in our lives are we trying to fill through spending even a nanosecond of time on celebrity culture, with its who-wears-what, who-cheats-on-whom gossip? What are the implications of knowing more about what's going on in the personal lives of celebrities than we do about our neighbors, coworkers, or, worse yet, our own family members?

The Soullessness of Popular Culture

If being human means possessing spiritual, intellectual, and creative capacities, we ought to be concerned about squandering popular culture's potential on a superficial, diversionary, mindless celebrity culture.

Critics and the general population often react derisively to the insipid gruel offered by entertainment culture, so why doesn't somebody make it better? Anyone who desires to change popular culture, to restore the soul of culture, will face a tough battle against the powerful forces driving it. Behind the scenes of popular culture are three partners united in a marriage of convenience: technology, marketing, and the age-old motivator, money.

Though often devoid of spiritual, intellectual, or aesthetic substance, popular culture nevertheless thrives because the sustaining forces of today's entertainment culture are technological and economic, not spiritual, ideational, or artistic. Despite its mind-numbing shallowness, popular culture appears alive and brimming with vitality because impersonal commercial interests are propping up and exploiting today's spiritually, intellectually, and artistically anemic enterprise.

Popular Culture Is Centered in Money

Andy Warhol quipped, "Buying is much more American than thinking,"[27] and Nobel-winning economist Milton Friedman apparently thinks it is in the economy's best interest to keep it that way: "Few trends could so thoroughly undermine the very foundations of our free society as the acceptance by corporate officials of a social responsibility other than to make as much money for their stockholders as possible. This is a fundamentally subversive doctrine."[28] The subversive doctrines of the 1960s gave way to America's addictive consumerism, and the result is a spiritually, intellectually, aesthetically bankrupt money machine called popular culture. "Greed is good," we learned from the film *Wall Street*.[29]

The core value in today's media culture is not a product's (song's, movie's, book's, game's) aesthetic quality nor its spiritual or moral advisability nor its usefulness to the individual or society; the core value is money. Money flows from the popular and as we have seen, the popular flows from the "mass-produced, low-cost, young, sexy, witty, transient, glamorous, gimmicky, expendable." The highest court of appeals is populated with P. T. Barnum's masses and suckers, and new ones are born every minute.

Profit motives drive marketers to create and exploit youth markets in particular because of youths' disposable income. It doesn't take a genius to see the devastating consequences of transforming teens from creative producers to consumers. Professional artist and occasional philosopher Robert Bateman puts it this way:

> For the last few decades we have been conducting an interesting social experiment in North America. We have been working on the creation of a new variety of human being I will call homo sapiens teenager consumerensis. . . . Teenagers are trained to have special needs . . . special foods, beverages, clothing, music, films. Eight year olds are persuaded that they are teenagers already and then the twenty-five year olds are convinced that they are still teenagers. This experiment is hurtling on apace using some of the most creative minds in our society and every modern technological and psychological tool, sparing no expense. Often sex, violence and greed are exploited to help sell products including TV shows and films. For the first time in the history of our species the most vital, active years of a person's growing life are dedicated to one major goal—self indulgence.[30]

It should be obvious that the situation Bateman describes is dehumanizing and inconsistent with Christian values. Thoughtful, creative Christians have always believed that humans should create a culture that reflects our highest and best achievements. Our art should glorify God and reflect our spiritual, intellectual, and creative capacities. We know that the love of money is the root of evil and that we are called to seek God's kingdom first, not material possessions. So where is the resistance to cultural conformity?

Popular Culture Is Spread by Marketing

In a few short decades, humans have been transformed from producers to passive consumers. In today's popular culture, we are but credit cards, targeted by marketers who reach us through new technologies that provide round-the-clock access to us.

The confluence of new sophisticated, research-based, demographically targeted marketing techniques, new technologies, and the creation of a well-defined youth market in the 1960s gave birth to what drives popular culture today—products aimed at specific demographics, especially youth. The driving force behind the emergence of popular culture, especially as it relates to youth culture, is not a love of artistry or the good, the true, and the beautiful; it is the cultivation of a sizable, wealthy, impulsive generation groomed to be consumers from the cradle to the grave.

Because of our economic prosperity, most young people in the Western world possess both time and money. They are energetically predisposed to the new, novel, and different. They are early adopters of new technology and are already wired in to the entertainment and information culture. They are susceptible to peer pressure. In short, they are the ideal consumer. In a frightening Public Broadcasting Service (PBS) special, "The Merchants of Cool," host and media analyst Douglas Rushkoff reports, "A typical American teenager will process over 3,000 discrete advertisements in a single day and 10 million by the time they're eighteen. Kids are also consuming massive quantities of entertainment media."[31]

MTV, the youth-oriented music entertainment network, trumpets youth culture's grassroots spontaneity, but in fact, large corporations calculatingly orchestrate what appears to be serendipitous. Robert McChesney, communications professor at the University of Illinois, describes their marketing muscle: "The entertainment companies, . . . a handful of massive conglomerates that own four of the five music companies that sell 90 percent of the music in the United States, . . . also own all the film studios, all the major TV networks, all the TV stations, pretty much, in the ten largest markets. They own all or part of every single commercial cable channel. . . . They look at the teen market as part of this massive empire that they're colonizing. Their weaponry are films, music, books, CDs, Internet access, clothing, amusement parks, sports teams."[32]

The savvy culture watcher is rightly distressed at the pervasiveness of affluenza, which PBS producer John de Graaf and his coauthors describe as "a painful, contagious, socially transmitted condition of overload, debt, anxiety, and waste resulting from the dogged pursuit of more."[33] We buy things we don't need, made by people who don't know or care about us, with money we don't have, to impress people we don't really like! Humans are called to produce, not just consume. When the mall becomes the center of social life, and young and old alike regulate their emotions through purchasing new stuff, we are looking at serious signs of dehumanization.

Popular Culture Is Sustained by Technology

In 1943, Thomas Watson, chairman of IBM, allegedly said, "I think there is a world market for maybe five computers."[34] Supposedly, he could not envision the rapidity of technological advancement and its social consequences just around the corner. Today's pervasive popular culture was born in a primitive age when people watched one of three channels on a black-and-white TV, played music on vinyl LP records, or listened to the radio in their car or while gathered around the RCA in the comfort of their own home. Since the 1960s, consumer products have expanded the distribution opportunities for popular culture, progressively offering more portability and accessibility, from transistor radios and mainframe computers to desktops to laptops to handheld PDA's; eight-track tapes to cassette tapes, CDs, MiniDiscs, and MP3 files; three network TV stations to thousands of satellite stations broadcast on high-definition color screens; rotary phones to touch-tone phones to cellular phones;

films in stand-alone local theaters to multiplexes to personal copies on videocassettes, laserdiscs, and DVDs.

Technology provides continual connectivity to a global village. An MCI commercial announces, "There will be a road. It will not connect two points. It will connect all points. It will not go from here to there. There will be no there. We will all only be here." Travel to the Middle East, and you'll see satellite dishes mounted on Bedouin tents. The Dayak people dwelling in the remote jungles of Kalimantan are exposed to MTV. This connectivity sometimes offers rich benefits: we can quickly discover others who share our passions and interests; we can pass along timely and important information instantly; we are no longer held hostage by bureaucratic gatekeepers. As a broadcaster, I knew things had changed when I learned about the Tiananmen Square rebellion through faxes sent by technically savvy students in China.

The savvy human is grateful for technology but is also aware of its potentially dehumanizing effects. In the 1960s, social scientist Marshall McLuhan warned, "All media work us over completely. They are so pervasive in their personal, political, economic, aesthetic, psychological, moral, ethical and social consequences that they leave no part of us untouched, unaffected, unaltered. The medium is the message. . . . Societies have always been shaped more by the *nature of the media* by which men communicate than by *the content of the communication*"[35] (italics added). How is media working us over completely? Technology allows constant connectivity to our diversionary, mindless, celebrity-driven popular culture, offering soul-numbing content around the clock. Technology creates the possibility of doing good faster but also speeds up the distribution of evil. For instance, when Apple announced the iPod's ability to play movies, the first large-scale application was pornography.

While it offers portentous benefits, technology also holds the potential to radically change human existence in detrimental ways. Technology is not a neutral force when placed in the hands of humans; it takes on a life of its own when combined with their propensities. Neil Postman said that we are becoming a "technopoly" that "consists in the deification of technology, which means that the culture seeks its authorization in technology, finds its satisfaction in technology, and takes its orders from technology. This requires the development of a new kind of social order, and of necessity leads to the rapid dissolution of much that is associated with traditional beliefs."[36] Technology focuses on continual improvement of process over improvement of content, on concrete information over conceptual ideas, and on change over tradition. These biases significantly affect youths who are early adopters of new technologies. Technology connects us as never before, but it also isolates us when we choose to be absorbed in entertainment or to interact with people who are not in our physical presence rather than those who are. A child listens to an iPod on the way to soccer practice while mom or dad drives and talks on the cell phone. Families sit passively in front of a TV instead of talking with each other.

The Power and Influence of Popular Culture

One might think, given its superficiality and soullessness, that popular culture would not play a significant role in our spiritual and intellectual life, but in fact, since the 1960s, popular culture rivals religion as preacher and teacher, as storyteller, and as identity and community shaper. We live mediated lives in which every aspect of our human existence is touched and influenced by a powerful, pervasive, and persuasive media culture.

Popular Culture Is a Preacher and Teacher

Popular culture systematically teaches and preaches, informing its audience about which issues matter most, fulfilling an educational role once occupied by schools and a spiritual role once filled by religion. Poet Carl Sandburg recognized this early, saying in the 1950s, "I meet people occasionally who think motion pictures, the product Hollywood makes is merely entertainment, has nothing to do with education. That's one of the darnedest fool fallacies that is current. Anything that brings you to tears by way of drama does something to the deepest roots of our personalities. All movies, good or bad, are education, and Hollywood is the foremost educational institution on earth."[37] Veteran religion editor Phyllis Tickle points out that since the 1960s, popular culture is where we explore our beliefs: "More theology is conveyed in, and probably retained from one hour of popular television, than from all the sermons that are also delivered on any given weekend in America's synagogues, churches and mosques."[38]

So much theology is derived from popular culture that many argue that it has replaced religion. A leading Jewish intellectual and commentator on culture, Rabbi Adin Steinsaltz, believes that popular culture actually *is* a religion: "Hollywood is not just a place—it is a world in itself. Hollywood has done something remarkable: it has created a great and very successful religion. Through its successful missionaries—the films produced in Hollywood—it has spread around the globe, gaining adherents faster than any other religion in the world. If it has not attained the stature of a full-fledged religion, at least it is a very strong cult."[39]

Every week, newly released songs, films, or books give voice to our common human concerns and probe the essential human questions: Is there a God? Who is God? Who are we? What is our meaning and identity? Where did we come from? What is our destiny? What is love? Why am I lonely? What will satisfy me and make me happy? Does anybody understand me? Is there any hope? These are the questions that Jesus engaged; today, they are the domain of popular artists. After the global tragedy in New York on September 11, 2001, one-time altar boy Bruce Springsteen's next album probed our common human angst. Of his calling, he said, "The band is like church. We're gonna shout that thing right in your face."[40] In the same vein, he also said, "I sometimes feel like a preacher; spiritual revival is a necessity and it has to be a communal experience. . . .

I think that fits in with the concept of our band as a group of witnesses. . . . That's one of our functions. We're here to testify to what we have seen."[41]

Popular Culture Is a Storyteller

Those who control the stories rule the world. Over time, storytelling has moved from the campfire to the printed word and now to digital bits of information delivered in today's movies, music, games, and TV programs. Stories have always played a central role in our communal life, and theologian Frederick Buechner points out that today, it is the producers of entertainment who supply the glue that binds us together through the stories they tell: "In a world where there are no longer books we have almost all of us read, the movies we have almost all of us seen are perhaps the richest cultural bond we have. They go on haunting us for years the way our dreams go on haunting us. In a way they are our dreams. The best of them remind us of human truths that would not seem as true without them. They help to remind us that we are all of us humans together."[42]

Jesus practiced the time-honored tradition of storytelling, and today, popular culture conveys messages through this most universally effective method of communication known to humans. Had Steven Spielberg lived in prehistoric days, he would have been the guy telling stories to people huddled around the fire at day's end. He would have been drawing pictures in the cave. Today, he makes movies because he is a born storyteller. Told well, truthful, wise stories can provide insight, understanding, and illumination for a path to a richer life for all who hear, understand, and embrace them; misguided stories, however, can lead an entire population astray. People who believe they know the truth need to realize that cultural influence requires more than knowing the story; it requires telling it thoughtfully and artistically. Never has there been a greater need for wise, gifted storytellers who understand the story we are in and can communicate a better way gracefully and truthfully.

Popular Culture Is a Community and Identity Shaper

Communities are formed around the things we hold in common. Since the beginning of time, families and religion have defined the development of identities within community. Today, it is popular culture that plays a key role in forming our identities and shaping our sense of community. Sociologist Todd Gitlin observes, "Popular culture summons improvisational communities—show audiences, fan clubs, chat groups. It saturates everyday conversation. It overlaps with politics. It circulates the materials with which people splice together identities. It forms the imagescape and soundtrack through which we think and feel about who we are or—as film critic Robert Warshow once put it—who we wish to be and fear we might become."[43]

Identity is often triggered externally and visually, through symbols rather than words, by a media that provides racks of identities, each complete with the tribal markings of dress, tattoos, brand of shoes, jewelry, hairstyle, and musical taste. Starting with James Dean's tight jeans in the 1950s and progressing to Annie Hall's baggy khaki pants in the 1970s and right through to today's fashion statements, celebrities in film, sports, and music influence what we wear and how we look. The choices we make form our image, which in turn determines the familiar group with which we associate. Marketers call these subgroups "tribal groups" and find them fertile territory for selling products of common interest to the tribe. Advertisers help consumers choose their tribe by offering a wide range of identities from which consumers may choose. They've learned that bored people find exotic and foreign tribal connections particularly interesting, so, for example, they might connect suburban kids with urban culture. Suburban American kids are hooked on anime; teens in Tokyo listen to American inner-city hip hop; and when Napoleon Dynamite's brother in the farmlands of Idaho hooks up with a big-city African American woman, he starts wearing heavy gold chains around his neck.

Choosing an identity differentiates us from others and provides entry into the desired tribe. Because popular culture is global, not local, you may have a stronger tribal connection with someone in Zurich than with your next-door neighbor. Online communities are forged by affinity instead of proximity and are displacing in-person encounters with less personal electronically transmitted ones. Identities were once formed almost exclusively through daily relationships with people we knew personally, whose internal core values were lived out in the local community. In the past, we imitated individuals who embodied our core values and whom we respected because we had observed their application of those values in everyday life. Today, our identities are often formed more superficially by adopting outward appearances and behaviors without regard for the internal values held by the originator, who, to us, is disembodied. Thus, people whom we do not know and cannot observe closely are influencing our life choices.

What are the implications of these shifts? Is deep selfhood being replaced by façade, with identities formed through the attaching of external features, like ornaments on a Christmas tree? Is it dehumanizing to displace face-to-face personal relationships with those conveyed electronically? What is the future of a society in which our identities are shaped by a multitude of impersonal, uncaring, commercially motivated forces instead of by people who know and love us? Arthur Kroker, who has been called the McLuhan of the twenty-first century, believes that western societies have abandoned both the external standards and the internal foundations necessary to form authentic identities and are panicked as a result.[44]

Edward Hallowell, psychiatrist and lecturer at Harvard Medical School, observes that while daily personal connections are required for longevity and happiness, in modern society, most people lack any substantial connection with someone who cares and listens attentively each day.[45] Unhappy, isolated people are bombarded by external media voices offering a myriad of identities, creating what academics call an age of "polyvocality,"[46] a phenomenon captured lyrically in Zero 7's song "In the Waiting Line": "Everyone's saying different things to me, different things to me."[47]

How is the saturated, isolated self to choose from among the many impersonal voices vying for attention? What are the implications for finding true community when humans reduce themselves to temporary façades seeking association with others who have temporarily chosen the same façade? Where is the authentic self who can enter into community with another authentic self? Who am I? In its concentrated focus on serving, satisfying, and shaping the self, has modern media destroyed the authentic self? Whatever happened to the human race?

Community and identity have always been mediated. In the past, the mediator was personal and local—families, religious affiliations, and neighbors. The printing press introduced a distant mediation, injecting foreign voices into local situations and thus enabling authors to influence identities and communities and to open up new worlds for their readers. The electronic media age is now only sixty years old, and like the printing press, it has introduced hoards of outsiders into our individual lives, and these hoards are relentless in their pursuit of access to us, bypassing reason with their entertainments and amusements, driven by cash more than ideas. While we are the recipients of this mediator's many benefits, we are just now becoming savvy about its potentially dehumanizing effects. Who will lead us through this era of fragmented, isolated selves to a new epoch of deeply grounded humans capable of genuine community?

The Spiritual Delusions of Popular Culture

The teacher and the preacher tell the stories. The stories shape our beliefs and values. The beliefs and values guide our choice of an identity. The identity determines our association with a community or tribe. This entire system was once the domain of religion, but today, media culture has displaced religion as the mediator of the spiritual journey. How reliable is this new guide?

Despite all the wondrous potential of popular culture and its occasional excellent contributions, since the 1960s, our spiritual sensibilities have for the most part been numbed by spiritual relativism. Today's spiritual delusions are the product of misguided beliefs embedded in the sixties credo: I am the supreme arbiter of all things. Experience is better than reason. Feelings trump traditional mores. If it feels good, do it. Relativism trumps absolutes. There is no truth; there is only what is true for you in a given situation. Expression is more important than imaginative capacity or beauty. All authority and every institution must be questioned. You can't trust anybody over thirty.

In his landmark study of teens, most of whom claimed Christianity as their religion, sociologist Christian Smith concludes that America now practices a shared religion that he calls "moralistic therapeutic deism," in which people are promised that therapeutic benefits, such as a happy life, can be achieved through good, moral, kind, nice, pleasant behavior. Teens believe in an uninvolved, undemanding God who is watching everything from above and is drawn into their lives rarely and only if necessary. In such a world, religion is inclusive yet peripheral, beliefs are held inarticulately and loosely, and each individual is the arbiter of what is true for them; there is no right answer. "Who am I to judge?" they might ask.[48]

Moralistic therapeutic deism is inconsistent with basic Judeo-Christian teaching and is the ideological offspring of the sixties, the misguided result of popular culture's mediation of our spiritual journey. Popular culture has fed us a veritable potluck of beliefs about God, heaven, hell, truth, sex, drugs, friendship, love, marriage, morality, and everything else under the sun. Today's individual is the blender into which are poured ingredients provided by television, movies, song lyrics, celebrities, friends, teachers, parents, advertisements, billboards, articles on the Web. Directions: add ingredients, press the button, chill, and serve.

Popular culture has become a mediator between God and humans—the role played by shamans in primitive cultures. The shaman was traditionally the medium between the visible and the invisible, the prophet and seer of the tribe. What are some of the common lessons taught by popular culture, this new shaman?

Spiritual Seeking Doesn't Require God

For centuries, humans have acknowledged God as our creator, the author of moral law, and the judge to whom we are accountable for our actions. Despite the pervasiveness of spiritual themes in Hollywood, a Biblically revealed deity such as that worshipped in the Judeo-Christian tradition is generally a nonfactor. Most treatments of the spiritual are either atheistic (there is no God) or agnostic (there isn't enough evidence to know for sure). Most commonly, in Hollywood films, God is a non-entity, silent, not mentioned, or referred to euphemistically as "the man upstairs." The view that God exists but is uninvolved in daily life is called *deism*, and as we've seen, it is the prevailing view of today's teens, even those who claim to be Christian. In a deistic worldview, humans, not God, are the central player on the stage—a view Tom Cruise articulates when he says, "People can create their own lives. . . . I decided that I'm going to create, for myself, who I am, not what other people say I should be. I'm entitled to that."[49]

Spirituality Is Good; Religion Is Bad

Throughout history, humans have conducted their spiritual journeys within the context of ancient religions, which were rich with lessons from the past and offered disciplines useful for growth and for the progression to maturity. At their worst, religions have been used to abuse and manipulate their adherents. But at their best, these loving, intergenerational communities have been the preservers of continuity, timeless truth, and practice. In Hollywood, spirituality is in and religion is out. Roma Downey, star of the 1990s TV series "Touched by an Angel," observes, "We have always reminded people that there is a God, that it's just the one God: the God of love. We were more spiritual than religious."[50] In one episode of "The Simpsons," son Bart asks his father, Homer, what his religious beliefs are. Homer replies, "You know, the one with all the well-meaning rules that don't work in real life. Uh, Christianity."[51]

Exception: Exotic Religions

While the entertainment culture often ignores or is critical of traditional Judaism and Christianity, Kabbalah, Scientology, or Buddhism usually get a free pass. Then there is Shirley MacLaine, who set up a mind, body, and spirit portal on a Web site that offered information on meditation, guided visualization, numerology, dream interpretation, astrology, chi energy, ESP, prophecy, a chat room for reincarnated people, a room for UFO witnesses, and spirituality for pets. Ancient forms of paganism have emerged everywhere. The singer Bjork reports, "I've always thought religion was really dodgy. I'm as anti-authority as ever. I think I'm pagan. I believe in nature."[52]

Eclectic Is Good

Historically, humans have believed that God exists with defined personal characteristics and qualities and that it is our task to discover God. Today, people construct God like they would a doll at a Build-A-Bear store, creating a mix-and-match deity designed to their own liking. David Kinnaman, vice president of Barna Research Group, says that Americans are "cutting and pasting religious views from . . . television, movies, conversations with their friends. Popular culture's general approach is this: you can probably put together a philosophy of life for yourself that is just as accurate, just as helpful as any particular faith might provide, so just do it!"[53]

There Is No Truth

For centuries, humans have believed that God has woven truth into the fabric of the universe, giving humans the capacity to discern truth from error. This is the basis of classic logic, which teaches that equal and opposite statements cannot both be true. In such a view, truth is objective and does not require the validation of our subjective affirmation. Irrationally, America's spiritual quest has become unlinked from truth. To be accurate, truth is actually out of favor in today's spiritual trek. Filmmaker Stephen Simon reports, "I do not believe that there can ever be a universal truth when it comes to matters of faith. Where I have a major problem is when I am told that I am wrong and that my beliefs are in violation of any 'true' faith. It is precisely that kind of bigotry that has started most of the major conflagrations of history. Once any group thinks they are the only true believers, people usually die for holding other beliefs."[54]

The contemporary erosion of belief in absolute truth affects both religious and irreligious people. Recently, a Barna Research study asked Americans if they believed in absolute truth. Seventy-six percent of Americans said there is no such thing as absolute truth. Sixty-seven percent of born-again Christians said the same.

There Is No Wrong or Right

Judeo-Christian traditions teach that God is holy and just and that from these character qualities flow timeless, inalterable moral expectations that are the essential guide for human behavior. The Ten Commandments are God's revealed moral laws, woven into the universe, absolute and universally applicable to all humans: You shall have no other gods before me. You shall not make for yourselves an idol. You shall not misuse the name of the Lord your God. Remember the Sabbath day by keeping it holy. Honor your father and your mother. You shall not murder. You shall not commit adultery. You shall not steal. You shall not give false testimony. You shall not covet (Exodus 20, paraphrased).

Such universal absolutes fly in the face of today's moral relativism. Since the 1960s, popular culture has increasingly depicted immoral behavior as normal, without judgment or consequences. In entertainment culture, sexually promiscuous people rarely contract STDs or get pregnant, and the aim of a new romance is to get laid. In this pretend world, casual drug users seldom become addicts and drunken parties are just plain fun—all part of expected rites of passage into adulthood. Violence is a way of life. Disobeying parents and disrespect for any authority is accepted.

There are numerous examples of work being done by thoughtful creatives that are not spiritually delusional. When culture watchers like Robert Johnston or Craig Detweiler and Barry Taylor[55] observe God showing up in popular culture, sometimes it is in commercially driven, entertainment culture, but more often it is in indie films or among local songwriters, poets, and artists. We need to be attentive to what contemporary thoughtful creatives are seeing and telling us. We must also admit that today's popular culture is frequently spiritually misguided, conveying spiritual seeking without God, intellectual pursuit without truth, and immoral behavior without consequences.

Misguided Popular Culture
Is Crippling People's Souls

To undiscerningly travel on the path of mindless popular culture is dangerous because it will never lead us to the spiritual life we need. As a matter of fact, this spiritual fog produces devastating consequences, as noted by filmmaker Andrei Tarkovsky, who warns that "modern mass culture, aimed at the 'consumer,' the civilization of prosthetics, is crippling people's souls, setting up barriers between man and the crucial questions of his existence, his consciousness of himself as a spiritual being."[56]

So here's the deal. The largest companies in the world are hiring smart people and spending billions of dollars to drive a diversionary, mindless, celebrity-fueled popular culture down the highway of new technologies and into our lives in order to sell us stuff we don't want or need. They don't care about us, what we believe, or how we want to live. Their ads and products regularly reduce women to sex objects and men to voyeurs and predators.

They are unconcerned with what is in our best interests spiritually or intellectually, and in fact, it is in their best interest to keep us spiritually desensitized and dumb. They play to our unhappiness, magnifying our feeling that we are missing something essential and that if we had this something they offer, we would be fulfilled. They then encourage us to shop, convincing us that shopping will do today what it failed to do yesterday—fill what French religious philosopher Pascal calls our God-shaped vacuum.

Today's superficial popular culture is symptomatic of our human malaise, and technology, marketing, and the lust for profits simply spread our addiction and disease faster and further. For the first time in history, it is possible for entertainment culture to distribute our spiritual sickness worldwide, producing a spiritual pandemic.

The 1960s gave rise to a general hopefulness that we were on the verge of a new age that would be ushered in by popular culture. Instead, we have produced a spiritually confused, superficial popular culture that is artificially sustained by technology, money, and marketing. If you believe, as I do, that humans possess innate spiritual, intellectual, creative, relational, and moral capacities, it seems clear that what we see today is a diminishment of God's image on the part of both the creators and consumers of popular culture. Where do we turn to find a better way? In a nation in which Christianity is the majority religion, conventional wisdom would point us toward the church, but as we will discuss in the next chapter, the bad news is that during the rise of popular culture, American Christianity marginalized itself by choosing to flee popular culture, fight it, or simply fall for it. American Christianity, which initially set out to transform culture, is itself in need of transformation.

2

THE CHRISTIANITY
WE ARE IN

I really struggle with American Christianity.
I'm not really sure that people with our cultural
disabilities, people who grow up in a culture that
worships pleasure, leisure, and affluence,
are capable of having souls, or being saved.[1]

RICH MULLINS, *AN ARROW POINTING TO HEAVEN*

What if we think we're at a high point in church history but are actually at a low point? Throughout history, Christianity has evolved, adapting to various ideological assaults, accommodating diverse cultural traditions, fragmenting into different denominations and factions. Culturally savvy Christians are savvy about their experience of Christian faith, realizing that it represents only one vantage point in the broad landscape of contemporary Christianity and is but a blip in two thousand years of Christian history.

Despite evangelicals' growing churches and increased economic and political clout, it is conceivable that the American Christianity that has risen up since the 1960s actually represents one of the low points in church history. If the seeds of popular culture's rise were planted in the sixties, so were the seeds for the shrinking influence of Christians. If a crisis is a dangerous opportunity, Christians faced one, and unfortunately, as we will see, for the most part have failed to avoid the threats and exploit the opportunities. While popular culture's influence has been rising, Christian influence has been shrinking, marginalized through three equally counterproductive ways of reacting to culture.

Cocooning from Culture

Cocoon: A protective case; a covering; something suggestive of a cocoon in appearance or purpose. To retreat from a harsh or unfriendly environment.

Religious people have always recoiled at the excesses of culture. In Jesus' day, a Jewish sect called the Essenes fled society, seeking safety in the secluded hills above the Dead Sea, believing that by avoiding contact with the polluted world, they could maintain their own purity. From the earliest days after Jesus, some followers have withdrawn from "the world" by slipping into a protective cocoon. Those who separate themselves from the world often defend their behavior as the Essenes did, by arguing that to be holy, believers must literally be separate from the rest of the world. Religious cocooning proceeds from the view that devoutly religious people are pure, holy seekers of righteousness and that everyone outside of their specific group is suspect.

Today, only a few groups, like the Amish, physically separate themselves from society, but many followers of Jesus have practiced cultural separation and chosen to live a balkanized existence, especially in relationship to entertainment and the arts. In the 1800s, Charles Finney attacked novels, saying, "I cannot believe that a person who has ever known the love of God can relish a secular novel. . . . Let me visit your chamber, your parlor, or wherever you keep your books. What is there? Byron, Scott, Shakespeare and a host of triflers and blasphemers of God!"[2] In 1930, even the mainline *Christian Century* opined, "There can be no doubt that the movies with their sensationalism, their false standards, their pornography, and their open exhibition of moral laxity and lawlessness are influencing our young people today far more than the church, and seriously counteracting the combined stabilizing influence of the school and the home."[3] In the 1960s, during the birth pangs of what became a cultural revolution, Christian youth were solemnly warned about the evils of rock and roll music and the young celebrities of the emerging popular culture, who were derided as long-haired, dope-smoking hippie freaks.

Today, many religious people react to the often polluting content of TV, movies, music, and games by withdrawing into a cocoon. In the early 1990s, Michael Medved, a movie critic and conservative Jew, rallied religious conservatives when, in *Hollywood vs. America*, he announced, "America's long-running romance with Hollywood is over. As a nation, we no longer believe that popular culture enriches our lives. Few of us view the show business capital as a magical source of uplifting entertainment, romantic inspiration, or even harmless fun. Instead millions of Americans now see the entertainment industry as an all powerful enemy, an alien force that assaults our most cherished values and corrupts our children. The dream factory has become a poison factory."[4] This view, widely embraced by many conservatives, is often combined with a nostalgic desire for a return to the entertainment culture of the past.

However, as we will see later in this book, though spiritually sensitive people often *are* aliens and exiles who experience dissonance with the arts and entertainment, Jesus clearly called his followers to discernment in the world, not dissociation from it. In his prayer for the disciples, he rejected the idea of cocooning, praying instead, "Father, I am not asking you to take them out of the world, but I ask you to protect them from the evil one" (John 17:15). When Christians cocoon themselves from culture, they violate the example and the teaching of Jesus and limit their ability to influence culture.

Worse yet, children raised in the protective cocoon are ill prepared to meet the challenges posed by the secular culture they will inevitably face one day. Thirty years ago, Francis Schaeffer warned, "I find that everywhere I go children of Christians are being lost to historic Christianity. . . . They are being lost because their parents are unable to understand their children and therefore cannot help them in their time of need. . . . We have left the next generation naked in the face of twentieth century thought by which they are surrounded."[5]

Combating Culture

Combat: A fight; a contest of violence; a struggle for supremacy. To resist; to oppose; to antagonize; to repel.

When a religious conservative does venture out of the cocoon and into culture, it is often to do battle. While it is true that the Apostle Paul warned that Christians are in a war, he was referring to a spiritual and ideological divide. Writer Harry Blamires observes, "Briefly one may sum up the clash between the Christian mind and the secular mind thus: Secularism asserts the opinionated self as the only judge of truth. Christianity imposes the given divine revelation as the final touchstone of truth."[6] What Paul viewed as a spiritual battle to be won with spiritual weapons like prayer, and Blamires viewed as a battle of ideas to be won on intellectual and theological grounds, many contemporary religious conservatives see as a political battle to be won at the ballot box.

Starting in the 1970s, many religious people were ripe for politicization in the wake of the cultural revolution because in the 1960s, they had witnessed the severe erosion of a civic culture once predisposed to Judeo-Christian values and beliefs. Groups like Jerry Falwell's Moral Majority in the 1980s and Pat Robertson's Christian Coalition in the 1990s worked to unite conservative Christians into a voting bloc able to wield power over the political process. In 1991, James Davison Hunter's book *Culture Wars: The Struggle to Define America* arrived, with the impact of a lit match to dry tinder.[7] Though it was actually an intellectually provocative book about worldviews, Hunter's book was heartily embraced by newly politicized conservatives, who especially liked the term *culture war*. They viewed the church as the final restraining force against evil and themselves as combatants enlisted in a life-or-death war against a secular, "godless"

culture. Although devout people of the Christian faith are represented on different sides of almost every political issue and polls
show that evangelicals are split between the Republican and Demo-
cratic parties, many moderate religionists who had rejected the
cocooning mentality of fundamentalists nevertheless were drawn
into the political arena and enthusiastically joined their more stri-
dent counterparts. While the culture war metaphor has some relevance, it is also easily distorted, conjuring up scapegoats and creating
images of demon-seed bad guys pitted against pure, angelic Christian
good guys. In such an us-versus-them political environment, hostile
talk is seen as justified and becomes commonplace. Loving enemies
seems a quaint and ill-conceived, Pollyanna-ish notion.

The political culture war has affected religious approaches to
popular culture. Combative religious conservatives destroyed products like Beatles albums in the 1960s and Harry Potter books in the
1990s. They boycotted films like *The Last Temptation of Christ* and
Marilyn Manson concerts. They attempted to legislate stricter
standards for music and films, developing rating and warning systems, publicly deriding producers and distributors of offensive content by name. Such activities are certainly the right of citizens in
a democracy but often are counterproductive when accompanied
by a self-righteous attitude and a hostile tone or when political
power displaces spiritual transformation as the primary basis for cultural restoration. Furthermore, many thoughtful Christians who
appreciate the arts are horrified that a pious, moralistic Christian
subculture that is defined by kitsch, that produces subpar music and
books, and that is addicted to artistic mediocrity would have the
audacity to speak out about the arts to the broader culture!

Today's religious conservatives are often the antithesis of the
Jesus they say they are serving. Jesus lived under a repressive Roman
authority and yet invested himself in the spiritual transformation of
the individuals he met each day. He said that *love* is the preeminent
commandment and the ultimate evidence of the genuineness of his
followers. Today, Jesus' politicized followers often come across as

nostril-flaring, "mad as hell and we're not going to take it anymore" people who detest unbelievers while glibly stating that they hate the sin but love the sinner. A watching population has only these reactionary Christians by which to gauge what it means to be Christian, and often, they do not see the Christian presence as a loving one. Combativeness, though understandable in a hostile culture, should never displace the Christian's primary call to love, serve, and bring good news to the world that God loves. The Apostle John's words are timely: God sent His son into the world not to condemn people but to save them.

Conforming to Culture

Conform: To be in accord or harmony; to comply; to be obedient; to submit; to be similar, be in line with; to adjust or adapt oneself.

We now turn to the evangelicals, who, in their quest to enter the world in order to influence it, have in many ways been more influenced by the world they desired to transform.

The Paradoxical Saga of Evangelicalism

In the early 1950s, a new movement was born, with appropriate, conciliatory, constructive engagement of culture as its stated intention. Believing that Jesus should not be disconnected from the spiritual, intellectual, or artistic world, adherents of this movement were well-intentioned individuals of the highest integrity, eager to penetrate and positively influence culture. They rejected cultural cocooning because they sensed that familiarity with culture's ideas was required to gain a hearing. They wanted to reach the masses, so they were prepared to employ new technologies and marketing approaches for the good. They also believed that their initiatives should be built on a solid theological and intellectual foundation.

They were called *evangelicals*, and they set out to transform culture on multiple fronts. Billy Graham was a telegenic, charismatic evangelist who could fill stadiums. Carl Henry was a respected journalist and a formidable thinker who, as founding editor of *Christianity Today*, intended to shape it into a credible counterpoint to the more liberal *Christian Century*. Harold John Ockenga was a graduate of Princeton Seminary, pastor of Boston's Park Street Church, and a driving force in the establishment of Fuller Seminary, the National Association of Evangelicals, and *Christianity Today*. The nascent movement gained momentum, and by the 1970s, it seemed clear that the center of gravity was shifting from the cocooning and combativeness of conservative fundamentalism to a conservative Christian movement aware of culture's threats but willing to take risks to seize the opportunities.

From the very beginning, evangelicals demonstrated an uncanny ability to use emerging technologies and marketing practices to make converts and raise money while embracing an accessible style and message. In the 1950s, William Randolph Hearst promoted Billy Graham's Los Angeles crusade after observing his charisma, celebrity, and ability to sell papers. Graham's message was homey, approachable, and not particularly intellectually demanding. Conversion involved making a public profession by going down to the stadium floor and then praying a sinner's prayer. The integration of technology in televised campaigns and of marketing techniques in direct-mail follow-up ensured Billy Graham's organization a flow of funds to support his growing ministry.

After his conversion, Bill Bright, a successful businessman, developed a simple presentation of the gospel called the "Four Spiritual Laws." It was a straightforward, uncomplicated, scalable way to equip a national and international "sales force" to present one-on-one what Billy Graham presented in the stadiums.

Using case studies drawn from successful mission ventures overseas, missiologist Donald McGavran suggested efficiencies for evangelizing that were analogous to marketing segmentation practices, demonstrating that by allocating resources to responsive demographics, bigger local churches could be produced. In what became known as the "church growth movement," these marketing principles became the basis for "seeker-sensitive" megachurches.

Locked Out of Mainstream Media. In the electronic media, evangelicals' attempts at entering the mainstream were relatively unsuccessful. By the time evangelicals were ready to pursue opportunities in radio and television, the major network affiliates had found more profitable uses of their airwaves and no longer needed to sell time to religious broadcasters, so evangelicals simply established a parallel universe by setting up their own media outlets. This development of a parallel culture became a pattern for a multitude of ministry or business niches: Christian camping, Christian counseling, Christian colleges, Christian bookstores, Christian men, Christian women, and Christian businesspeople, along with specialized associations for each niche. Christian TV, Christian radio, Christian publishing of books and periodicals, Christian film companies, and Christian contemporary music have all experienced rapid growth and, in many cases, enviable profits. But by developing their own subculture, evangelicals often veered, unintentionally, I believe, into the cocooned approach they had sought to break out of.

Subculture or Marketing Niche? Soon, evangelicals became plentiful enough to be viewed as a voting bloc by politically active groups like the Moral Majority and the Christian Coalition, who desired to engage culture politically and stridently—a style more characteristic of fundamentalists than evangelicals. Deciding to become co-belligerents in political causes against common "enemies," evangelicals, who had set out to be constructive, not combative, were now often embroiled in a culture war, with all that that entailed: enemies, hostile us-versus-them talk, and substantial funds in financial war chests, available on a moment's notice to fund specific battles.

By the late 1990s, their sheer numbers made evangelicals attractive to retailers, and soon, most Christian music labels and book publishers were bought out by mainstream companies eager to seize their piece of a growing market. Evangelicals were seen as a sizable market segment with higher-than-average income and education and a willingness to buy stuff like everybody else!

Mel Gibson exploited the potential of megachurches as a retail distribution channel for his film *The Passion of the Christ*. Though Gibson viewed the film as a work of art, his company learned early in the process that to effectively tap the expansive evangelical market, they would need to allow evangelicals to position the film as an evangelistic opportunity. So they did. A spokesman for Gibson, Alan Nierob, explained the outreach efforts as "more in the interest of marketing than evangelism."[8] In one interview, a Gibson spokesman observed that a Disney movie can benefit from fast-food toy tie-ins, and *The Passion of the Christ* needed a similar boost; fast-food toys seemed inappropriate, so they looked for a ubiquitous distribution outlet and found one in churches. Just as there was a McDonald's on every block, there was a church on every block; evangelical churches were the equivalent of a fast-food distribution outlets, without the toys. Rick Warren engaged his network for this worthy cause, enthusiastically describing the process in *Fortune* magazine: "All of it depends on the network. If I want to rally people, I push a button, and boom!"[9] Soon thereafter, Warren pushed the button for his book *The Purpose-Driven Life*, and boom, it sold over 32 million copies.

The Seductiveness of Popularity. Unfortunately, it seems that in stylistically mirroring popular culture, evangelicalism was becoming increasingly *like* popular culture. A large segment of evangelicalism evolved into what might be called "pop Christianity," characterized by the broader culture's breezy superficiality and anti-intellectualism; it too was becoming a celebrity culture sustained by marketing and technology.

Many evangelicals who once had been rooted in a tradition of deep spiritual growth became obsessed with growth as measured by numbers of conversions and increased church attendance. Increasingly and often uncritically, they relied on technology and marketing to generate successful numeric and economic growth. The art and craft of marketing are built around appeals to self-interest, offering individuals something they want and desire. Conventional marketing wisdom advocates taking the path of least resistance in order to achieve success. Christian marketers embraced this approach, mastering it in order to raise money and sell the gospel. The result was often a Christianity that, on the surface at least, looked and sounded as driven by a focus on the self as the rest of American culture.

The same phenomenon occurred when evangelists and preachers constructed a more palatable "sales pitch" in presenting the gospel. Gone were warnings about the narrow way, denying yourself, repenting of sin, and taking up a cross. The gospel was marketed like a product by presenting features, advantages, and benefits; people were offered personal contentment, a happier family, and more success in their career and finances. Call the toll-free number on your screen, receive Jesus, and it can all be yours! Dietrich Bonhoeffer's *The Cost of Discipleship*, written during his imprisonment by Nazis, was widely known but seldom read or applied. Bonhoeffer had said, "We [Lutherans] have gathered like eagles around the carcass of cheap grace, and there we have drunk of the poison, which has killed the life of following Christ. But do we also realize that this cheap grace has turned back upon us like a boomerang? The price we pay today in the shape of the collapse of the organized church is only the inevitable consequence of our policy of making grace available to all at too low a cost."[10]

Marketing-driven church growth strategies resulted in large, event-driven churches serving individuals' felt needs through well-crafted programs and products fronted by winsome personalities—the evangelical celebrities. At one time, churches and denominations had sought out thoughtful biblical expositors to serve as pastors, but now they recruited entrepreneurs and magnetic personalities who could establish new churches or develop strategies to reach target markets. Pastors were expected to be CEOs and leaders who operated their local churches like franchises, submitting statistical reports to regional managers who evaluated the health of a church by its numbers.

Is the Evangelical Experiment a Success?   Americans understand the standards used to measure success in business, and by those standards, conservative Christianity is a runaway success, with its megachurches, growing colleges, electronic and print media empires, political influence, and wealth. Sociologist Alan Bloom went so far as to report that "we are back to a situation in which evangelicalism dominates our culture."[11] Oddly, despite evangelicalism's success as judged by American business standards, there is little evidence that this highly visible brand of Christianity is transforming culture. If evangelicals are dominating American culture, why is our culture in such bad condition spiritually, intellectually, morally, relationally, and aesthetically?

Christianity is always susceptible to adaptation to the culture in which it takes root. It is inevitable that any religion seeking to operate within a culture will be influenced by that culture. This is what missiologist Lesslie Newbigin meant when he said, "There is no such thing as a pure gospel if by that is meant something which is not embodied in a culture."[12] An authentic Christian presence in culture requires avoiding culture's threats when its values are dissonant with faith and seizing its opportunities at points of resonance. By almost every measurement, in the evangelical quest for cultural relevance, it appears that the influence of culture on evangelicals has been far greater than evangelicals' influence on culture.

Christianity-Lite

I want to make it clear that today, one can still find a robust remnant committed to reflecting the image of God through spiritual, intellectual, artistic, relational, and moral vitality in every movement within Christianity—Catholic, Orthodox, mainline Protestant, fundamentalist, and evangelical. Unfortunately, the predominant energy within American Christianity is in what I call "pop Christianity" or "Christianity-Lite." This brand of faith tastes great but is less filling, and wherever it prevails, it is a source of impoverishment of faith and culture. Christianity, when it takes on these characteristics, is an imposter. People are seeking the way home to God, but pop Christianity cannot provide it. Yet for many today, Christianity-Lite is all they know, and the consequences are serious for both the religious and the irreligious.

Christianity-Lite's cultural accommodation poses severe consequences for today's spiritual seeker. When seekers become disenchanted with a diversionary, mindless, celebrity-driven, and well-marketed but unsatisfying popular culture, if they turn to contemporary Christianity, they will often find those same qualities. We are witnessing the marketing of a Christianity-Lite that produces conversions instead of disciples. Dallas Willard reminds us of something anyone who reads the New Testament knows, Jesus never called anyone to be a Christian; he only called people to be disciples, individuals who would learn from him and obey all that he commanded.[13] In place of Jesus' call to self-denial and promise of persecution and sacrifice, today's consumer-oriented, commoditized Christianity offers heaven in the future and fulfillment of the American dream now.

The sobering contrast between historic Christianity and Christianity-Lite is illustrated by my recent experience in China. There, I heard the testimony of an underground church leader who had spent eighteen grueling years in prison, where he was beaten, chained, and subjected to physical torture and psychological torment, all because of his profession of faith in Jesus Christ. His captors lied to him, fabricated stories about infidelity on the part of his wife and a suicide attempt on the part of his son, offering to release him if he would denounce Jesus Christ as Lord. He showed us the purple grooves in his wrist where the chains had penetrated his rotting, infected flesh, rubbing it down to the bones.

He wept as he told us of how close he had come to denying his faith so that he could avoid the escalating torture and be reunited with his family. Yet he resisted betraying his faith by concentrating on the example of Jesus, who, as the Apostle Paul said, "emptied himself, took upon himself the form of a servant and made himself obedient even to his own death" (Philippians 2:7–8). Though severely tempted, the Chinese Christian could not turn his back on Jesus, who had suffered so much for him. In China, the house church movement has grown, despite persecution, because of the deep faith of Christians like this man, who view their suffering for their faith as normative, not heroic.

The day I returned to the United States, I found at the top of my stack of mail a postcard from a new seeker-sensitive church. It pictured a convict in black and white striped prison garb, a ball and chain attached to his ankle. I flipped the card over to read the message on the back: "Does going to church feel like going to prison? Not anymore!" The card went on to offer the seeker comfortable, stadium-style seating at a local cineplex, complete with popcorn, face painting and other fun and games for the kids, and, best of all, no preaching—just multimedia presentations and an inspirational talk designed to lead to greater success in life!

Is the gospel offered by this seeker-sensitive church the same as the gospel preached in China but adapted to our very different cultural milieu, or is this a completely different gospel? Is this simply a strategic accommodation that will produce a vibrant local church with the same kind of spiritual depth and maturity that I witnessed among Christians in China? The answer seems obvious. Christians are called to be light of the world, not the lite of the world.

What kind of culture is today's popularized Christianity producing? Again, the answer seems obvious. Instead of creating a robust, authentic culture, Christianity-Lite simply imitates the broader popular culture's aesthetic in form and content. A friend of mine who was departing the pastorate after twenty years told me, "I embrace evangelical doctrine; I just can't stomach its culture." My friend Ralph Mattson once put it this way to me: "If Christians were going to create a subculture, why did they have to create one that is so boring, imitative, and uninspiring?"

Vibrant faith involves understanding Scripture, employing reason, benefiting from the lessons of tradition, and engaging in a profound personal experience of God. From this kind of spiritual intensity flows cultural transformation. I once heard a seminary professor summarize historian T. R. Glover's explanation about the influence of early Christians on culture this way: the early Christians out-thought, outlived, and out-died their pagan counterparts. This certainly cannot be said of pop Christians.

Illiteracy in Faith. There is ample evidence that in attempting to influence culture, Christians have jettisoned basic, historic Christian beliefs. Not only does Christianity-Lite fail to advance Christian beliefs and practices, but it has forgotten what they are! How else can you describe a situation in which most church-going adults reject the accuracy of the Bible, claim that Jesus sinned, believe that good works will persuade God to forgive their sins, and describe their commitment to Christianity as moderate or even less firm?[14] Our numbers indicate strength, but our shallowness betrays our weakness. We are a mirror image of the moralistic therapeutic deistic culture that I described in Chapter One.

In the first century, Paul chided the church at Corinth because it was more influenced by pagan culture than able to influence it. In his book of Revelation, John complained that the church at Ephesus had "lost its first love" and warned the church at Laodicea that although it thought of itself as "rich, prosperous, and in need of nothing," that it was in fact "wretched, pitiable, poor, blind, and naked . . . lukewarm, neither hot nor cold" and would be "spit out of God's mouth" (Revelation 3:15–17). Such a church cannot influence culture, and Christianity-Lite is producing such a church. Yale University's Louis Dupré laments, "On a fundamental level the West appears to have said its definitive farewell to a Christian culture. . . . Christianity has become a historical factor subservient to a secular culture rather than functioning as the creative power it once was."[15]

When sociologist Alan Wolfe described evangelicals as a dominant culture, they seized on it with excitement and pride, but Wolfe's extremely significant clarification was often unreported. Wolfe continued, "But that doesn't mean 'fundamentalist.' It means revivalist, personalist, therapeutic, entrepreneurial—the mega-church."[16] Similarly, when the press covers evangelicals, a pattern is emerging: evangelical strength is usually calculated by the size and number of churches, church attendance, economic clout, or political muscle or by its enviable breadth of distribution outlets and educational institutions; the press does not generally find evangelicalism noteworthy for its spiritual depth, intellectual rigor, aesthetic richness, relational health, or moral purity. I've never heard cultural observers describe contemporary Christianity as a profoundly spiritual movement offering deep union with a transcendent God or as the basis for a spiritually inspired, intelligent, and aesthetically rich cultural renewal.

Cultural Imitation. All my cautionary observations about evangelicals grieve me, for it was within evangelicalism that I got my start with Jesus. My critique is meant to be constructive and corrective, and I am not alone in my concerns. Within evangelicalism, many thoughtful people are troubled about the price we have paid for our "success." Some believe that in our quest for numeric growth, we have grown big but are shallow, producing an American Christianity three thousand miles wide but two inches deep. Others observe that our apparent success has been accomplished by conforming to American culture rather than transforming it, pointing out, as Alan Wolfe observed, that instead of theological, it is therapeutic; instead of intellectual, it is emotional and revivalist; instead of emphasizing a serving community, it is consumeristic and individualistic; instead of producing spiritual growth and depth, it is satisfied with entrepreneurialism and numeric growth. Instead of being a moral and spiritual beacon, evangelicalism is viewed as an important political and economic niche.

None other than the late Carl Henry, an early founder of evangelicalism and its intellectual champion, expressed alarm at the accommodation to culture. Near his death, he wrote, " 'I have two main convictions about the near-term future of American Christianity. One is that American evangelicals presently face their biggest opportunity since the Protestant Reformation, if not since the apostolic age. The other is that Americans are forfeiting that opportunity stage by stage, despite the fact that evangelical outcomes in the twentieth century depend upon decisions currently in the making.' *The Biographical Dictionary of Evangelicals* states that toward the end of his life, Henry was concerned that the movement he had helped shape was losing its identity due to uncritical accommodation."[17] Our forfeits take many forms. Certainly, popular culture has played an important, shaping role in Christianity-Lite's conformity that is reflected in Christians' media consumption, beliefs, and behavior and in their media creation.

Media Consumption, Beliefs, and Behavior. Ted Baehr, author of *The Media Wise Family*, reports, "Extensive research indicates that most Christians have the same media diet as non-Christians, though many Christians complain about the entertainment media. The same percentage of Christian teenagers as 'non-Christian' watch R-rated movies with the same frequency."[18] Researcher George Barna has also documented the increasing role of popular culture as an influencer in the life of evangelicals; he reports that born-again adults spend "an average of seven times more hours each week watching television than they do participating in spiritual pursuits such as Bible reading, prayer, and worship. . . . They spend roughly twice as much money on entertainment as they donate to their church. And they spend more time surfing the net than they do conversing with God in prayer."[19]

In his book *Hollywood Worldviews*, Brian Godawa correctly observes that most Christians are on the extremes in their consumption of popular culture. They are either "cultural anorexics," cut off from culture completely, or "cultural gluttons" who uncritically consume anything that comes along.[20] My friend Russ Ward adds a third category, "cultural bulimics," who indiscriminately gorge themselves on the worst of pop culture and then purge themselves through vociferous condemnation of those who produce it (and others who consume it)!

George Barna's research consistently exposes Christianity-Lite's conformity to culture's beliefs: "Only four percent of Americans hold to a biblical worldview," defined simply as "believing that absolute moral truths exist; that such truth is defined by the Bible; and firm belief in six specific religious views. Those views were that Jesus Christ lived a sinless life; God is the all-powerful and all-knowing Creator of the universe and He still rules it today; salvation is a gift from God and cannot be earned; Satan is real; a Christian has a responsibility to share their faith in Christ with other people; and the Bible is accurate in all of its teachings."[21]

Barna's research also indicates troubling trends in behavior among the "born-again population," including a higher divorce rate than the general population and patterns of consumerism matching the general population. Evangelicals condemn abortion and sexual immorality but are relatively silent about the accumulation of wealth and concerns for the poor. He notes particular concerns about the next generation: "The emerging generation of parents is the least likely of any demographic subgroup in the nation to possess—and, therefore, to transmit—biblical moral values. They will naturally impart to their children their own beliefs, and model and reinforce behaviors that fit their own values. Within the next quarter century we will likely see a state of radical moral amnesia in America."[22]

Media Creation. Today, thousands of companies offer Christians cocooned options in radio, TV, Web sites, film, games, books, magazines, cruises, retail stores, clothing, resorts, retirement communities, insurance, amusement parks. Virtually every aspect of life can be experienced without the messiness of interactions with unbelievers. However, the Christian entertainment culture (Christian TV, movies, music, and books) is often characterized by the same spiritual confusion, intellectual superficiality, and marketing- and money-driven values as the broader popular culture. I will deal with this issue more extensively in Chapter Nine where I discuss artists who are Christian, but at this point, I simply note that Christian use of the media has been primarily imitative, striving to look like and sound like mainstream media while adapting the lyrical and moral content to the reductionist, feel-good gospel of pop Christianity. Generally, it lacks spiritual depth, intellectual firepower, and artistic originality, and for the most part, it is satisfied with being a counterpart to the popular culture: entertaining and mindless and driven by celebrity, technological competence, good marketing, and, above all else, profitability.

Many contemporary Christian musicians and young authors aren't personally or stylistically predisposed toward cocooning, yet they are partnered with a vast network of Christian radio stations and distributed through a network of Christian retailers that advertise themselves as places where listeners will never hear anything "offensive" and will always feel "safe." The result is a diversion from reality and the perpetuation of feel-good Christianity-Lite.

As it goes mainstream, pop Christianity tends to aim low. When Bud Paxson started PAX TV, there was a surge of hope followed immediately by dismay when he made comments like "I wish there were the kind of programs that could get huge ratings, like wrestling, and yet bring people into the Kingdom."[23] Pop Christianity aims for family values programming and ends up with sentimental shows that are ineffective at connecting with today's younger generation. Many religious conservatives revered the TV series "Touched by an Angel," but in a reader survey in *Maxim*, a magazine geared toward eighteen-to-thirty-four-year-old men, 75 percent said they would rather kill themselves with a steak knife than watch an episode of "Touched by an Angel."[24]

In his book *All God's Children and Blue Suede Shoes*, cultural observer Ken Myers warned that popular culture might swallow up evangelicals: "It might seem an extreme assertion at first, but I believe that the challenge of living with popular culture may well be as serious for modern Christians as persecution and plagues were for the saints of earlier centuries. Being thrown to the lions or living in the shadow of gruesome death are fairly straightforward if unattractive threats. Enemies that come loudly and visibly are usually much easier to fight than those that are undetectable."[25]

Christianity-Lite and the Image of God. A strong case can be made that in trying to seize the opportunities offered by culture, contemporary followers of Jesus have been overwhelmed by its threats. Having rejected both cocooning and combat, a majority of today's Christians have slid from a conciliatory and constructive engagement of culture to an attempt at relevance resulting in conformity. Christianity-Lite is not in a position to restore and transform culture because it is too enamored of it and enmeshed in it. Alan Wolfe observes, "American culture is an enormously powerful force. It will change religion, just as religion will change culture." Already, he says, evangelicals "are far more shaped by the culture than they are capable of shaping it to their own needs."[26] *New York Times* columnist Walter Kirn puts the final nail in the proverbial coffin: "Christianity doesn't compete with pop culture. It is pop culture."[27]

This overall assessment of Christianity-Lite leads to a staggering conclusion. It seems fair to say that Jesus would not recognize the message and practices of Christianity-Lite. When it comes to finding God, in the words of the Beatles, "once there was a way to get back homeward,"[28] but today, the very ones who claim to know the way, the truth, and the life are obscuring the path. Again, I believe that humans possess innate spiritual, intellectual, creative, relational, and moral capacities, and it seems clear that what we are seeing in Christianity-Lite is a diminishment of God's image on the part of followers of Jesus. But we're all in the same boat; today, irreligious and religious seekers each face a losing proposition: either the popular culture's blender style of spirituality or Christian religion in the form of Christianity-Lite. This is a grim scenario, because every human since the dawn of time has intuitively sensed that, in the words of Joni Mitchell, "we've got to get ourselves back to the garden."[29] How does the noble idea of every human being created in God's image—with spiritual, intellectual, creative, relational, and moral capacities—relate to Christianity-Lite? If neither culture nor contemporary Christian faith can show us the way, where can we turn?

3

THE STORY
WE ARE IN

The significance (and ultimately the quality) of
the work we do is determined by our understanding
of the story in which we are taking part.[1]
WENDELL BERRY

And so here we are, religious and irreligious alike, intuitively
believing that there is more to being human, wallowing in the
squalor of superficiality in both faith and culture, unsatisfied by
mindless diversions and spiritual delusions. The symptoms of spiritual hunger—our sense of meaninglessness and heartache—are
everywhere. The poet Goethe called it our "holy longing," philosopher Søren Kierkegaard referred to "sickness unto death," and pilgrim poet Basho searched for "a glimpse of the under-glimmer,"
similarly described as "the undersong" by Ralph Waldo Emerson.
Gauguin cries out through his art, "Why are we here? Where do we
come from? Where are we going?" Joni Mitchell sings, "We've got
to get ourselves back to the garden."[2] Jim Morrison's voice cries out
from beyond his Parisian grave, "Let me tell you about heartache
and the loss of god. Wandering, wandering in hopeless night."[3]

In the early 1900s, an archaeologist came upon the ancient
gravesite of an old-world explorer. Etched in the stone were the
words of a man who was curious to the very end. "Stand on my
grave and tell me what you see," his epitaph implored. As we depart
the twentieth and embark upon the twenty-first century, a myriad
of seers and futurists stand on the graves of the past, peering into
the future—and this is what they see: every human, religious or not,
is burdened by a residual recollection of wholeness and wellness, to

which we yearn to return. This deep human yearning is inescapable. Augustine says, "God has made us for Himself and our hearts are restless until they find their rest in Him."[4] Pascal refers to every human's "God shaped vacuum" that only God can fill."[5] Songwriters, poets, and artists recall it most clearly, feel the loss most deeply, and, through the centuries, have passed bits and pieces of the saga from village to village and age to age. What was once drawn on the walls of caves is now projected as bright digital bits in darkened rooms. For centuries, humans have gathered at day's end by the fireside to tell their tales. Recall poet Robert Graves's lamentation: "Much snow is falling, winds roar hollowly, the owl hoots from the elder. Fear in your heart cries to the loving-cup: sorrow to sorrow as the sparks fly upward. The log groans and confesses: There is one story and one story only."[6]

One Story and One Story Only

We know intuitively that beneath all myths and religions and metaphysical explorations, there is what C. S. Lewis and J.R.R. Tolkien called "the one true myth." Our one story and one story only is the narrative of our loss of God and longing to get back to God. We organize our lives against the sad backdrop of this story, knowing that our loss is the source of the loneliness and angst we feel in a lonely crowd. Our one story and one story only mourns our lostness; it is why we need a compass, why we believe we are off the trail, and why we have concluded that without God, meaning and significance are always somewhere else. Meant to be aglow with God's image, our lamp is dim, the image faded, obscured and seen through a glass darkly. We deceive ourselves into believing that things are getting better; but then poignant tragedies from which our collective eyes cannot be diverted clarify our human dilemma. After the horrific events of September 11, 2001, I recalled W. H. Auden's haunting "September 1, 1939," written in New York City on the day that he learned that the Nazis would invade Poland. In that poem, he describes our avoidance of the very real truth that we are "children afraid of the night" who are "lost in a haunted wood."[7]

Our way back, our only hope, is to know the universal story we are in, to understand where we are in it, and to write a better outcome than the one we now find ourselves expecting. Like every good story, ours consists of a beginning, a middle, and an end. Our story's beginning is an auspicious one, because there we learn of God's spiritual, intellectual, creative, moral, and relational capacities, which were bestowed uniquely on humans as the sole bearers of God's image.

The Story of Creation

Fully Human: The Image of God

Joni Mitchell's "Woodstock" lyrics recall your story and mine: "I came upon a child of God. . . . We are stardust. We are golden . . . billion-year-old carbon."[8] Our tale begins in a magical garden in a time when we were fully human, aware that we were God's image bearers, stardust and golden, made of the stuff of earth yet endowed with godlike capacities. To this day, though separated by generations from our first ancestors, we retain a primal, residual awareness that we are more than billion-year-old carbon.

The story of the Garden of Eden has passed from generation to generation and still survives today. We are told that God breathed into dust and made it live. Various theories have been advanced to harmonize this teaching with modern science, and we may differ on the details about how and when, but God's involvement in human creation is and always has been the foundational article of Jewish and Christian orthodoxy.

The ancient story reveals that just before He created the first human, God said, "Let us make humans in our image." The implications are profound: we, uniquely among all creation, possess a reservoir of godlike capacities. Because of this, our only hope for personal and cultural transformation is in rediscovering these rich, fertile roots as image bearers of God. Any successful search for true human identity begins by understanding the revealed truth conveyed in this ancient story. Without God's mysterious involvement in creation, we can only conclude that we are accidental bits of billion-year-old carbon. Without reference to God, in whose image we are created, our pursuit for meaning is futile.

Human purpose and our path to meaning and satisfaction are rooted in the fact that God *was* involved in creation. From the beginning of time, we were created to pay tribute to our creator by fulfilling our godlikeness, and when we fully express God's image, we experience the pleasure of being fully human. This is the truth conveyed in the film *Chariots of Fire*. Eric Lidell realizes that he is called to be a missionary to China, but he also says, "When I run, I feel God's pleasure!"[9] Experiencing God's pleasure requires becoming fully human, and because we are created in God's image, becoming fully human requires expressing our individual spiritual, intellectual, creative, moral, and relational capacities.

Reflecting Five Qualities of God Imprinted on Humans: Toward Becoming Fully Human

To Be Fully Human Is to Be Creative

> In the beginning, God created the heavens and the earth.
> —Genesis 1:1

Dorothy Sayers once said that if all we knew about God was the first five words of the Bible, all we would know is that God is creative.[10] When in the first words of the Bible, we discover God's identity as a creator, we get a glimpse of our own identity as humans who possess creative capacities.

Genesis 1 reveals the dimensions of God's creative process, which, not surprisingly, given our creation in God's image, is replicated in human creativity. *In the beginning, God created.* God brings something out of nothing and order out of chaos. *The earth was a formless void.* God is a seer who can envision something others cannot and then imaginatively reveal the new reality as a unique, distinct entity. *God saw what He had made and it was good.* Like God, the good artist strives for excellence, not just expression, and the spiritual, intellectual, and imaginative quality of the work is the measurement by which we determine the worth of our art. *The heavens declare the glory of God,* and the human artist seeks to relate and communicate through his or her art.

Our human creativity originates in God's creative image, which is imprinted in our genetic code. Whereas God created out of nothing; humans create out of what exists. So Igor Stravinsky observes, "Only God can create. I make music from music."[11] Great artists will tell you that their imaginative inspiration comes from some unknown place. Filmmaker Ang Lee confesses that when things work, they *come* to him; they are not what he has willed.[12] Mark Doty says that a good poem is something he *finds,* not something he makes.[13] Imagination cannot be manufactured or willed into being, yet it is at the heart of the creative enterprise. God creates from a known place, Himself, and at God's core, you find an imaginative being.

Imagination reflects originality, intuition, and the hitherto unseen, and so we evaluate our individual and cultural health by looking for evidence of our imaginative capacity to deliver the new and fresh, which elicits and illuminates deeper, transcendent meanings.

As image bearers, we are designed with a creative capacity.

To Be Fully Human Is to Be Spiritual

> And the Spirit of God swept over the waters.
>
> —Genesis 1:2

Our universal human quest for the spiritual also springs from God's image in us, for from the beginning of time, we have known that God is spirit. Jesus affirmed this to the Samaritan woman at the well: "God is spirit, and those who worship him must worship in spirit and truth" (John 4:24). The spirit is unseen; it moves with the unseen force of the wind or the fluidity and grace of a dancer.

The spirit is elemental, or as composer John Tavener says, it is primordial.[14] It existed before the creation of matter. In the mythology of the film *Star Wars*, the force is the most essential element of all being, yet it is unseen. Likewise, our human spiritual dimension is real, though we cannot see it or touch it. Our spiritual sensitivities are reflected in our art, which flows from the spiritual and then becomes material. The spiritual is the unseen nothingness from which comes something.

In Hebrew, Greek, Sanskrit, and Latin, the word for "spirit" is the same as the word for "breath." In the Bible, human life specifically is singled out as having been breathed out by God. In his poem "The Creation," James Weldon Johnson describes God "like a mammy" bending over her baby, shaping the dust into His image, blowing the breath of life into the clay that then becomes a living soul.[15] Our spiritual capacities are as essential to the soul as breathing is to the body, and absent the spiritual, humans are like asthmatics, gasping for fresh, pure air.

The spirit brings life, energy, and movement, and so we evaluate our individual and cultural wellness by looking for evidence of our individual and cultural spirit, asking whether it is good, pure, and loving.

As image bearers, we are designed with a spiritual capacity.

To Be Fully Human Is to Be Intelligent

> The Lord by wisdom founded the earth.
>
> —Proverbs 3:19

In a society that treats intellectual pursuits as optional and the domain of stuffy, elitist academics, it is important to remember that Jesus commanded, "You shall love the Lord your God with all your heart and with all your soul and *with all your mind*" (Matthew 22:37, italics added). We will never be satisfied with a steady diet of mindless entertainments, because, created in God's image, we possess intellectual capacities.

The universe itself flowed from a reasoned intelligence, an idea captured by the Apostle John, who said, "In the beginning was the word, and the word was with God, and the word was God. . . . All things came into being through him [the word]" (John 1:1). At first glance, the idea that "the word" was there in the beginning seems like a reference to God speaking the heavens and earth into existence ("and God said"). When you read further in the Apostle John's writing, however, you realize that "the word" to which he refers is Jesus: "The word became flesh and dwelt among us" (John 1:14). John is establishing that Jesus participated in the creation of the heavens and the earth and that he is, in fact, God.

More important for our purposes, John's metaphorical use of "the word" reveals an important aspect of God's creative nature. The Greek term John uses for "word" is *logos*, the root of our word *logic*. The ancients saw God's intelligence in creation, so the writer of Proverbs says, "The Lord by wisdom founded the earth" (Proverbs 3:19). The Apostle John attests that there was a cosmic intelligence woven into creation from its very beginning. Creation reveals God's complex logic at work. Mathematicians see hints of this because the laws of nature are consistent and follow preestablished rules. Equations are elegant because they come from a beautifully ordered mind. As scientists begin to comprehend the language of DNA, they are discovering the intricate, surpassing intelligence embedded in this ancient code. Art, whether audible, written, tactile, or visual, is similarly the expression of a mind at work. This is why St. Thomas Aquinas called art "reason in the making," a definition described by Flannery O'Connor as cold but beautiful and unpopular today only because "reason has lost ground among us."[16]

Intelligence reflects order, logic, and sensibleness, and so we evaluate our human and cultural wellness by asking whether our individual lives and our culture are intelligent, orderly, understandable, and reasonable.

As image bearers, we are designed with an intellectual capacity.

To Be Fully Human Is to Be Relational

> And God said, "Let us make man in our image, after our
> likeness" . . . and so male and female he created them.
>
> —Genesis 1:26–27

Humans yearn for relationships because we are created in the image of a relational God. It is significant that the Bible, which is rigorously monotheistic, declaring that there is but one God, nevertheless describes a plurality within the person of God from the very beginning. "Let us make man in our image, after our likeness." God exists in community and created humans for relationship in community. One God in three persons—the creator God, Spirit hovering over the waters, and Jesus the Logos—was there at the creation in the beginning. Our relational nature mirrors the very nature of God. The fact that expressing God's image required both a male and a female is an astounding revelation. We should not be surprised that a further footnote declares, "It is not good that the man should be alone" (Genesis 2:18). Our human capacity for the relational extends not only to our need for an active relationship with God but also to our need for interdependent relationships with each other as well.

Jewish theologian Martin Buber brilliantly depicts the human need for relationship in his classic book *I and Thou:*

> Here is the infallible test: Imagine yourself in a situation where you
> are alone, wholly alone on earth, and you are offered one of the
> two, books or men. I often hear men prizing their solitude but that
> is only because there are still men somewhere on earth even though
> in the far distance. I knew nothing of books when I came forth from
> the womb of my mother, and I shall die without books, with
> another human hand in my own. I do, indeed, close my door at
> times and surrender myself to a book, but only because I can open
> the door again and see a human being looking at me.[17]

Of all our godlike capacities, the relational seems closest to the core of God because the essence of God is love, and love is expressed in relationship. When the ancients were most conscious of God's involvement in their lives, they often referred to God's steadfast love, steady and dependable. When Jesus summarized the entire Hebrew law, he reduced it to our human capacity to love God and our neighbor.

Our deepest human wellness requires that we evaluate our individual and cultural health on the basis of our relationships and the centrality or absence of love as the defining quality in them.

As image bearers, we are designed with a relational capacity.

To Be Fully Human Is to Be Moral

> You may surely eat of every tree of the garden, but of the tree of the knowledge of good and evil you shall not eat, for in the day you eat of it you shall surely die.
>
> —Genesis 2:16–17

Humans possess an innate moral capacity to obey or disobey, to do good or evil. These qualities also derive from our creation in God's image. In the Garden of Eden, God revealed both a behavioral expectation and our freedom to choose when he communicated to Adam and Eve that they could eat of any tree but one and then commanded them to not eat of it.

Woven into the universe from the beginning were natural and moral laws that govern our well-being. Natural laws govern the well-being of the physical universe, and moral laws govern the well-being of humans created in God's image. These moral laws are the basis for human health and wellness. Just as violating natural laws results in disaster, violating moral laws also has consequences.

I still remember, in the turbulent moral confusion of the 1960s, reading for the first time Moses' advice to the next generation of Jews as they were about to enter the Promised Land. Moses elegantly and simply shared the timeless lessons he had learned about the moral life and reminded them of the consequences of their choices:

> For this commandment that I command you today is not too hard for you, neither is it far off. It is not in heaven, that you should say, "Who will ascend to heaven for us and bring it to us, that we may hear it and do it?" Neither is it beyond the sea, that you should say, "Who will go over the sea for us and bring it to us, that we may hear it and do it?" But the word is very near you. It is in your mouth and in your heart, so that you can do it. See, I have set before you today life and good, death and evil. . . . Therefore choose life, that you and your offspring may live, loving the Lord your God, obeying his voice and holding fast to him, for he is your life and length of days. [Deuteronomy 30:11–20]

We are created in God's image as moral beings, and so we evaluate our individual and cultural wellness on the basis of our compliance with the unchanging moral laws of the universe.

As image bearers, we are designed with a moral capacity.

Human Potential and Purpose

In all the created order, nowhere is the potential of creating for God's glory and receiving God's blessing more profound than in humans. From the beginning, we were destined to occupy a unique place in the created order, a place described in Psalm 8 as just a little lower than the angels. Our purpose is to showcase God's glory, enjoying full, unhindered intimacy with God and each other, creating a rich culture and exercising dominion over the entire created order on earth.

And so we see that the creation story explains our universal unfulfilled longings, for humans, uniquely in all of God's creation, are bearers of God's own creative essence, with spiritual, intellectual, creative, relational, and moral capacities. When we fail to develop and express those capacities, we are less than fully human.

Our Full Humanity Is Revealed in the Culture We Create

When we fail to develop and express our godlike capacities, we are less than fully human and the culture we create reflects our incompleteness. This is because God placed His imprint on humans and then commanded us to place our imprint on the earth by creating culture: "Let us make humans in our own image, and let them have dominion over . . . the earth" (Genesis 1:26). To be fully human simply means to express God's image fully in our lives.

Because God is infinitely creative, woven into the core of our being and blended together in combinations unique to each of us is a pattern, a complex of innate talents and personality traits, ensuring that each of us is a distinctive, one-of-a-kind creation. Our individual genius means that each of us will visualize things that others do not see, hear things others don't, conceive of ideas or calculations or ways of doing things that seem obvious to us but to which others are oblivious! The seeds of our creativity are manifest in the things we make and do, and when we are exercising our uniqueness, we have an irresistible, passionate drive to make everything we do good.

Culture is created when humans pool our talents and combine our creations for the broader community. Culture is simply the composite of the patterns, arts, beliefs, institutions, and other products of our human work and thought. Ideally, diversely gifted people, fully aware that we are all created in God's image, would work interdependently, each making contributions that flow from his or her own distinct competencies. The result would be a rich culture characterized by the harmonious blending together of uniquely gifted, creative, intelligent humans.

We intuitively sense that God, the source of our universal human creativity, is the gold standard by which our spiritual, intellectual, and aesthetic pursuits should be measured, individually and collectively. This is why when we observe humans deriving their standards from contemporary mediocrity instead of the criteria exemplified by the highest and best, we instinctively know that the human race is falling short of our potential.

The culturally savvy Christian understands that our human story begins with great promise. We are made for deep relationship with the living God and created in God's image, with the potential to create a culture resplendent with God's image. The reason that neither today's religious nor its irreligious cultures can satisfy us in their current superficial condition is that we were made for so much more. We're reaping the rewards of a popular culture dominated by people who have lost the connection between building culture and glorifying God and of a Christian subculture that has lost the connection between glorifying God and building a richer culture.

Any hope of restoring culture starts with restoring the individuals who make culture, and any hope of restoring individuals starts with rediscovering the origin of our capacities in the one who made us.

The next part of our story reveals how humans displaced God as the object of our affection and worship and how, in so doing, became less than fully human, dulled and tarnished reflections of God's image.

The Story of Our Revolt

Though humans have been gloriously created in God's image, we are limited in significant ways. Unlike God, humans are physical and occupy a specific place. We live within time and are bound by chronology. We can create out of something but cannot create out of nothing. Because we are part of the created order, we are at best co-creators with God or, as Tolkien described us, "sub-creators."[18] Though we are formed in God's image, humans are substantially unlike God, whose otherness is described by eleventh-century mystic Hildevert of Lavardin:

God is over all things,
under all things,
outside all,
within, but not enclosed,
without, but not excluded,
above, but not raised up,
below, but not depressed,
wholly above, presiding,
wholly without, embracing,
wholly within, filling.[19]

Wholly unlike God, we nevertheless are God's image bearers. Wholly unlike God, we nevertheless are like God in another important way in that we are free beings. Knowing that true love is chosen, not imposed, God gave humans the gift of freedom—freedom to choose either to glorify God, as creatures who honor their creator, or to usurp God's rightful place, choosing to glorify ourselves, the created ones. Human destiny was concentrated in a test of allegiance when Adam and Eve were warned of the consequences if they chose to revolt against God: "You may surely eat of every tree of the garden, but of the tree of the knowledge of good and evil you shall not eat, for in the day that you eat of it you shall surely die" (Genesis 2:16–17).

Today, we yearn to fulfill our destiny as image bearers, to create and dwell in a richer culture, yet everywhere we see evidence of our individual and communal shortcomings. Though we are created in God's image and therefore are the unique recipients of God's creative capacity, our human ability to reflect that image has clearly been diminished. Why?

Displacing God

What went wrong in the garden? Genesis starts by describing our extraordinary potential and then tells the sad story of our self-inflicted unraveling. The Apostle Paul says humans are "God's workman-ship" (Ephesians 2:10), using the Greek word *poeme*, from which we derive our word *poem*. If we read contemporary life as a poem or glance at the collective snapshots of our existence, it is obvious that something has gone terribly wrong. Designed to be bearers of God's image, we have become what poet T. S. Eliot described as "hollow men,"[20] lamenting our loss, universally longing, and inconsolably lonely. We seem unable to find meaning or a sense of identity or purpose. Writer Christopher Lasch describes twenty-first-century humans as "plagued by anxiety, depression, vague discontent and a sense of inner emptiness."[21]

At the heart of our universal story is our revolt against God, a rebellion in which the human race displaced God as the center of our life and replaced God with ourselves. Rather than choosing to enjoy unending fellowship with God, Adam and Eve took the lead in what poet John Milton called the "foul revolt."[22] They enthroned themselves in place of the creator; not satisfied with their godlike-ness, they wanted to *be* god. This phenomenon persists today. Like the tower of Babel, the culture we build today is a monument to human greatness, not God's greatness, and our art and architecture is a tribute to ourselves, not God. Mystery writer Nevada Barr re-turned to faith after her walk on the wild side, saying, "It was a number of years of crashing and burning before I made the discov-ery that I was not God. . . . Finally I realized that though I was not God, I was *of* God."[23]

Seduced by the Dark Side

Our ancestors did not leave God on their own; they were seduced by outside influences, enticed by the dark forces that still deceive us today. In the prototypical story, Adam and Eve were lured to the dark side by the crafty, lying serpent. By asserting their indepen-dence from God, they rushed headlong in the wrong direction, away from God and toward the oppressive, unfulfilling bondage of the dark side. Even now, when we seek to restore God to the place of supreme importance in our lives, we inevitably meet resistance from a powerful force at odds with God. Bob Dylan clarified our human struggle, singing, "You got to serve somebody," whether it is the devil or the Lord.

Literature is rich with metaphors about Satan, the Devil, or Lucifer. The dualistic "dark side," personified by Darth Vader in George Lucas's brilliant *Star Wars*, is a common metaphor for our wanderings off the right path. The seductions of the dark side are explored in songs like Wilco's "Hell Is Chrome," in which front man Jeff Tweedy, fresh out of rehab, contemplates how good people can be drawn into doing bad things. Modernity has not diminished our belief in the truth of these stories; on the contrary, the evidence of the dark side all around and within us make the stories ring truer than ever.

These thematic stories of the garden, a tempting serpent, and our human decline maintain a strong grip on the human psyche because they tap into the deepest truth of human existence. When Adam and Eve made the choice to defy God, they displaced God as the central object of their affection, and they paid the price. So do we.

Fallen Humans, Faded Images

As the ancient story goes, having rebelled against God, humans were banished from the garden lest they eat of the tree of life and live in their corrupt condition forever. With their defiance, our great unraveling began: separation from God, hierarchy and dissension in marriage, pain in childbearing, thorns in the fertile fields, sweat in work, animosity between humans and the animal kingdom, abuse and disregard for the earth, and, most significantly, death itself.

Created to glow with the presence of God by reflecting God's image, we usurped God's rightful place in our lives, and our center, once radiant with God's presence, became dim as the once-bright image of God began to fade. Humanity's residual memories of God and our longing for the restoration of God's image remain, but humans are lost. Jim Morrison's haunting lyric still resonates: "Let me tell you about heartache and the loss of god. Wandering, wandering in hopeless night."[24]

Our human dilemma following Adam and Eve's fall can be summarized quite simply: we yearn for restored fellowship with God, but in our fallen condition, we continue to want it on our own terms. During an interview with National Book Award winner Robert Stone about his book *Damascus Gate*, I mentioned reading somewhere about his abandonment of the Catholicism of his youth, about how he initially felt free but woke up twenty years later feeling like "half his head was missing." Stone replied, "I think it happens to a lot of people. You leave religion with a tremendous sense of liberation, and then, years later, you discover that something really important is missing . . . and you either start all over again and go back and try to reclaim it or else you substitute something else for it." He went on to say, "There is that element of man; as Pascal said, 'the world everywhere gives evidence of a vanished God, and man in all his actions gives evidence of a longing for that God.' So you make do in small ways. One way or other, you've got to fill that space somehow."[25] After movingly confessing that something central is missing, Stone accurately described the barrier between humans and our restoration with God, namely that we try to fill the "God space" with something other than God!

The Story of Reunion and Restoration

Sickness unto death infects each dimension of our lives as God's image bearers. Everything once straight is bent. Everything clear is now clouded. Our spirit, made to glow with God's iridescence, is dimmed. Our mind, once employed to discover and enjoy harmony with God's intelligence, is deceived, debased, and diminished. Our creativity, once dedicated to the Great Artist and passionate in its pursuit of excellence, truth, and beauty, now descends to express our lessened, fallen state. Our relationships, once flowing to and from God, who is love, are tinged with self-seeking, bitterness, and dissension. Our moral compass, once set on the good, now swings erratically to evil, undiscerningly calling evil good, confusing light and darkness, rationalizing, justifying, and obscuring. Deterioration, diminishment, darkness, lies, deception, ugliness, death, and hostilities: these are the marks of the dark side. Our image, which once reflected God, now mirrors the evil one. In *Crime and Punishment*, Fyodor Dostoevsky, a Russian Orthodox novelist, renames God's image bearers: "Come forth, ye drunkards, come forth, ye weak ones, come forth, ye children of shame! . . . and we shall stand before Him. And He will say unto us, 'Ye are swine, made in the image of the Beast and with his mark.'"[26]

Yet God is good, God is love, and God will find a way. The luster of God's image *can* be restored to our spiritual, intellectual, creative, relational, and moral capacities, so that we embody God's presence in faith and culture. We've discussed our universal story of creation, revolt, loss, and longing; now let's hear the rest of the story as told by Jesus, commonly referred to as the "story of the prodigal son":

The beginning. A young man was born into a home in which he lacked nothing.

The revolt. Nevertheless, the young man grew tired of being his father's son and wanted to make a name for himself. Unwilling to wait for his father's death to receive his full inheritance, he decided to act as if his father were already dead, saying, "Give me what is coming to me, and give it to me now." He went to a far country, where he was free to do his own thing. Soon, he squandered all that he had in partying and riotous living, and he fell into poverty. The young man who once had worn the finest clothing and gold jewelry now wore tattered clothes and took a job feeding pigs. Eventually, things got so bad that he was eating a steady diet of pig slop.

The reunion. One day, the young man came to himself; he "got it." He recalled the earlier time when he had lived in his father's home. He realized that with his father, he had had everything he needed. Because of his shameful revolt and wasted life, he felt unworthy to return and ask forgiveness of the father he once had wished dead. But he overcame his pride, rose up, and began to make his way back home. Before he arrived home, he saw his father running toward him. The father's compassion was obvious, and the two embraced and kissed.

The restoration. Not content to simply welcome his son back into his home, the father began to restore everything the son had lost when he ran away from home. He clothed his son in the finest robes, had shoes custom-made for his weary feet, and slipped a finely crafted gold ring on his hand. He prepared a bounteous banquet and invited all his friends to celebrate his son's homecoming.

The prodigal's story is Jesus' imaginative retelling of the universal human story. Ours is the story of fantastic potential as God's children, crafted in God's image. It is the saga of our foul revolt and the longing that results from our loss. But ultimately, ours is a love story, a universal and deeply personal story of God's loving, transforming presence repeatedly extending forgiveness and restoration to all who will receive it.

Even though humanity rejected God in the garden, we need not feel unrelenting shame. In fact, John Milton describes our turn from God as the "fortunate fall"[27] because those who have lost something of great value can enjoy it more fully when they have found it again. God extends an offer to restore us to wellness. In the words of Julian of Norwich, "All shall be well and all shall be well and all manner of thing shall be well."[28] Such wellness flows from God's restorative presence, and is available to any who will declare God's supreme importance in their life. Our impoverished faith and culture bear witness to a culture in full *revolt* against God and a faith community satisfied with a *reunion* with God and future hope of heaven, but without the radical spiritual, intellectual, creative, relational, and moral wellness that comes through the *restoration* of God's image now. Our metamorphosis from fallen human to fully human enables us to transform culture and such wellness is a gift reserved for those who are serious about faith.

SERIOUS

The culturally savvy Christian is

serious about faith,

savvy about faith and culture,

and skilled in relating the two.

4

GOD'S DEEP PRESENCE

God created us for union with himself.
This is the original purpose of our lives.[1]
BRENNAN MANNING

While I was writing this book, people would sometimes ask what it was about. I would say something like this: "We live in a superficial popular culture, soulless, spiritually delusional, and driven by celebrity. Today's Christianity has taken on those same qualities. Because we are created in God's image, with spiritual, intellectual, creative, moral, and relational capacities, we will never be satisfied with a superficial, mindless culture or religion; the result is that religious and irreligious people alike are experiencing deep spiritual hunger."

Virtually everyone seemed to agree with my assessment of our situation. Many went on to energetically cite specific examples of superficiality in both popular culture and religion. Because this book doesn't just analyze the problem but offers a solution, I would then repeat what a wise man once said: "If we desire fresh, cool water, we must dig a deeper well. We will not find pure, refreshing water by digging many shallow wells." Twenty-first-century humans are masters of digging shallow wells spiritually, intellectually, and creatively, and it is killing us. We know that we must dig a deeper well toward God, but don't do it.

God: The Destination of True Spiritual Journey

After hearing me tell the story of the deeper well, one student wrote the following passage in his journal (and later gave me permission to publish it): "Deep faith is a tough issue for me. I was seriously wanting to avoid this conversation altogether. I hate talking about it because I know I don't have it. I've tried to convince myself many times that I had deep faith, and that it was just different than what most people consider it to be. But that's garbage. I know I don't have it and what's even worse is that I WANT IT. But that might be a lie too, because if I truly wanted it I would be searching for it. I don't search for it."

This young man has a problem. When he was a boy, he was told that his spiritual needs would be met if he received Jesus as his personal savior. He "became a Christian," yet is still unsatisfied. Today, whether his hungry soul turns to culture or to Christianity-Lite, his restless spirit will find the same spiritual, intellectual, and aesthetic impoverishment.

It hasn't always been this way. Throughout history, there have been Christians who addressed human longings authoritatively. Augustine said of God, "You have made us for yourself and our hearts are restless until they find their rest in you."[2] Pascal said only God is able to fill our "God-shaped vacuum."[3] These devout Christians were able to provide assistance to individuals exploring the spiritual life or seeking to deepen their Christian faith, because they actually knew God, drank personally from the deep, fresh springs of living water, and ate the sustaining bread of life. For most people, seeker and religious alike, those days are long gone; devout Christians full of God's presence are rare.

Sociologist Peter Berger has observed, "If anything characterizes modernity it is the loss of the sense of transcendence—of a reality that exceeds and encompasses our everyday affairs."[4] This is certainly true in our culture, and fifty years ago, A. W. Tozer warned of the same trend in the church, saying, "Worship is the missing jewel in modern evangelicalism. We're organized; we work; we have our agendas. We have almost everything, but there's one thing that the churches, even the gospel churches, do not have: that is the ability to worship. We are not cultivating the art of worship."[5] Tozer recognized that our worship only goes as deep as our knowledge of the holy. As a pastor, Tozer failed to implement any of the principles of church growth. He wasn't seeker-sensitive; he knew nothing of tailoring his message to felt needs; and he was the furthest thing from an entrepreneur. Thus, if he had wanted to be a pastor today, he might have had a hard time finding a church that would have him, and if he had pastored a church, in today's superficial culture, it likely would not have grown. However, in his time, Tozer did offer the one thing that mattered; he knew God. He practiced the daily presence of God and was qualified to help his parishioners find God, too. His church may not have grown in attendance, but the people in it grew deeply.

There is reason to believe that we need fewer entrepreneurial pastors and more pastors who actually know God deeply. If the next generation is any indication, our spiritually, intellectually, and aesthetically impoverished popular culture and the corresponding vacuousness of Christianity-Lite are taking their toll. Despite occasional glowing articles about teenage spirituality, research shows that teenagers are leaving religion and usually replacing it with nothing. A University of Chicago study reveals that in 1999, only 16 percent of eighteen-to-twenty-two-year-olds had ongoing regular contact with the faith of their family.[6] The signs of disinterest begin in high school or earlier. One of George Barna's studies concluded, "American teenagers are widely described as deeply religious individuals who have integrated their religious beliefs into their lifestyle and their thinking. . . . Neither their behavior nor their beliefs support the notions that they are deeply spiritual or truly committed to Christianity. Although their spirituality is more overt than that of their elders, teenagers are even less committed to Christianity than are the Baby Boomers."[7] The number one reason the younger generation leaves the church is sobering; *they never experienced God there*.

Historian Arnold Toynbee refers to "a time of troubles"[8] in discussing historical periods characterized by instability, rapid change, and signs of unraveling. We are in such an age, religiously and culturally; the roots of it are essentially spiritual, and for the most part, the Christian church is not positioned to do anything about it. Christianity-Lite lacks spiritual depth, knows little about deep union with God, and therefore is unable to resolve a spiritual crisis characterized by the loss of God and a longing for a deeper spirituality. Furthermore, Christianity-Lite has abandoned the mandate to build a richer intellectual and aesthetic culture on earth, choosing to settle for a mindless, insipid, imitative artistic subculture instead. Combined with spiritual superficiality, the abandonment of our mandate to build a rich culture severely limits contemporary Christianity's ability to participate in resolving the cultural crisis. Paradoxically, for seeker and believer alike, the way out of this spiritual and cultural malaise is the same. We need to rekindle our deep connection to the transcendent God.

Today, we hear a lot of talk about spiritual seeking. Popular culture believes that the destination is personal fulfillment, and the church generally teaches that the destination is heaven. In fact, our destination is God, and what we seek is not our inner self, nor do we seek some future bliss; what we seek is reunion with God now.

Ten Truths You Need to Know
About God's Deep Presence

I want to tell you some of what I have learned about experiencing God's presence, but I want to warn you that some of it—maybe *all* of it—may seem familiar. As you read the ten truths that follow, you may feel that you already know these basics of experiencing a deeper relationship with God. Yet most people who say they know these truths also say they lack a sense of deep union with God. I would suggest that either we are mistaken and do *not* know these truths, or we know them but have not applied or experienced them. This is partially because in the Western world, we believe we know something if we comprehend it factually or intellectually. We forget that Jesus was a Mediterranean Jew for whom knowledge was a holistic blend of head and heart. For Jesus, an individual's personal behavior and experience was the evidence of what they truly knew and understood. Do not read this chapter as a selection of intellectual facts to be mastered but rather as numinous truth to be intuited and experienced. In addition, remember G. K. Chesterton's quip: "The Christian ideal has not been tried and found wanting; it has been found difficult and left untried."

As I've tried to find an image that captures the true nature of digging a deeper well and experiencing God's presence in our lives now, I am drawn to the excitement and magic described in Christmas music as it celebrates the arrival of God's presence on earth. At Christmas, we thrill to the news that God has arrived in the person of Jesus. Today, every disciple of Jesus should experience the same enchanted elation with the arrival of Jesus in their life through the indwelling Holy Spirit.

"Joy to the World, the Lord Is Come"

The most joyous season in the church calendar is Christmas, when we celebrate Jesus' arrival on earth. That same spirit of enthusiasm and irrepressible merriment should characterize each of us who welcome God's presence into our life each day. Consider the lyrics of the classic carol "Joy to the World" as a celebration of God, whose presence in Jesus was announced in the season we celebrate as Christmas and whose presence in our lives today is secured through the indwelling Holy Spirit.

Joy to the World

Joy to the world, the Lord is come!
Let earth receive her King;
Let every heart prepare Him room,
And heaven and nature sing,
And heaven and nature sing,
And heaven, and heaven, and nature sing.

Joy to the world, the Savior reigns!
Let men their songs employ;
While fields and floods, rocks, hills, and plains
Repeat the sounding joy,
Repeat the sounding joy,
Repeat, repeat, the sounding joy.

No more let sins and sorrows grow,
Nor thorns infest the ground;
He comes to make His blessings flow
Far as the curse is found,
Far as the curse is found,
Far as, far as, the curse is found.

He rules the world with truth and grace,
And makes the nations prove
The glories of His righteousness,
And wonders of His love,
And wonders of His love,
And wonders, wonders, of His love.[9]

Those who are prepared to dig a deeper well will find God. The cool, fresh restorative springs of living water are found only in the deeper reaches. Only those who go deeper can experience the deep wellness that comes from reunion with God, and only deeply well people can produce a well culture. This is because the spiritual, intellectual, and creative health of a culture begins with the spiritual, intellectual, and creative health of the individuals who make it. Are we prepared to dig a deeper well? If we dig within the depths offered by Jesus, we will never reach the bottom, for the wellspring of our faith is the unfathomable, eternal God.

What does it mean to dig a deeper well? What does it mean to experience the deep presence of God?

"Let Every Heart Prepare Him Room": Three Preconditions for God's Deep Presence

1. God Is Present When We Hunger for Him. Hunger is a basic human condition, and hungering for God is our most basic hunger. Our appetites define us. Jesus said, "Blessed are those who hunger and thirst after righteousness, for they will be filled" (Matthew 5:6). In the same sermon, Jesus commanded his followers to seek first the kingdom of God and His righteousness (Matthew 6:33). This is reminiscent of King David's priorities: "One thing I asked of the Lord, that will I seek after: to live in the house of the Lord all the days of my life, to behold the beauty of the Lord, and to inquire in his temple" (Psalm 27:4).

In the story of the loaves and fishes, Jesus feeds the five thousand, and the size of the crowd increases. When he ups the ante by teaching that he will suffer and die, many disciples turn away and desert him. Jesus turns to the Twelve, his most devoted disciples, and asks, "Are you going to leave too?" The impetuous Peter yearns for the "bread of life" and the spiritual sustenance it offers. He is single-minded in his hunger for God, and he cries out, "Lord, where would we go? You alone have the words that give eternal life. We believe them and we know you are the Holy One of God" (John 6:68–69).

Our heart's capacity for God is infinite, and the measure of God's presence in our life is gauged to the size of our appetite for God. Those who seek God with passionate, reckless abandon will find that their appetite for God increases as God's presence increases.

2. God Is Present When We Invite Him to Reside in Our Lives. The Apostle John describes Jesus' entrance into our lives as a man standing at the door and knocking, waiting for an invitation to enter. He imagines Jesus standing at the door, saying, "Listen! I am standing at the door, knocking; if you hear my voice and open the door, I will come in to you and eat with you, and you with me" (Revelation 3:20). Evangelicals often use this verse to explain what happens when a person is first deciding whether to become a Christian. Actually, this verse describes Jesus' relationship with the church of Laodicea, where they were already Christians but were lukewarm in their spirituality, neither hot nor cold. Jesus is asking to enter their lives like a friend invited in for a meal and a warm, intimate event among friends.

In his book *My Heart—Christ's Home*, Robert Munger took this metaphor to another level, showing what it is like to invite Jesus to enjoy permanent residency in our whole life, using the analogy of a guest who is given unlimited access to every room in our home. Munger moves room by room: in the living room, we meet Christ daily; in the dining room, we examine our appetites, which control us; we even invite Christ into the secret closets in our lives, asking Christ to help us clean them out.[10] This image captures the holistic and comprehensive nature of Christ's presence in our life, reminding us that if God is not of central importance, God is of no importance at all.

Many irreligious people seek spiritual experience without seeking God—a ludicrous proposition. Today's Christians have done something just as ridiculous. Christians have reduced the gospel to a sales pitch in which becoming a Christian is achieved through "praying a simple prayer," instantly resulting in the person "becoming a Christian," which is defined as asking Jesus into your heart so that you can go to heaven when you die. Pastor A. W. Tozer rejected the distorted image of individuals deciding whether or not to accept Christ, while almighty God stands at the door, nervously tossing his hat from hand to hand, waiting for the "customer" to decide whether to invite him in or leave him standing on the porch. Tozer declared that the gospel is really about whether God our Creator and Savior will accept us. (He will.) The gospel is about God moving into our lives through the Holy Spirit as a resident, taking charge of our lives and then radically transforming us from the inside out through the Holy Spirit.

3. God Is Present When We Invite Him to Preside in Our Lives.

The third precondition of God's presence is our willingness to allow God not only to reside in our life but to *preside* over our life. In *The Divine Conspiracy*,[11] writer and philosopher Dallas Willard reminds us that Jesus never called anyone to become Christian; he called us to be disciples, which requires denying ourselves, taking up a cross, and following him.

If God is the destination of our journey, and if deep union with God through Jesus Christ and the indwelling Holy Spirit is the promise for those who seek and find God, how do we begin the process of going deeper in God? Theologian Karl Barth once said, "Tell me your Christology, and I will tell you who you are." Our lives will be radically changed or not changed, starting with our decision about who Jesus is. Who we believe Jesus is determines whether we will allow him to take the central place in our life. C. S. Lewis progressed from atheism (believing that God does not exist) to agnosticism (believing that God might exist but that there is insufficient evidence one way or another) to theism (believing in the existence of God). He then explored what various religions believe about God. It was when he fully examined the life of Jesus and the seemingly outrageous claims Jesus made about himself that Lewis decided to follow Jesus to God:

> People often say about Him: "I'm ready to accept Jesus as a great moral teacher, but I don't accept His claim to be God." That is the one thing we must not say. A man who was merely a man and said

the sort of things Jesus said would not be a great moral teacher. He would either be a lunatic—on a level with the man who says he is a poached egg—or else he would be the Devil of Hell. You must make your choice. Either this man was, and is, the Son of God: or else a madman or something worse. You can shut Him up for a fool, you can spit at Him and kill Him as a demon; or you can fall at His feet and call Him Lord and God. But let us not come with any patronizing nonsense about His being a great human teacher. He has not left that open to us. He did not intend to.[12]

Liar, lunatic, or Lord? If we choose to believe Jesus is lord, or ruler, we are accepting his right to rule over the universe and his authority over our life.

From the moment humans were expelled from the Garden of Eden, we have longed to get back to God. Rejecting God's rule resulted in the loss of our intimate relationship with Him, and our only way back to union with God is through yielding the authority of our lives back to God, then making Jesus lord of our life. Many people say, "Jesus is Lord," even in Christianity-Lite, where glib choruses heartily proclaim Jesus' supremacy. But the evidence of Christ's lordship is seen in our daily allegiances and in our transformed life, not in our words. What Richard Niebuhr observed in liberal Protestantism is now ominously descriptive of Christianity-Lite: "A God without wrath brought men without sin into a kingdom without judgment through the ministrations of a Christ without a cross."[13] Jesus' followers are loyal subjects who allow Jesus to preside as lord and king of their lives because he has earned our allegiance through his death on the cross.

"He Comes to Make His Blessings Flow": Three Blessings in the Nature of God's Presence

4. God's Essential Presence. In Chapter Three, I mentioned my interview with Robert Stone, whose departure from religion left an unfilled hole in his life. One line in the interview haunts me to this day: "You leave religion with a tremendous sense of liberation, and then years later, you discover that something really important is missing."[14] I don't think most people believe that God is essential to human life and experience. They don't think something really important is missing. How else do you explain the phenomenon of so-called Christians for whom God is on the periphery of their life, called on only in times of crisis or on special occasions? We have somehow gotten the idea that deep faith is for a special few monastics, people who are very serious about God, devoting their life to pursuing and pleasing God. We think such devotion is optional and definitely not expected of mere mortals like us!

This view overlooks the essential, core role that God plays in human existence. Knowing God and being known by God are the very reason we exist. If we fail to fulfill our reason for existence, we will not be well and will suffer what Kierkegaard described as a sickness unto death. This is an apt description of our situation today. Created to be God's image bearers, we are surrounded by a superficial popular culture and a version of Christianity that have forgotten our very purpose. We instinctively know that we need to go deeper in God, yet we fail to make space for God to go deeper in us. Visit even the most devout follower of God, secluded in the monastic life, someone whose every moment has been devoted to knowing God deeply, and they will confess that the more they know God, the deeper is their desire and capacity for God; the more they know God's indwelling presence, the more they want God to occupy them more fully.

I've spent a lot of time observing today's Christian enterprise. I see people obsessed with evangelism and discipleship, or passionate about the intellectual and artistic restoration of culture, or committed to engaging the culture politically. But for culturally savvy Christians, there is only one worthy obsession: God. Only God's deep spiritual, intelligent, creative presence in us will draw people to him. Only the presence of deeply well people will transform popular culture, and only by going deep in God can we be restored to deep wellness.

5. God's Completing Presence. God is essential to the fully human life, and God's presence makes us complete. Jesus told the parable of a vine and its branches, saying, "I am the true vine, and my Father is the vine grower. Abide in me as I abide in you. Just as the branch cannot bear fruit by itself unless it abides in the vine, neither can you unless you abide in me. I am the vine, you are the branches. Those who abide in me and I in them bear much fruit, because apart from me you can do nothing" (John 15:1–4). Any branch disconnected from the central vine will die, and apart from the vine, the branch is incomplete.

In the film *Jerry Maguire*, a sports agent falls in love with the fragile, trusting Dorothy, who is won over when he utters the following memorable lines: "We live in a cynical world. And we work in a business of tough competitors. I love you. You . . . complete me."[15] While humans can fill certain gaps in each other, there is only one being who truly completes us, and that is God. God is home, now and in the future. Giorgio de Chirico's painting "Nostalgia for the Infinite" finds its satisfaction in the infinite because God is the infinite one we seek. When we find God, we say, as writer Isak Dinesen did of Africa, "This is where I ought to be."[16] In God alone, the restless soul finds its rest, and only God fills the God-shaped vacuum to overflowing. Listen to the testimony of St. Teresa of Avila: "Let nothing disturb you. Let nothing frighten you. All things are changing. God alone is changeless. Patience attains the good. One who has God lacks nothing. God alone fills our needs."[17]

6. God's Mystical Presence. Theologian Karl Rahner predicted, "In the days ahead, you will either be a mystic who has experienced God, or nothing at all."[18] When Jesus came to earth, his purpose was to restore us to full and complete intimacy with God and to restore God to the central place in our life; through accomplishing this task, Jesus would glorify God: "I glorified you by finishing the work that you gave me, by giving them eternal life; and this is eternal life, that they may know you, the only true God, and Jesus Christ whom you have sent" (John 17:4).

Christians often confuse eternal life with a future life in heaven, but Jesus said that the kingdom of God is *now*, offering us intimacy with God comparable to the intimacy he experienced with God the Father while he was on earth: "I in them and you in me, that they may be completely one" (John 17:23). When we are reunited with God, we enjoy divine presence in the present while looking forward to a more complete union in the future, when we go to the place with the Father that Jesus has prepared for us.

Only union with God satisfies and restores our deeper longings. When asked "Why does life seem like great weariness, vanity and striving after wind?" Orthodox Christian writer Frederica Mathewes-Green replies, "Because although God knows us, we do not know God very well. We are vacant inside, deafened by the continual wind of our emptiness, and only God's presence can fill us. Yet we fail to know God well. Sometimes this is because we don't want to know Him and sometimes because we don't know how."[19] I can hear her prayerful refrain: "Lord Jesus have mercy on me."

How do we find our way homeward to God? Jesus' answer was unambiguous: "I am the Way to the Father" (John 14:6). To convey how he reunites us with God, Jesus painted vivid and colorful images to help us visualize our new life in union with God: in God, we find springs of living water, the sustenance of daily bread, light in darkness, truth, the guidance of a shepherd leading his sheep, abundant life beginning now, and, after death, a resurrection that extends this new life into eternity.

Because Jesus is one with the Father, our union with God is often described as mystical union with Christ. The Apostle Paul refers to this mystical indwelling of Christ 164 times! Union with God is the normative experience to which every follower of Jesus is called; it is not reserved for super saints or the exceptional few. Jesus explained that he would be present in each of his disciples, even after his ascension. The Apostle Paul promised the same, saying,

"Christ *in* you is the hope of glory!" (Colossians 1:27; italics added). You may think of yourself as a rationalist for whom faith is an intellectual proposition; you may be the furthest thing from a mystic; and you may be frightened by those who claim ecstatic experiences, but it is obvious that the indwelling of Christ is an essential, mystical experience expected of every follower of Jesus. Jesus didn't call us to know about God, he called us to know and experience God directly.

Jesus explained that he would be present in every disciple through his indwelling Holy Spirit. He promised that when he returned to the Father, he would not leave us comfortless but would send the Holy Spirit, "who will dwell with you and *be in you*" (John 14:17; italics added). The Holy Spirit, the spirit of truth, will "guide us into all truth," "teach us all things," "bring to remembrance the things Jesus has said," and "bear witness" about Jesus (John 14–16). Do you know God's presence intellectually or experientially? Annie Dillard experienced reunion with God in Christ and described it this way: "Something broke and something opened. I filled up like a new wineskin."[20]

"The Glories of His Righteousness": Three Wonders of God's Love

7. *God's Life-Giving Presence.* In the film *The Sixth Sense*, a little boy announces, "I see dead people." Without God's presence, we are the dead people. God's presence is the only reason that we can experience life. If the roots of our discontent were simply idolatry, we could, in theory, resolve this problem by restoring God to a central place in our individual lives. Unfortunately, ours is a more serious, even life-threatening problem. On the day Adam and Eve ate the forbidden fruit, God warned that they would die, which we have come to understand was a twofold death, physical and spiritual. Adam and Eve's spiritual death began instantly, in the very moment they rebelled. Years later, the Apostle Paul taught early followers of Jesus that because of sin, theirs and ours, each human suffers a spiritual sickness that leads to death (Ephesians 2:1).

This spiritual sickness unto death is the source of our deep unwellness. In *The Lord of the Rings*, J.R.R. Tolkien uses the tragic figure of Gollum to illustrate the death and dying process associated with idolatry. Obsessed with the very ring that is causing his illness, Gollum, through his personal deterioration, depicts the effects of spiritual sickness. Who can forget Gollum's sad, pathetic, haunting whispers as he pleads for his idolized ring: "precious, . . . my precious." Anyone looking at Gollum's emaciated body wasting away can see that his obsession with the ring is killing him, yet he can't give up his powerful affection. When Tolkien read this story aloud, he hissed like a snake when Gollum said the word "precious," an audible mimicking of the serpent in the Garden of Eden. Satan promises well-being to those who displace God, but Satan is a liar, capable of making us sick but not well.

The cross is central to our personal story, because Jesus offers to bring spiritually dead people to life through the cross and through the resurrection by which he signified that he had conquered death. The Apostle Paul goes so far as to say, "If anyone is in Christ, he is a new creation" (2 Corinthians 5:17). The cross means that our old human nature will die; the resurrection announces that we can get a fresh start. Spiritually dead people cannot produce life, but Jesus offers restoration. Just as seeds are destined to produce certain outcomes, the kind of seed determining whether it will produce an oak tree or maple, those in the lineage of Adam and Eve, according to Judeo-Christian theology, are destined to bear the marks of the fall. We cannot become "fully human" as God's image bearers through our own efforts.

Through Jesus, God introduced a dramatic plot twist into the human story. Jesus is fully God and fully human and does not bear the marks of the fall; therefore, he is able to provide a new start for the human race. Unlike a run-down house needing a simple remodel, our only solution is to tear down the old house of our life and start all over by building a brand-new life. Jesus gives us that opportunity because he is "the image of the invisible God, the firstborn of all creation. . . . He is the beginning, the firstborn from the dead" (Colossians 1:15). C. S. Lewis describes the significance of Jesus' role in our transformation: "In Christ a new kind of man appeared; and the new kind of life which began in him is to be put into us. . . . Jesus Christ is the new seed from which new human life may spring. Jesus did not come to make us better; he came to make us new."[21]

New people are alive with God's presence because they sink deep roots. Jesus told a parable about a farmer planting seeds. Some of the seeds fell along the path and never took root. Other seeds fell on rocky ground and began to grow, but withered away when the sun came up. Other seeds fell among the thorns and were eventually choked out by the weeds. Finally, some seeds fell on good soil and grew to be healthy plants. Jesus used this parable to teach an important lesson about spiritual life. It is not enough for the earth to receive the seed; healthy plants grow deep roots in fertile soil. Jesus warned that many who receive him are like shallow soil in which seeds will never take root. Some will hear the word and receive it with joy, but will fall away due to tribulation. Others will hear the word, "but the cares of the world and the deceitfulness of riches and the desires for other things will enter in and choke the word" (Mark 4:3–19). God's presence brings life; deep roots sustain our new life.

8. God's Nurturing Presence. Jesus used many metaphors to convey God's nurturing presence in our lives. "I am the bread of life. Whoever comes to me will never be hungry, and whoever believes in me will never be thirsty" (John 6:35). Jesus said to the woman drawing water from the well, "If you knew the gift of God, and who it is that is saying to you, 'Give me a drink,' you would have asked him, and he would have given you living water."

Jesus was fond of the image of sheep and their shepherd, and he used it often. "I am the good shepherd. I know my own and my own know me. The good shepherd lays down his life for the sheep" (John 10:11, 14). This same imagery was used of God by King David, a man after God's own heart, who penned our twenty-third Psalm. In it, David describes the intimate participation of God in his daily life. David's God is deeply personal: "The Lord is my shepherd, I shall not want." David's God is present in every activity of his daily life: "He makes me lie down in green pastures. He leads me beside still waters. He restores my soul. Even though I walk through the valley of the shadow of death, I will fear no evil, for you are with me; your rod and your staff, they comfort me. You prepare a table before me in the presence of my enemies; you anoint my head with oil; my cup overflows."

These rich metaphors convey God's intimate, personal presence, which nurtures us, restores and feeds us, guides and protects us. In an age when every soul is battered, relationships are bruised or broken, and spirits are without hope, God's presence offers healing, restoration, and hope.

9. *God's Good, True, and Beautiful Presence.* God is the source of goodness in human life. Most of us think of ourselves as good people who on rare occasions do bad things, generally concluding that we are better than most people and therefore OK with God. Unfortunately, the test of how we are with God does not start by asking what we have done; it starts by asking whom or what we love and whether God is and always has been of supreme importance to us.

One time, a very religious young man came to Jesus and asked, "Good teacher, what must I do to inherit eternal life?" Jesus said, "Why do you call me good? No one is good except God alone." After Jesus reminded him of the Ten Commandments, the young man said, "Teacher, all these I have kept from my youth." At this point, the author of the text inserts a very interesting comment: "And Jesus, looking at him, *loved him*." It is likely that the purpose of this insertion is to acknowledge to readers what all the disciples knew, which is that nobody has kept all the commandments and, furthermore, that Jesus had just told the young man none but God is good! Instead of quibbling with the young man about which particular sin he had committed, Jesus went to the heart of the matter by testing whether God was of supreme importance to the young man. Jesus said, "You lack one thing; sell all that you have and give it to the poor and you will have treasure in heaven; and come, follow me." The story ends with the observation that the young man was "disheartened by the saying." "He went away sorrowful, for he had great possessions" (Mark 10:17–22). Our goodness flows from God's presence taking its rightful place as central in our life.

God in us is the source of truth, a rare commodity these days. In the 1990s, I interviewed Marlo Morgan, a midwestern woman who, in her fifties, had found that her life lacked excitement. She claims that she made a trip to Australia, where aborigines allegedly kidnapped her, stripped her, and issued her a loincloth. As they wandered in the desert, they entrusted her with 30,000 years' worth of ancient wisdom. She returned and told her story in a book titled *Mutant Message Down Under,* which she eventually sold to a publisher as nonfiction. When the publisher couldn't verify parts of her story, they informed her of their plans to publish it as fiction. I asked her about this, and she told me it didn't matter to her because "what is true for me is true for me, and what is true for you is true for you!" Her response reminds me of the cartoon in which Ziggy stands in a bookstore in front of three bookshelves. One says "Fiction," the second says "Nonfiction," and the third says "Not Sure." After revelations of fabrications in James Frey's *A Million Little Pieces* and ludicrous claims by Dan Brown that his novel *The Da Vinci Code* is based on accurate documentation, we are more aware than ever of the need for and importance of truth. Jesus said, "I am the truth" and described Satan this way: "There is no truth in him. When he lies, he speaks according to his own nature, for he is a liar and the father of lies" (John 8:44). An honest and true person is a priceless gem in this age of equivocation. I recall a survey a few years ago that concluded that the vast majority of us tell some little white lie almost every day. A life lived transparently and truthfully attracts attention by sheer virtue of its contrast to a culture marked by insincerity and chronic deceit. When Jesus arrived on this planet, people were amazed because he spoke as one having authority (Matthew 7:29). When he arrives in our lives, the one who said, "I am the way, the truth, and the life" (John 14:6) brings into the core of our being the authenticity and authority of truth as a way of life. God is the source of truth.

God is the source of the beautiful. My grandmother was an imaginative Bible teacher who generated extra income for her family as a seamstress. Her marvelous, detailed, well-crafted work meant that she was sought out for custom work even when she was in her eighties. She herself was a tall, dignified, elegant woman who, because of her skills, always dressed fashionably. In the kitchen, she took great care to prepare home-cooked meals that were not only nourishing but colorful and attractive. I remember her commenting about the rich contrast of apple pie with a deep orange slice of sharp cheddar cheese. When she died, I was given her Bible and discovered in it her favorite verse from the Bible: "And let the beauty of the Lord our God be upon us: and establish thou the work of our hands upon us; yea, the work of our hands establish thou it" (Psalm 90:17 KJV). Those who discover the beauty flowing from the Great Artist will create beauty themselves.

On the fifth anniversary of the September 11 attacks, I was transported into God's good, true, and beautiful presence by the intellectual, spiritual, and creative collaboration of Gabriel Fauré and soloist Jeanette Thompson at St. George's in NYC. As her glorious soprano voice brought to life "Pie Jesu" from Fauré's *Requiem*, art, craft, spirit, soul combined as Fauré's apt lyrics flowed into our hearts: "Merciful Lord Jesus, grant them rest, rest everlasting." Overwhelmed by the beauty, truth, and goodness of the moment, I asked myself, Why would we exchange this rich bounty for the emaciated spiritual, intellectual, and artistic imposters that pass as art and music today? Before we can create a good, true, and beautiful culture, we must each again experience the good, true, and beautiful in our own life, and this comes only through God.

"He Rules the World with Truth and Grace; Let Heaven and Nature Sing": The Eternal Now and Forever

10. God's Permanence. God is not just central in our life. God is the ruler of the universe; He rules the world, heaven and nature. And the reign of God is eternal. The writer of Hebrews reports that Jesus says "I will never leave you or forsake you" (Hebrews 13:5). David's twenty-third Psalm extends God's provision and care beyond the grave and into eternity: "Surely goodness and mercy will follow me all the days of my life, and I will dwell in the house of the Lord forever."

When I think of the permanence of God's presence, I think of two memorable hospital visits that I made to visit dying patients. One was to Roger, a man in his eighties. As I entered his room, the nurse told me that she did not expect him to live much longer, so I was surprised to see him sit up and start talking as I approached his bed. This aging spiritual man who, moments before, had been in a comatose condition was suddenly animated, grinning broadly, pointing upward, and saying excitedly, "I'm going home!" And he did. Immediately after his enthusiastic, smiling outburst, he laid his head down and died in my presence.

A few months later, I visited Phyllis, a woman who was dying of cancer. She was in extreme pain and quite agitated, her entire body shaking violently. Her distressed husband, Jack, asked for more medication, but the nurse said there was nothing they could do. I asked Jack whether I could pray with her, and I took her hand as it waved erratically in the air. I prayed the twenty-third Psalm, and something amazing happened. As I reached the sentence "Even though I walk through the valley of the shadow of death, I will fear no evil, for you are with me; your rod and your staff, they comfort me," Phyllis became completely still and calm. She died a few weeks later, but I'll never forget the experience that afternoon, when a woman found relief and hope in God's comforting and eternal presence, now.

"No More Let Sin and Sorrow Grow; Repeat the Sounding Joy"

God's deep, abiding presence is available to us, yet we say that we seek but do not find. As an observer of America's popular and religious culture, I find it curious that the absence of the deeply spiritual is a consistent theme. If 82 percent are seeking, I wonder why so few are finding? Why do we think seeking without finding is acceptable or even admirable? Jesus told many parables about seeking, but the seeker always found something. The woman found the lost coin; the shepherd found the lost sheep; the prodigal son and his father were reunited. The rich presence of God will only be found by those who seek with the aim of truly finding. Today, most of what we call spiritual searching is in fact a sham and a vain exercise better described as pseudo-seeking. We seek and do not find because we seek a God who will improve our life and make us happy without making any demands on us. Author Rick Moody told me that in his spiritual journey, "All this talk about the spiritual was kind of vague and squishy,"[22] so he returned to the disciplines and community provided by religion. C. S. Lewis confessed that prior to his conversion, he was not truly seeking God, adding, "Amiable agnostics will talk cheerfully about 'man's search for God.' To me, as I then was, they might as well have talked about the mouse's search for the cat!"[23] The wise person knows that God is like a consuming fire, intent on purifying us like gold passed through heat and fire.

We seek and do not find because our superficial culture trivializes all that it touches, including our ideas of God and the spiritual. Euphemisms like "the man upstairs," vagaries like "higher power," print ads for a product named "Eternity," a TV ad for Direct TV announcing that "someone up there is watching you," a commercial for a resort claiming that it is "like heaven without the long-term commitment," or any one of hundreds of inane interviews with celebrities about their latest faddish dalliance with the "god in me"; all these shallow glosses on God and the spiritual obscure what is truly involved in the deep inner wellness available through the pursuit of a transcendent yet imminent deity.

We seek and do not find because we are aimless seekers, not pilgrims willing to pay the price to reach our destination. At one point, the working title of this book was "Pilgrims Through This Barren Land," a title that some of my friends and advisers found too dark and negative. I like the word *barren* because it conveys the spiritual impoverishment of popular culture and religion in our so-called Christian nation. I like the word *pilgrim* because it touches on the metaphorical contrast between today's superficial seeker and the more substantial image of the pilgrim. Traditionally, a pilgrim is a traveler on a purposeful journey with a destination, someone who is focused, prepared, attentive, seeking something that matters deeply, improving by enduring and overcoming tests, progressing by meeting challenges on the way. Mircea Eliade, an expert on world religions, reminds us that "every real existence reproduces the 'Odyssey' and [provides a] chance to become the 'new Ulysses.'"[24] Each of us must decide whether we will embrace a real existence by undertaking a rigorous pilgrimage toward wellness or settle into a pseudo-existence by being satisfied with the shallowness and spiritual impoverishment of the typical life.

The well soul is available to the pursuer of God's presence, but not to the halfhearted, superficial seeker. God responds to pilgrims who seek the hidden meaning of their wanderings, undergoing the initiation trials and obstacles on the journey. The pilgrim seeks the center, the warmth of home and hearth, in God. And the true seeker will find all that he or she needs in the deep presence of God.

5

GOD'S TRANSFORMING PRESENCE

Theology has to stop explaining the world
and start transforming it.[1]

JOSE MIGUEL BONINO, ARGENTINE THEOLOGIAN

Like any child of the 1960s, there was a time when I wanted to change the world; now, I am content to simply ask God to change me.

As a young follower of Jesus, I was taught that Jesus had commanded his disciples to go into the world and make disciples. It is true. He did. However, I began to notice that while many mission-driven, transform-the-world types were passionate about making a difference in the world and effecting change in other people's lives, they often failed to invest the same energy in transforming their own life. When they did make personal adjustments, it was often motivated by their desire to be more effective in their world changing. It began to occur to me that if the God of the universe has truly taken up residence in us, radical changes in us should be inescapable. No gardener takes over a new plot and doesn't remove the weeds, prune the trees, and introduce and nurture new, more appropriate, and beautiful plants. It also occurred to me that as a world changer, Jesus was not very strategic. He arrived in a small, somewhat inconsequential country, spent three years with twelve uninfluential men and a broader gathering of unknown men and women, and oh, by the way, changed the world. I decided that either Jesus was doing something wrong or contemporary world changers were.

All the big programs we designed and money we raised and strategies we employed to change the world were actually rather ineffective, and more significantly, they often satisfied our type A drives but not our souls. I witnessed and participated in numerous campaigns designed to "win the world for Christ," which were executed by weary, ragged workaholics who traveled the globe but had no time for their own families or the neighbor across the street. One time, in a prayer meeting with a bunch of my well-intentioned, mission-motivated friends, a variation on the question in Mark 8:36 ran through my head: "What does it profit a man if he gain the whole world and lose his own family?"

The more I thought about it, the more I realized that Jesus did not come to earth to change the world. Jesus came to earth to do the will of the Father, which in Jesus' case meant a local ministry of healing, teaching, preaching, and, eventually, crucifixion. Jesus' obedience was by way of a short life followed by a brutal death, burial, and resurrection. Jesus' daily obedience to God's will gave birth to the global movement that bears his name today.

I came to realize that my desire to do something grandiose for God was driven more by a grand global vision to "win the world" than my own inner transformation or a sense of God's will for me personally. I began to see that God wanted to dwell in me and change me. I also began to see that God wanted to restore everything about me to an expression of God's image—spiritual, intelligent, creative, moral, and relational. The word *well* comes from a root word meaning "whole." Compartmentalized people—those who develop capacity in one area of their life to the exclusion of others—aren't well. I know a violinist who has developed her creative and aesthetic abilities but is a moral scoundrel; I know of NBA players who are illiterate; and I know mission-driven Christians who want to win the world for Christ but ignore their family in the process of doing it. I came to realize that God didn't want my partial transformation; He wanted to make me a completely well person. I saw that God wasn't interested in transforming me so that I could transform the world; God wanted to transform me so that

I could become fully human. Transforming the world is the by-product, not the aim of being fully human, and it only occurs when transformed individuals seek and do God's will as Jesus did.

Jesus was able to know and do God's will because God was central in his life and, as a result, he was not conformed to the religious or irreligious culture around him. Jesus thought differently about virtually everything and then stood out from the crowd as the embodiment of the winsome human being who is firing on all cylinders, spiritually, intellectually, creatively, morally, and relationally. Our theology textbooks say it all: Jesus was fully God and fully human. Jesus is the definition of what it means to be fully human.

God's transforming presence will change us, not so we can transform the world, but so we can experience God's presence more deeply and be restored to God's image more completely. When fully human people do God's will, they move into the neighborhood as a loving, transforming presence, like Jesus did. If there is to be a renaissance of faith and culture, and I pray that there will be, it will be a by-product of God's transforming presence in our individual lives. Cultural enrichment proceeds from enriched individuals, and there is but one aim for our transformation: *God intends to transform us from fallen humans to fully human*.

Jesus: The Source of Our Transformation

Becoming fully human requires restoring God to the central place in our life and then allowing God to transform us into the spiritual, thinking, creating, relational, and moral creatures we were meant to be. God is the path to the peak of Abraham Maslow's familiar pyramid depicting the hierarchy of human needs; moving beyond our physiological needs and our needs for esteem and belonging, we find ourselves actualized, learning and creating at the highest levels of our human potential.[2] When God is central and our full humanity is developed for God's pleasure, we find ourselves more fulfilled than we would have had self-glory or personal gratification been our aim.

The gospel, the good news, can be stated this way: in Christ, God has begun to restore all that unraveled in the fall, restoring God's image and making us fully human. Though born in the lineage of the fallen Adam, those who follow Jesus can be "born again" in the lineage of Jesus. This is what the Apostle Paul meant when he said, "If anyone is in Christ, there is a new creation; everything old has passed away; see, everything has become new" (2 Corinthians 5:17). Jesus did not come to make us better; he came to make us new.

Fully Human: The Goal of Our Transformation

In today's Christianity-Lite, salvation often refers to the reunion we experience with God when we "become a Christian." Experiencing forgiveness, being welcomed into God's fellowship, and receiving the promise of our future perfection in heaven are no small matters, but they are only the first part of the story. Art historian and L'Abri theologian Hans Rookmaaker reminds us of a fuller story when he makes the jarring claim that "Jesus did not come to make us Christian; Jesus came to make us fully human."[3] There are hints of what this means in the story of the prodigal son. You'll recall that in Jesus' parable, the son was reunited with the father (analogous to "becoming Christian"), but that was only the prelude to the next part of the story— the prodigal's restoration. After their reunion, the father restores the son to his pre-rebellion condition, putting new shoes on his feet, placing a ring on his finger, and preparing a celebratory banquet.

Sometimes we focus on the good news of the reunion with the Father but then neglect the holistic, restorative transformation that is supposed to follow. In this reductionist scenario, the prospective follower of Jesus "accepts Jesus," receives forgiveness for sin, makes a commitment to live a morally upright life, and is then charged with the task of helping other people become Christians. This emphasis on good, heaven-bound people taking on the task of evangelizing (telling others the good news) is a good start, but it is an incomplete version of the purposeful life. The only way we can please God is by fulfilling the purpose for which we were originally created. God's original purpose is not our salvation or the evangelization of others; it is that we glorify God by reflecting God's image through expression of the spiritual, intelligent, creative, moral, and relational capacities uniquely imprinted on humans. This creation mandate has never been rescinded.

Genesis 1 and 2 tell the story of God as creator and of humans made in God's image. Genesis 3 tells the story of human rebellion and reveals God as our loving savior. The Christianity we see today often focuses on God as a savior for fallen humans and emphasizes reunion with God and the transformation of our moral and relational qualities but overlooks the importance of the creator God's intention to restore His image in us. This truncation has produced a Christianity that is generally disinterested in art and the mind and that emphasizes morality and evangelism. A more complete view of salvation starts with the creation story, in which we learn that because humans are made in God's image, we possess intrinsic intellectual, spiritual, and artistic qualities. In this holistic gospel, saving us means that God intends to revitalize our capacity to again reflect His image, starting now and into eternity.

Any Christianity that knows God as savior but not as creator will produce Christians who are less than fully human, as will any Christianity that knows God as creator but not as savior. God is not content with such limitations on our transformation. Transformation without attentiveness to the mind, spirit, and creativity is like the prodigal story without the banquet! God intends to radically change us into prime examples of full humanity, because only by becoming fully human can we bring glory to God. As St. Irenaeus said, "The glory of God is man fully alive!"[4]

Transformation to Full Humanity: The Process

Jesus' resurrection from death was miraculous, as is our rebirth from spiritual death in the lineage of Adam to spiritual life in the lineage of Jesus. Once we are spiritually alive, God intends another miracle, our transformation from fallen human to fully human. The Greek word for "transformation" is *metamorphosis*, exemplified by the process of a caterpillar entering the cocoon and exiting as a completely different thing, a butterfly. The Apostle Paul articulated the radical path to our metamorphosis: (1) present your body as a living sacrifice; (2) do not be conformed to this world; (3) renew your mind (Romans 12:1–3). The Apostle Paul teaches that these three actions are the path to our transformation into disciples who can know God's will. We are told to follow in the steps of Jesus, who exemplified each of these qualities and is the only human to ever perfectly understand and do God's will.

Restore God to the Central Place in Your Life by Presenting Your Body as a Living Sacrifice

"God is of no importance unless He is of supreme importance," writes Abraham Heschel.[5] Our transformation begins when we decide that the central purpose of our life is to please God and, consequently, subordinate our will to His. In the 1800s, Danish philosopher Søren Kierkegaard observed the superficiality of the Danish church and culture and sounded a clarion call for a single-minded commitment on the part of true believers. In his book *Purity of Heart Is to Will One Thing*, he included this prayer: "Oh, God that gives both the beginning and the completion, may You early, at the dawn of day, give to the young man the resolution to will one thing. As the day wanes, may You give to the old man a renewed remembrance of his first resolution; that the first may be like the last, the last like the first, in possession of a life that has willed only one thing."[6]

What does it mean to will one thing? Jesus said that the initial requirement for becoming his disciple is to deny yourself. Similarly, the Apostle Paul taught that our transformation begins by presenting our bodies as a living sacrifice. Paul is using what was at the time a common image of ritual animal sacrifices to show how our metamorphosis to full humanity begins with the daily act of dying to self, laying our life down as a sacrifice is laid on the altar in a religious ceremony. By presenting our body to God, we acknowledge the death of the self's rule and its replacement with God's central rule over our entire life, body, mind, personality, and will. This act is an appropriate response to Paul's admonition that "you are not your own; you've been bought with a price" (1 Corinthians 6:20).

In a self-oriented culture, yielding to God is foreign and profoundly countercultural, yet for the person pursuing deep faith, knowing and doing God's will must be his or her first desire. Jesus modeled this practice during his time on earth, saying his will was to do the will of the Father. He expects no less from us, even teaching us to pray "Father, your will be done on earth as it is in heaven" (Matthew 6:10). It is impossible to nurture God's presence or to experience a personal transformation to our full humanity without acknowledging God's centrality in each moment of each hour of each day.

When God is central, our life can again be aglow with God's presence. Think of an old kerosene lamp that, once lit, sends out bright rays of amber light. God fuels the glow of human life; when God is present and at the center of our life and when we are listening for and doing God's will, we become the light in darkness described by Jesus. The further God moves from the center of our life, the dimmer becomes the light of God's image that is reflected through us. When John the Baptist encountered Jesus, he grasped the supremacy of Jesus immediately and said, "He must increase, that I may decrease" (John 3:30). This should be our prayer today.

Stop Conforming to the World

The transcendentalists had a saying: "What lies behind us and what lies ahead of us are tiny matters compared to what lies within us."[7] I like to paraphrase this by saying, "What lies behind us and what lies ahead of us are tiny matters compared to *who* lives within us." God is all-powerful and dwells within us, and God is the source of immeasurable hope. As the Apostle John said, "He who is in you is greater than he who is in the world" (1 John 4:4). But the Apostle

Paul also warned that to know and do God's will requires dealing with the external forces all around us and therefore commands that we "no longer conform to the world" (Romans 12:2).

Asking us to not conform to the world is like asking a fish to swim without water. This world is the ocean we've swum in all our lives; it is all we know. Yet Jesus sent us into the world to replicate his loving, transforming presence and said that our presence would be transformative, like salt and light. Both of these metaphors capture the image of Jesus' followers as a transforming presence wherever they go; light pierces darkness, and salt adds flavor and preserves food. Jesus also recognized that this world that we are to transform also threatens to transform us and warned that some people who set out to follow him will eventually be lured away by the "cares of the world and deceitfulness of riches" (Luke 8:14).

Jesus' disciples warned us of the difficulties of being in the "midst of a crooked and twisted" generation that is pursuing the desires of the flesh, desires of the eyes, and the pride of possessions (1 John:2:16). The Apostle John bluntly commanded Jesus' followers not to love the world or the things in the world, warning that this world is still under the power of "the evil one" (1 John 5:19). Despite the evil one's threat to our faith, Jesus did not want us to withdraw from the world, and he specifically asked God *not* to remove us from the world but to protect us from the evil one while we are still in this world (John 17:15). Renegotiating our relationship with the world and its systems of thinking and behaving is one of the biggest challenges we face when we seek to become fully human and reflect God's image.

Each generation is exposed to a dominant system and way of thinking that defines their era—the zeitgeist, or spirit of the age. As we've seen, ours is an age of the enthroned self, devoid of absolute truth or a binding morality. Our dominant culture is spiritually delusional, consumeristic, and intellectually and aesthetically superficial, and this impoverishment has even overwhelmed the church, distorting a once-deep faith into a shallow, superficial Christianity-

Lite. None of us should be deceived into thinking we are immune to the seductive spirit of our age. Our minds have been squeezed into the mold of the thought patterns, beliefs, values, and behaviors of our fallen culture. They are the old familiar ways, and though they are utterly at odds with God's elevating purpose for our life, we are blind to them, vulnerable to them, and even addicted to them.

Our transformation requires a deliberate decision to stop conforming to our culture's zeitgeist. While there are many worthy elements in our culture, our nonconformity must start with the assumption that certain aspects of both the faith and the culture around us are at odds with God's will. This means developing the habit of consciously evaluating our faith and culture and resisting those that are incompatible with God's expectations for our life. It also means changing our daily practices to reflect the priority of pursuing God first and fully. If we spend hours consuming popular culture each day and only a few minutes nurturing our spirit, how can we expect to avoid conforming to the thought patterns of our age?

Nowhere is our nonconformity more necessary than in our relationship with popular culture, which, as we've seen, is intentionally calibrated to make us conform. As we resist conformity, we will become highly sensitized to culture, recognizing the superficial, mindless diversions and seeing through the shallowness of celebrity. Attempts to reduce us to unproductive consumers will be obvious and odious. We will wake up to the impoverished aesthetic in faith and culture, developing a new appetite for the highest and best, spiritually, intellectually, creatively, relationally, and morally.

Anyone who chooses to resist conformity is inevitably launched on an exciting adventure, but those who take the road less traveled will also find that it can be a lonely path. You may discover, as I have, that very few people are actually determined to resist conformity while also pursuing the creation of a richer culture. Over time, you will discover the work of thoughtful creatives and find among them a remnant of Jesus' followers. You will pursue God in the company of such friends.

Jesus' call to self-denial is similar to Paul's challenge to present our bodies to God as a living sacrifice. Once we lay our life down and begin the reckless pursuit of God, we have set our life's course on the path of nonconformity. Taking the road less traveled is the equivalent of taking up your cross, for if you truly follow Jesus, you will experience what he did. You will seem too irreligious to your religious friends ("Why is Jesus partying with the drunkards and prostitutes?") and too religious for your irreligious friends ("Why is Jesus obsessed with God?").[8] You will become, as I explain in my book *Too Christian, Too Pagan*, too Christian for your irreligious friends and too irreligious for your Christian friends.

Nonconformity is the right and good path, but it requires a death of self and a steadfast commitment like that of Japan's kamikaze pilots in World War II, who each received and participated in a complete funeral service prior to leaving on their mission. One of my friends has a saying: "The only good Christian is a dead Christian!" (It gets a great laugh when delivered to people who have been antagonized by Christian misbehavior!) However, he is not referring to the Christian's physical death but to the death of the old self so that Christ's life in that Christian becomes preeminent in creating a new person. This is one aspect of what the Apostle Paul meant when he said, "For me to live is Christ, to die is gain" (Philippians 1:21).

Renew Your Mind

The caterpillar is disappearing, and the butterfly is beginning to spread its wings, but there is yet another step in our process of becoming fully human: "Be transformed by the renewal of your mind" (Romans 12:2). A renewed mind helps us reject our old ways and discover and embrace the new and richer ways of one who is fully human. As you might suspect, your mind has been so affected by the world's way of thinking that God plans to erase its hard drive and install a brand-new, completely different operating system!

Immersion in today's highly influential, mindless, soulless, spiritually delusional popular culture has resulted in our high literacy in popular culture and low literacy in our faith. Most of us cannot recognize the contrast between the ideas and values that dominate our culture and those consistent with our faith, because our primary education has been in the ideas and values of our age and we remain illiterate about Jesus' expectations for our life.

As we've already seen, many of today's cultural ideas and values have their recent origin in the 1960s, but in many ways, the rebellion of the sixties is just a modern version of the original revolt in the Garden of Eden. The credo of the sixties rippled through all of human history from that legendary garden, where our ancestors declared, "We are the supreme arbiter of all things. There is no truth; there is only what is true for us in a given situation. All authority must be questioned." By Noah's day, the "thoughts of humans were evil only continually" (Genesis 6:5). In the first century, the Apostle Paul observed "futile thinking by people who think they are wise, but whose minds are completely debased" (Romans 1:28) and who were pseudo-intellectual rebels who "knowingly exchange the truth of God for a lie" (Romans 1:25). These descriptions are eerily accurate depictions of today's age. Unless we commit ourselves to the renewal of our minds, we may easily be lulled into breezy acceptance of Eden's values and behaviors, for they are routinely parroted in today's popular culture. Those born since the 1960s are particularly vulnerable because their minds have been shaped and formed in the amniotic fluid of popular culture. Post-sixties generations have been weaned from childhood on a spiritually confused, intellectually vacuous diet of superficiality and untruths, worked over completely by technology, served a soulless aesthetic, bombarded by biblically illiterate packages of sound bites, and subtly encouraged to be consumers rather than creators.

After years upon years of filling our minds with words and images conveying this age's values and behaviors, to become a completely new person requires not just rethinking everything but a complete and radical change of mind. Such renewal of the mind is not instantaneous; it requires time, patience, and a devotion to study and prayer. There are no shortcuts. Even Jesus, though literate in the Scriptures as a young man, had no public ministry until he was thirty. The highly educated Apostle Paul experienced a dramatic conversion but then disappeared for twelve years of study, reflection, and mind renewal before he began his ministry as a teacher.

Recognizing and appreciating the mind of Christ after twenty, thirty, or forty years of cultural bombardment requires radically reconstructing our ways of thinking. Pop Christianity is not up to the challenge of facilitating this deeper, personally renewing faith, and sometimes even our most promising new experimental churches are led by sincere, devoted Christians who themselves are captivated by our age and are in need of a radical transformation. We can't see what we can't see, and we can't fix it if we don't see it! Seeing requires that we commit to a countercultural life and begin the process of transforming our mind. Centuries of experience have taught us that rich renewal in faith and culture comes through individuals who have pursued the deep path of nurturing God's presence, denying self, and rejecting conformity to our age—in other words, individuals whose minds are immersed in God's thoughts and ways. This is the challenge for the church and the leadership of the next generation.

I cannot overstate the severity of our situation. A spiritually, intellectually, and aesthetically impoverished church and culture require a radical renaissance that can only come through completely transformed individuals who no longer conform to the values of this age. All the excitement about new paradigms, enthusiasm for relevance, and the sincere desire to transform church and culture will amount to nothing unless they are accompanied by the deep faith that produces transformed people.

Today, we are called to renew our minds in an age inattentive to the mind. Our culture, devoted to entertainment and amusement, will not encourage us down this path, nor will most churches.

Historian Mark Noll concluded that "the scandal of the evangelical mind is that there is so little of the evangelical mind." Without renewed minds, we are doomed.

How do we renew our minds so that we can calibrate our will to God's and become fully human? Jesus practiced a set of disciplines for nurturing God's presence, renewing the mind, and knowing God's will, and he passed them on to his disciples, who have passed them on from generation to generation. These are the practices through which we can maintain God's transforming presence in our life and learn to think God's thoughts.

The Mind of Christ:
Jesus' Spiritual Practices

Because we have been raised in an undisciplined culture that makes few intellectual or spiritual demands on us, we need to be prepared for the challenge and hard work of renewal. While each of the disciplines described in this section is rewarding, they are more demanding then watching TV, listening to music, or playing an electronic game. Going deeper in God requires understanding how the shallows of today's culture have conditioned us toward superficial living. Society's passionate quest for self-fulfillment has led many of us to an unrewarding personal emptiness. In the age of "me," we have lived as if our self is the arbiter of all things. We have rejected "taking up a cross," choosing instead to do what feels good. We have recoiled at the idea of following anyone else, believing that the highest virtue is to seek our own way. Now Jesus is giving us an opportunity to return to the age of God by living a new kind of life.

Digging the deeper well requires learning the disciplines of Jesus. The Apostle Paul compared the practices leading to spiritual maturity to those of an athlete in training who exercises each day to enhance skills and strengthen endurance. Practicing these disciplines in everyday life produces spiritual health and maturity by calibrating our daily life on earth to the will and perspective of the eternal God. They are the practical way to fulfill the prayer Jesus taught us: "Thy will be done on earth as it is in heaven." I will briefly describe each of the practices. For a more detailed and systematic approach, I strongly recommend Richard Foster's book *Celebration of Discipline*.[9]

Four Private Disciplines

Jesus practiced four disciplines in his private life: prayer, study, meditation, and fasting. *Prayer* takes us out of this world and puts us in God's world, an exercise through which we become equipped to be put back in this world for useful service. Jesus awoke early in the morning and prayed. It is impossible to replace the voices of culture with God's voice unless you are actively engaged in prayer, which is why the Apostle Paul said we should "pray without ceasing."

Jesus *studied* the Scriptures, and at the age of twelve, he stunned the rabbis of the Temple in Jerusalem with his knowledge and insight into the Scriptures. Every Jewish child understood that Scripture was as essential as food, milk, and meat to sustain life. Only when our minds are saturated with the words of God can we avoid conformity with the words and images of our culture. To study means we understand Scripture by asking what the writer is saying, interpret it by asking what the author means, evaluate it by asking whether it rings true, and apply it by asking how it should change our life. We understand that study is not an academic exercise to make us smarter but a path to deeper union with God. Trappist monk Thomas Merton said, "We read the Gospels not merely to get a picture or an idea of Christ but to enter in and pass through the words of revelation to establish, by faith, a vital contact with the Christ Who dwells in our souls as God."[10]

Our study is deepened by *meditation*, the practice of quiet, focused concentration on God. Meditation centers our life in the eternal, now. In today's cacophonous and frantic world, few practices are more difficult to maintain or more necessary for our spiritual health and well-being than mind-renewing meditation. "On the glorious splendor of your majesty, and on your wondrous works, I will meditate" (Psalm 145:5). The Psalms were Jesus' prayer book, and they are full of admonitions to meditate.

Jesus *fasted*, abstaining from food, for the spiritual purpose of hearing God more clearly. Spiritual men and women throughout history have fasted, including a veritable who's who from the Bible: David, Elijah, Esther, Daniel, Paul. Fasting allows us to concentrate on God and on the spiritual over the physical. Fasting reveals what controls us and focuses our heart and mind to ensure that God is of central importance. We think nothing of consuming a steady diet of popular culture each day. Do we spend an equal or greater amount of time devoted to daily prayer, study, and meditation? Do we set aside time for fasting on a regular basis? Aspiring to align our mind with the mind of Christ and becoming fully human require that we follow these practices of Jesus.

Four Public Disciplines

Jesus also practiced four public disciplines: simplicity, solitude, submission, and service. By *public disciplines*, I simply mean that they can be observed by others.

Simplicity means that our inner life is consistent with our outer life, our God-shaped vacuum is filled, and we are no longer dependent on or possessed by outward things. Our consumeristic age is the enemy of simplicity, and so, like fasting, simplicity has become countercultural. Jesus taught that simplicity flows from a life that seeks God's kingdom first. Psychologists talk about cognitive dissonance, the difference between what we believe and how we behave. In contrast, simplicity flows from a renewed mind that seeks to harmonize what we know to be God's will with our daily behavior.

Jesus practiced *solitude*, or restorative aloneness, because he knew that his active public life required a concentration on God's presence that is best achieved in times of quietness and aloneness.

"Early in the morning, while it was still dark, he departed and went out to a desolate place and there he prayed" (Mark 1:35). How can we find the mind of Christ if our entire day is spent with a cacophony of electronic interventions and human demands?

The renewed mind is a mind that has been brought into *submission* to God. Paul urges us to let the mind of Christ dwell in us and reminds us that Jesus, "though he was in the form of God, did not regard equality with God as something to be exploited, but emptied himself, taking the form of a slave, being born in human likeness. And being found in human form, he humbled himself and became obedient to the point of death—even death on a cross" (Philippians 2:6–8). In our culture dominated by power, Jesus' timely message is this: the greatest power is demonstrated by those who restrain themselves from wielding it and who, when called upon to do so, will even yield it.

The renewed mind thinks of *serving* instead of being served, and this too reflects the mind of Christ. "The Son of Man came not to be served but to serve, and to give his life as a ransom for many" (Matthew 20:28). On the evening before his crucifixion, Jesus did not ask the disciples to attend to his needs; he washed their feet, modeling servanthood to the very end. The Apostle Paul said, "Let no one think more highly of themselves than they should" (Romans 12:3) and referred to the humility of Christ's mind.

Four Communal Disciplines

Jesus practiced four disciplines communally: confession, worship, guidance, and celebration. The renewed mind does not rationalize sin but *confesses* it. The New Testament word for "confess" comes from the Greek word *homologeo*, which means "to agree, assent, or reach the same idea." Confession is only possible when our mind recognizes the dissonance between our behavior and God's expectations. A mind filled with the values of a morally relativistic age won't recognize the need to confess because it cannot even recognize sin when it occurs. Confessing our sin requires an elevated awareness of God's standards and expectations, agreeing with God when we have sinned, and confessing to others when we sin against them. Jesus said to the disciples, "If you forgive the sins of any, they are forgiven them" (John 20:23); James urged Jesus' followers to "confess your sins to one another" (James 5:16); and John reminded us that "If we confess our sins, he who is faithful and just will forgive us our sins and cleanse us from all unrighteousness" (1 John 1:9).

Worship is the practice of adoring, reverencing, and honoring. Conformed to the values of this world, today's mind is bound to accept some level of self-worship as normal. The renewed mind knows that God is central and worships God as a way of life, recognizing that worship is, as Wheaton Conservatory's Harold Best said, "a continuous outpouring in response to a continuously outpouring God."[11] A. W. Tozer said, "No religion has ever been greater than its idea of God. Worship is pure or base as the worshiper entertains high or low thoughts of God."[12] As our mind is renewed with clearer images of God, our worship reflects it.

A Christian with a renewed mind seeks *guidance* in making decisions and determining a course of action by reading Scripture, praying, and seeking the counsel of trustworthy brothers and sisters in community, instead of relying solely on his or her own understanding.

Renewing the mind also involves *celebration*—observing special festivities to mark significant events. A Christian observes the Eucharist because it is a way of remembering and focusing the mind: "As often as we eat the bread and drink the cup, we proclaim the Lord's death until he comes" (1 Corinthians 11:26). The deeper spiritual way of Jesus is a celebratory one, and our life in community should reflect God's peace, joy, and love as a way of life.

Privately, publicly, and communally, we practice the disciplines of Jesus to renew our minds, and as our minds are refreshed and restored, we find ourselves resisting the negative force of conformity to the world while experiencing the joy that comes through knowing and doing God's will.

God's Glory: The Evidence
of Being Fully Human

To become fully human means that we are spiritually, intellectually, creatively, morally, and relationally alive. Jesus is our example of this fully human life; he attracted attention because he so exquisitely reflected God's image in his daily activities. Healing bodies, nurturing spirits, challenging minds, turning water into wine, enjoying great meals, provoking spirited conversations—everything about Jesus crackled with life, energy, and love, all evidence of a life aglow because of God's presence, radiating His image.

We too should glorify God in every activity of daily life. C. S. Lewis said, "Christianity does not exclude any of the ordinary human activities. St. Paul tells people to get on with their jobs. He even assumes Christians may go to dinner parties, and what is more, dinner parties given by pagans. Our Lord attends a wedding and provides miraculous wine. Under the aegis of His church, and in the most Christian ages learning and the arts flourish. The solution to this paradox is, of course, well known to you: 'Whether ye eat or drink or whatsoever you do, do all to the glory of God.'"[13]

With God's glory as our goal and guide, we seek to become fully human in the following ways:

We nurture God's spiritual presence in our daily life, knowing that, as Jesus said to the woman at the well in Samaria, God is spirit and those who worship God do so in spirit and truth (John 4:24). We cooperate with the indwelling Holy Spirit, knowing that this produces the best qualities of the fully human person: "love, joy, peace, patience, kindness, generosity, faithfulness, gentleness, and self-control" (Galatians 5:22–23). We also know that when God is not central and when we are conformed to the world, we are incapable of fully reflecting God's image and are prone to substandard human behavior as described by the Apostle Paul: "fornication, impurity, licentiousness, idolatry, sorcery, enmities, strife, jealousy, anger, quarrels, dissensions, factions, envy, drunkenness and carousing" (Galatians 5:19–21).

We renew our mind, learning and stretching it to the fullest of our individual, intellectual capacity. We love God with our mind, realizing that it is our capacity to reason that separates us from the rest of the creative order. Blaise Pascal said, "Truth is so obscured nowadays and lies so well established that unless we love the truth we shall never recognize it."[14] We actively pursue the good, the true, and the beautiful, reading, thinking, "taking every thought captive," as the Apostle Paul admonished us to (2 Corinthians 10:5), and learning to reason and discern, developing our intellect as a way to glorify God.

We exhibit excellence in our everyday creativity. Like Jesus, the master storyteller, we become masters of creativity in endeavors arising from our distinct gifts, talents, and calling. We are emboldened to believe that God has called us to build a glorious culture by reflecting His image, and we will devote our days to intelligently and imaginatively creating a life and a culture that reflect God's creativity and excellence. During the building of the tabernacle for the ark of the covenant, God said, "I have given to all able men ability, that they may make all that I have commanded"; He called on a variety of craftsmen who were filled with the spirit of God and endowed with all the knowledge and ability of their craft, to devise artistic designs; to work in gold, silver, and bronze; to cut stones for setting; and to carve wood for the tabernacle (Exodus 31).

We live morally upright lives as individuals and promote a higher ethic of justice for society, knowing that the evidence of our renewed mind is the ability to do as the Apostle Paul said: "Let love be genuine; hate what is evil, hold fast to what is good; love one another with mutual affection; outdo one another in showing honor. Do not lag in zeal. Be ardent in spirit. Serve the Lord. Rejoice in hope. Be patient in suffering and persevere in prayer. Contribute to the needs of the saints; extend hospitality to strangers" (Romans 12:9–13). We will be attentive to the "least of these," looking after orphans and widows in their distress. We will strive to keep ourselves from being polluted by the world (James 1:27).

Sociologist Rodney Stark discusses the societal impact of early Christians, whose changed lives changed society: "Christianity revitalized life in Greco-Roman cities by providing new norms and new kinds of social relationships able to cope with many urgent urban problems. To cities filled with the homeless and impoverished, Christianity offered charity as well as hope. To cities filled with newcomers and strangers, Christianity offered an immediate basis for attachments. To cities filled with orphans and widows, Christianity provided a new and expanded sense of family. To cities torn by violent ethnic strife, Christianity offered a new basis for social solidarity. And to cities faced with epidemic fires and earthquakes, Christianity offered effective nursing services."[15]

Our every relationship is characterized by love. We recognize that a renewed mind is a humble one, and we follow the Apostle Paul's instructions: "For by the grace given to me I say to everyone among you not to think of yourself more highly than you ought to think, but to think with sober judgment, each according to the measure of faith that God has assigned" (Romans 12:3). We will strive to give evidence of the transformed life as commanded by the Apostle Paul, who said, "Bless those who persecute you; bless and do not curse them. Rejoice with those who rejoice, weep with those who weep. Live in harmony with one another; do not be haughty, but associate with the lowly; do not claim to be wiser than you are. Do not repay anyone evil for evil, but take thought for what is noble in the sight of all. If it is possible, so far as it depends on you, live peaceably with all. Beloved, never avenge yourselves, but leave room for the wrath of God; for it is written, 'Vengeance is mine, I will repay,' says the Lord" (Romans 12:14–19).

"I Am Not Done with My Changes!"

Through the process of presenting our lives to God, rejecting conformity to this world, and allowing God to renew our minds, we can
become deeply well people and, therefore, better prepared to be the
loving, transforming presence God wants us to be in a culture that
desperately needs it. Aleksandr Solzhenitsyn captured the severity
of the world's situation and our calling in it: "If the world has not
approached its end, it has reached a major watershed in history,
equal in importance to the turn from the Middle Ages to the
Renaissance. It will demand from us a spiritual blaze; we shall have
to rise to a new height of vision, to a new level of life."[16]

Burning bushes attract attention, and so do humans aglow with
the presence and image of God. Some people hear Solzhenitsyn's
words as a rallying cry for changing culture, but it is a call first and
foremost to go deep in God. Pray that your life will become a snap-
shot of God's presence and that it will be said to you, in the words
of Oscar Wilde, "Life has been your art. You have set yourself to
music. Your days are your sonnets."[17] Only people who find the
deeper well can become deeply well, and only such people can be
an enriching force in creating a well culture. In your pursuit of God
and a complete transformation, do not be discouraged when you
experience setbacks, because our call to become fully human is a
direction, not a promise of perfection. The hopefulness of the
process is captured in "The Layers," written by the late poet laure-
ate Stanley Kunitz: "Though I lack the art to decipher it, no doubt
the next chapter in my book of transformations is already written.
I am not done with my changes."[18]

6

GOD'S LOVING PRESENCE

To love at all is to be vulnerable. Love anything, and
your heart will certainly be wrung and possibly broken.[1]
C. S. LEWIS, *THE FOUR LOVES*

Deep wellness results from allowing God's presence to transform us, a metamorphosis that is graced from beginning to end by God's loving presence.

In a day when hearts have grown cold, we need the warmth of God's love more than ever. Despite all the talk about love in today's movies, books, and songs, religious and irreligious people alike suffer from a severe love deficit. This love deficit is crucial to our universal angst, because nothing is more central to being fully human than love, and nothing diminishes our humanity more than an inability to give and receive love. Jesus' arrival two thousand years ago signaled a change in the human story we are in and addressed the love deficit head on. Jesus embodied God's love for a love-hungry world and then sent us out to do the same, saying that his followers would be recognized by their love.

Yet today, people in both culture and church are equally hungry for deep, loving relationships. Power, wealth, the acquisition of more stuff, entertainment, liberated sex, and a revolving door of relationships have proven inadequate substitutes for the love we need. The popularity of a TV show like *Friends* signals a culturewide hunger for friendship. Christians, on a quest for absolute knowledge, ever-increasing ecstatic experiences, faith that moves mountains, political and economic power, bigger churches, and relevant, hip messages, seem to have forgotten that "if we have all these and don't have love, we are nothing" (1 Corinthians 13:1–3). *Community* has become a hollow buzzword in Christian circles; every church offers it, but almost nobody experiences it. Instead of delivering the love for which people yearn, we build bigger and better facilities and programs, which become gathering places for increasing numbers of lonely, isolated, unconnected people.

"God is love," said the Apostle John. Unfortunately, as any honest child of the 1960s will tell you, conversations about love can easily drift into meaningless platitudes. The Beatles glibly sang, "All You Need Is Love," but their bickering led to their breakup soon thereafter. William Morris's poem titled "Love Is Enough" reportedly received a short review summarized in two words, "It isn't."[2] Wherever we look, the story is the same: we need more *than* love, more *of* love, or a *different kind* of love.

God offers the different kind of love we need, and though we know God *is* love, it is even more important to understand the nature of God's love.

The Nature of God's Love: Four Kinds of Love

A population obsessed with love cannot find the love that satisfies because although we are created with a capacity for love, we are unaware that the only love that will satisfy, God's love, is very different from the love we are accustomed to offering and receiving. In C. S. Lewis's classic book *The Four Loves*, he describes three natural loves: affection, friendship, and eros. *Affection* is the relationship we have with familiar people, regardless of common interests or attractiveness. *Friendship* "arises out of mere companionship when two or more of the companions discover that they have in common some insight or interest or even taste which others do not share and which, till that moment, each believed to be his unique treasure (or burden)."[3] *Eros* (the Greek root from which we derive the word *erotic*) is what we commonly call "being in love," which includes sexual attraction but is not limited to it.

Almost all portrayals of love in popular culture concentrate on natural love. Our movies, songs, and magazines have reduced friendship to witty repartee in sitcoms and eros to a one-night stand. In the best of circumstances, natural love is insufficient, but in our age, we are witnessing the parody and vulgarization of love. The me-first, free love movement of the 1960s has produced broken homes and children who hunger for and simultaneously fear love. The sexual liberation of the sixties has reduced eros to pornography. The sinking sand on which we build our romantic relationships is illustrated in celebrity magazines, which chronicle a cyclical pattern that predictably starts with the excitement of finding new love ("I've never been happier; I've found my soul mate"), followed by a period of dissolution, accusation, and deterioration ("I found him with another woman," "Her career is more important than having a family"), and ending with "an amicable separation and divorce."

Because we are created in God's image, we possess a capacity to give and receive a fourth kind of love, which Lewis calls *charity*. This kind of love is mirrored in the natural loves but also transcends them. "Charity is *(like affection)* undiscriminating, loving even those who do not seem loveable. It is *(like friendship)* free of jealousy, ready to receive the outsider. It is *(like eros)* selfless, devoted to the good of the beloved."[4]

Agape: Love That Gives

Lewis's fourth love is sometimes referred to as *agape* or sacrificial love, because agape is about giving, not getting. Recall the Apostle Paul's memorable description of agape: "Love [agape] is patient and kind; love does not envy or boast; it is not arrogant or rude. It does not insist on its own way; it is not irritable or resentful; it does not rejoice at wrongdoing, but rejoices with the truth. Love bears all things, believes all things, hopes all things and endures all things. Love never ends" (1 Corinthians 13:4–8).

When Jesus commanded his disciples to love one another, he used the Greek word *agape*. "I give you a new commandment, that you love [agape] one another. Just as I have loved [agape] you, you also should love [agape] one another" (John 13:34). Describing agape, Jesus taught, "No one has greater love [agape] than this, to lay down one's life for one's friends" (John 15:13).

This is the love to which we aspire and to which we are called but which we often seem incapable of producing, a problem that was familiar even to Jesus' disciples. Prior to the crucifixion, Peter pledged that he would never betray Jesus, and Jesus asked, "Will you lay down your life for me? Truly, truly, I say to you, the rooster will not crow till you have denied me three times" (Matthew 26:34). After his crucifixion and resurrection and just before his ascension to heaven, in Jesus' final conversation with Peter, he asked, "Do you love me more than these?" (John 21:15). Peter replied, "Yes Lord, you know that I love you." Jesus then said to Peter, "Feed my lambs." This exchange is repeated a second and third time (John 21:16–17). The Greek text explains the repetition. Jesus is asking "Do you love me?" using the Greek word *agape*. Peter is answering that he loves Jesus using the word for friendship (*phileo*). Jesus is calling Peter to the higher agape, while Peter is extending only phileo, the love of a friend.

In each of his exchanges with Peter, Jesus makes it clear that the love he has commanded, expects, and deserves is agape, which transcends our natural loves (affection, friendship, and eros). Jesus expects all of his followers to practice agape love, for he said, "By this everyone will know that you are my disciples, if you have love [agape] for one another" (John 13:35). Like Peter, we often offer each other friendship and affection but not agape. We long for true community but cannot achieve it with natural love alone; we need agape.

Fortunately Peter's story did not end with that final conversation with Jesus. After Jesus ascended into heaven, he sent the Holy Spirit to dwell within his followers, transforming Peter so radically that although once he could offer only friendship, his agape love eventually led him to sacrifice everything for Jesus.

Today, our love deficit is due to our God deficit. Agape, the only basis for true community, is impossible without God's indwelling presence in our life because God is the source of agape love. By nurturing God's agape, His loving presence, we will be able to transcend our capacities for natural love and become deliverers of agape to others who need it.

Transforming Love: Love That Improves

God's agape love welcomes us unconditionally but also transforms and continuously improves us in some very specific ways that we will now examine.

Transforming love is truthful love. In the familiar story of the woman caught in the act of adultery, the Pharisees were prepared to stone her to death, but Jesus intervened and said, "Let anyone among you who is without sin be the first to throw a stone at her." Aware of their own sin, they slipped away one by one, until just Jesus was left with the woman. Jesus, the only one without sin, the only one who could rightfully cast a stone, did not, saying instead, "Where are they? Has no one condemned you? Neither do I condemn you." In light of her obvious guilt, Jesus' forgiveness displayed God's extraordinary, unconditional agape love and forgiveness. But there is more to the story. Jesus turned to the woman and added these important words: "Go your way and from now on do not sin again." Jesus was the perfect holistic blend of love and truth. He showed the woman love by publicly protecting her from the judgmental Pharisees, and he told her the truth by privately admonishing her to change her behavior. The Apostle John said that when people saw Jesus, they saw God's glory, because Jesus was "full of grace and truth" (John 1:14). In all his encounters with spiritual seekers, Jesus did not sacrifice either love or truth, because he was the full embodiment of both.

Christians need such holistic fullness today. We tend to err on the side of grace or truth. We either love people unconditionally, not delivering the truth about their need to change, or we deliver the truth without showing them unconditional love. Jesus' approach can be summarized as follows: Truth without grace is legalism. Grace without truth is romanticism. Truth with grace is dynamism. Jesus demonstrated that loving a person does not require us to abandon the truth, nor does truth demand that we neglect love. Jesus was full of both grace and truth, and when Jesus is at work within us, our lives will display this same exquisite fullness.

In today's highly divisive culture war, Christians have become characterized as those who know or claim to know the "right answers," or truth, rather than being known for our love. We cannot escape the Apostle Paul's admonition, "If I speak in the tongues of men and of angels, but have not love, I am a noisy gong or a clanging cymbal. And if I have prophetic powers, and understand all mysteries and all knowledge, and if I have all faith, so as to remove mountains, but have not love, I am nothing. If I give away all I have, and if I deliver up my body to be burned, but have not love, I gain nothing" (1 Corinthians 13:1–3). If we are genuinely transformed by God's love, our agape should drive us out of our cocoon and into the world, out of combat and into compassion, and out of conformity and into transformative truth, but above all, we will be known by our love.

Transforming love is practical, need-meeting love. Jesus taught the disciples to ask God for their daily bread. King David compared God's love to the shepherd who provides for his sheep: "He makes me lie down in green pastures. He leads me beside still waters" (Psalm 23). Jesus picked up on this theme, teaching that prayer is what activates God's loving provision: "Ask, and it will be given you; seek, and you will find; knock, and it will be opened to you. For every one who asks receives, and he who seeks finds, and to him who knocks it will be opened. Or what man of you, if his son asks him for bread, will give him a stone? Or if he asks for a fish, will give him a serpent? If you then, who are evil, know how to give good gifts to your children, how much more will your Father who is in heaven give good things to those who ask him!" (Matthew 7:7–11).

In our consumeristic age, when most people are unable to distinguish want from need, the words of Jesus are hauntingly resonant: "Do not be anxious about your life, what you will eat or what you will drink, nor about your body, what you will put on. Is not life more than food, and the body more than clothing? . . . Do not be anxious, saying, 'What shall we eat?' or 'What shall we drink?' or 'What shall we wear?' . . . But seek first the kingdom of God and his righteousness, and all these things will be added to you" (Matthew 6:25, 31, 33). "Do not lay up for yourselves treasures on earth, but lay up for yourselves treasures in heaven. For where your treasure is, there your heart will be also" (Matthew 6:21). As we experience God's agape love through the provision of our daily bread, we are expected to show agape love by helping those who hunger and thirst. How would the world be different if we acknowledged and were content with God's provision for our basic needs and then dedicated our lives to fully pursuing God and showing agape for others, including those whose basic subsistence needs go unmet? God's extraordinary love compels us to invest in "the least of these" and to accept God's forgiving love when we fail, as noted by Madeleine L'Engle, who, as she reached old age, said, "We have much to be judged on when he comes, slums and battlefields and insane asylums, but these are the symptoms of our illness and the result of our failures in love. In the evening of life we shall be judged on love, and not one of us is going to come off very well, and were it not for my absolute faith in the loving forgiveness of my Lord I could not call on him to come."[5]

Transforming love is restoring and healing love. King David the psalmist declares, "He restores my soul. . . . Even though I walk through the valley of the shadow of death, I will fear no evil, for you are with me; your rod and your staff, they comfort me" (Psalm 23). The lyrics of our classic hymns also pick up on the nature of God's transforming love, like this one from George Matheson, written in 1882: "O Love that wilt not let me go, O light that followest all my way, O Joy that seekest me through pain, I rest my weary soul in thee." Matheson's life had been a difficult one: he was blind, had lost his one true love in a broken engagement, and was concerned about the ideological impact of Darwinism. He said, "[I was] suffering from extreme mental distress, [and] this hymn was the fruit of pain." Charles Wesley reflected on "Love Divine, All love excelling," saying, "Jesus Thou art all compassion, pure unbounded love thou art, visit us with thy salvation, enter every trembling heart, breathe oh breathe thy loving spirit into every troubled breast."

Our deepest needs can only be met by the healing presence of God's mystical, loving presence. Today, we are battered and shaken by firsthand exposure to love's failings in our closest relationships and are disillusioned by the superficial substitutes offered by popular culture and most churches. As encumbered as they are with Elizabethan language, the old hymns nevertheless reflect the experience of an earlier generation that knew the deep satisfaction of God's healing, restoring presence in the midst of life's disappointments. Only God's deep love brings such deep healing. When God's agape enters our lives, it transforms us, meeting our needs, restoring and comforting us, telling us the truth, and disciplining us so that we can experience a metamorphosis like a caterpillar turning into a butterfly. We can be transformed into deeply loved, fully human individuals capable of extending that same love to others.

Dependable Love: Love That Stays

Paraphrasing Augustine, C. S. Lewis advised, "Do not let your happiness depend on something you may lose. If love is to be a blessing, not a misery, it must be for the only Beloved who will never pass away."[6] Natural love is limited by time and human frailty, and we cannot ultimately depend on it. Because we are imperfect, even the finest of humans will sometimes fail at love. God's love is limitless and transcends time; it knows no beginning or end. The Apostle Paul captured this magnificently, saying, "If God is for us, who can be against us? Who shall separate us from the love of Christ? Shall tribulation, or distress, or persecution, or famine, or nakedness, or danger, or sword? No, in all these things we are more than conquerors through him who loved us. For I am sure that neither death nor life, nor angels nor rulers, nor things present nor things to come, nor powers, nor height nor depth, nor anything else in all creation, will be able to separate us from the love of God in Christ Jesus our Lord" (Romans 8:31–39).

It is our rootedness in God's eternal, limitless love that sustains us through life's cruel disappointments. Horatio G. Spafford was a successful attorney in Chicago, the father of four daughters, and a loyal friend and supporter of evangelist Dwight. L. Moody. In 1873, when Moody left for Great Britain on a speaking tour, Spafford decided to take his family on a vacation to Europe, where they could join Moody on his tour. When he was detained by urgent business, Spafford sent his wife and four daughters as scheduled on the S.S. *Ville du Havre*, planning to join them soon. Halfway across the Atlantic, the ship was struck by an English vessel and sank in twelve minutes. All four of Spafford's daughters were among the 226 who drowned. Mrs. Spafford was among the few who were miraculously saved. Later, Horatio Spafford stood hour after hour on the deck of the ship carrying him to rejoin his sorrowing wife in Cardiff, Wales. When the ship passed the approximate place where his precious daughters had drowned, Spafford received sustaining comfort from God and he wrote the words of the hymn "It Is Well with My Soul," which begins with the lines, "When peace, like a river, attendeth my way, when sorrows like sea billows roll; whatever my lot, thou hast taught me to say, It is well, it is well with my soul."

Our individual lives and the culture we produce could be made well if we would build on the sure foundation of God's love instead of the vagaries of natural human love. We derive a certain level of happiness from the rich benefits of human affection, friendship, and romantic love, but soul wellness is ours only when the indwelling God, whose love is eternally available and utterly reliable, sustains us.

God's Love Enfleshed

The most surprising development in the story we are in is the enfleshment of God's love in Jesus. "In the beginning was the Word, and the Word was with God, and the Word was God. And the Word became flesh and lived among us, and we have seen his glory, the glory as of a father's only son, full of grace and truth" (John 1:14). Jesus was God's love enfleshed.

I have learned that the best intellectual argument for faith pales by comparison to simple observable acts of kindness and sacrifice. I'd like to take a personal detour for a moment to illustrate how I came to believe this.

Though I love ideas and find abstract concepts fascinating, I was wooed, not reasoned into faith, by love enfleshed. From the womb, I was taught that the essence of God is love, but I did not understand the significance of that love until I saw my parents' response when my brother Timmy was born with brain damage when I was ten. Before he was born, I remember my excitement at the thought of playing catch with a brother who could also join me in my personal calling, the tormenting of my two younger sisters. When my parents brought Timmy home from the hospital, I don't remember being told that anything was out of the ordinary, but I knew that there would be no playing catch when I was awakened at 2 A.M. by the sound of Timmy's first grand mal seizure as he thrashed and clawed in the crib just a few feet from my bed.

My journey toward God was dealt a serious blow that night, for I reasoned that no loving God could allow such a tragedy. Years later, I thought of this when interviewing literary giant Norman Mailer, who, on the basis of the Holocaust, had concluded that God could not be both all-loving and all-powerful because, logically, this would mean that God chose to allow innocent people to die unjustly. He opted for God being all-loving but not all-powerful.

I saw the power of God's love in my parents' care for my brother, and in their daily acts of love toward Timmy, they saved his life and mine. They saved my life because they forced me to think more

deeply about the theological implications inherent in God's grant-
ing humans free will and in the universal consequences for humanity's displacing God as central in our lives. More important, they
saved my life by displaying God's sacrificial love in their observable
unwavering agape love for my brother. I learned that the most effective argument for the existence of God is the embodiment of God's
loving, transforming presence in a fully human life.

Until I was disarmed by an image of God's love in action, I was
unwilling to move on to the logical, rational consideration of the
intellectual issues before me. I remember my dad reading William
Blake to my brother:

> Little lamb, who made thee?
> Dost thou know who made thee?
>> Gave thee life, and bade thee feed
>> By the stream and o'er the mead;
>> Gave thee clothing of delight,
>> Softest clothing, wooly, bright;
>> Gave thee such a tender voice,
>> Making all the vales rejoice?
> Little lamb, who made thee?
> Dost thou know who made thee?
>
> Little lamb, I'll tell thee;
> Little lamb, I'll tell thee:
>> He is called by thy name,
>> For He calls Himself a lamb,
>> He is meek, and He is mild,
>> He became a little child;
>> I a child, and Thee a Lamb,
>> We are called by His Name.
> Little lamb, God bless thee!
> Little lamb, God bless thee![7]

It seemed odd to me that my father could read a poem about
God, the creator, to his son, for whom the process of creation had

taken such a grotesque turn, but I knew that my dad loved this God, and so I sought a deeper understanding. I discovered the Jesus who was a "man of sorrows and acquainted with grief" (Isaiah 53:3 KJV), born in a stable and filled with compassion for the lame, blind, infirm, and all those feeling harassed and helpless. Jesus' love began to heal me.

Only those who experience God's loving presence in the deepest places of their soul can be a loving presence in the souls of others. When touched by God, our deepest wounds can become our deepest well of compassion for the sorrows of others. So the Apostle Paul says, "Blessed be the God and Father of our Lord Jesus Christ, the Father of mercies and God of all comfort, who comforts us in all our affliction, so that we may be able to comfort those who are in any affliction, with the comfort with which we ourselves are comforted by God" (2 Corinthians 1:3–4).

The Evidence of God's Love

Now, here is the amazing conspiracy of the divine: the God who enfleshed love in Jesus in order to love a love-hungry world plans to enflesh love in us so that we can enter the world as a loving, transforming presence, displaying to the world what God is doing in us:

Our response to God's love is gratitude and appreciation. As Charles Wesley's hymn proclaims, "What shall I render to my God for all His mercy's store? I'll take the gifts He has bestowed and humbly ask for more. The sacred cup of saving grace, I will with thanks receive, and all His promises embrace and to His glory live."

Our response to God's love is obedience. Love is not a concept or an abstraction; love is action. As Jesus said on numerous occasions, we know that we have come to know God if we keep His commandments. If you love me, you will keep my commandments. It is our disobedience, our sin, that blocks the flow of God's love, not because God no longer loves us when we sin but because God gives us the freedom to turn away from His love. Our obedience is the key to nurturing God's loving presence, so the writer of Hebrews urges us "to set aside the sin that weighs us down" (Hebrews 12:1).

Our response to God's love is embodiment. Our transformation is the result of God's presence in our life, and the evidence of God's presence is our embodiment of God's love.

Society displays human fallenness in its mindless, soulless, spiritually delusional popular culture. Today's Christians are often a mirror image of popular culture, wanting to transform the world without being transformed, wanting to prove Christianity intellectually without displaying the love that is the proof we are Jesus' disciples. The only way to enrich our culture is to be enriched personally, which comes when we experience God deeply and then embody God's loving presence. The culturally savvy Christian is serious about faith, and savvy about faith, culture, and the story we are in. The culturally savvy Christian's goal is to embody God's loving, transforming presence in the world. The culturally savvy Christian is fully human, displaying God's image holistically—spiritually, intellectually, creatively, morally, and behaviorally. In the chapters that follow, we'll see how culturally savvy Christians are skilled in embodying their three roles in culture: countering culture, creating culture, and communicating within it.

Most important, the culturally savvy Christian knows that the glow of God's presence is fueled by love. As the Apostle Paul, the great intellectual apologist, advanced in years, he reached the conclusion that love is the Christian's one essential quality: "When I was a child, I spoke like a child, I thought like a child, I reasoned like a child. When I became a man, I gave up childish ways. For now we see in a mirror dimly, but then face to face. Now I know in part; then I shall know fully, even as I have been fully known. So now faith, hope, and love abide, these three; but the greatest of these is love" (1 Corinthians 13:13).

C. S. Lewis: Snapshot of
the Culturally Savvy Christian

Just as the word *love* is an abstraction until we see it embodied, so the idea of a culturally savvy Christian is an abstraction until it is enfleshed, a realization that led to my appreciation of C. S. Lewis. A few years ago, I began an association with the C. S. Lewis Foundation that resulted in my spearheading a campaign to raise the money to convert Lewis's Oxford home, the Kilns, into a year-round study center. As I thought about why it is important to extend Lewis's legacy to the next generation, I began to see him as fully human in his spiritual, intellectual, creative, relational, and moral pursuits. Furthermore, I observed that as Lewis's life became enriched and aglow with God's presence, he enriched culture by countering culture, communicating within it, and also creating it. As I met people like his stepson Douglas Gresham and others who had known Lewis personally, I began to realize how the embodiment of love in daily life is what gave his private life such authenticity. In short, I began to see Lewis as a metaphor for the culturally savvy Christian—a Christian who is serious, savvy, and skilled, possessing a deep, culturally enriching faith fueled by love.

The Culturally Enriching Faith of C. S. Lewis

Following his 1943 BBC radio talks, C. S. Lewis's voice became the second most recognized in all of England, surpassed only by that of Winston Churchill, who, with Lewis, was attempting to lift the spirits and deepen the resolve of the nation against the very real, ominous threat of Nazi occupation. Churchill's was a political, military task and Lewis's a spiritual and intellectual one. Fifty years ago, those talks were published as *Mere Christianity*, Lewis's classic masterpiece, in which he says of all Christians, "At the center of each there is something, or a Someone, who against all divergences of belief, all differences of temperament, all memories of mutual persecution, speaks with the same voice."[8]

Lewis died on November 23, 1963, the day of John F. Kennedy's assassination and Aldous Huxley's death. Yet in 2005, Lewis books sold a few million copies and the film *The Lion, the Witch, and the Wardrobe* was a box office sensation. In the same year, *Time* magazine reflected on this world-renowned Oxford and Cambridge scholar and best-selling author: "In 1947, a *Time* cover story hailed Lewis as 'one of the most influential spokesmen for Christianity in the English-speaking world.' Now, 58 years later (and 42 years after his death, in 1963), he could arguably be called the hottest theologian of 2005."[9] J.R.R. Tolkien, Lewis's friend, also retains his popularity; his trilogy, *The Lord of the Rings*, was voted the most influential of the twentieth century in four separate polls, and the third installment of its film adaptation by director Peter Jackson, *The Return of the King*, won the Academy Award for best picture.

It is not unreasonable to ask why the popularity of a couple of tweedy Oxford dons is on the rise all these years later. For anyone concerned about the current superficial state of both American Christianity and popular culture, it is an essential and core question. In my view, the future of faith and culture lies in a renaissance of the spiritual, intellectual, and imaginative legacy embodied in these two men and available to you and me today.

Lewis: Serious About Deep Faith

C. S. Lewis was raised in a Christian home, but as a young boy, his belief was shattered when God "failed to answer" his prayers for his dying mother. As a teen, his atheism found intellectual legs under the tutelage of a brilliant atheistic mentor, and by the time he finished Oxford, he was a thoroughgoing unbeliever. His progression from atheism to theism came through a series of events, but his progression from theist to Christian came very specifically through a careful examination of the underlying truth of the claims of Christ.

I've mentioned that until I was disarmed by an image of God in action, I was unwilling to move on to the logical, rational consideration of the intellectual issues before me. The same thing happened to the intellectual logician Lewis, who, after attending Oxford for a short time, realized that the friends he admired and spent the most time with were Christians. It was conversations with those friends—J.R.R. Tolkien, Hugo Dyson, and Owen Barfield—that led to Lewis's conversion.

We've already seen that Lewis became convinced of the truth of Jesus' claim to be Lord, and he understood that to follow Jesus meant self-denial and a radical transformation of his thoughts and behavior. In short, he was deeply devoted to Jesus Christ and pursued God vigorously, engaging in a rigorous study of Scriptures, accompanied by a life of prayer and service.

Lewis expert Paul Ford summarizes Lewis's deep spirituality as "a rhythm of worship, work, reading, and leisure, an unfrantic response to God, who is, as Lewis insisted, always a courteous Lord." Ford says Lewis exemplified an "English style of spirituality in which lifestyle is revealed by the use of time: what is given place and space; what is included and what, therefore, is excluded. In Lewis's life we see his steady involvement in his parish church; the quiet regularity of his Bible-reading and prayers; the natural large place for his main work of study and writing; the large blocks of time for leisurely conversations with special friends; and the importance of letter writing, especially with those who sought his help in the matter of Christian pilgrimage. For all of his immense output of literary work, his life is marked by a spacious, unfrantic rhythm of worship, work, conversation, availability, and intimacy."[10] Lewis and Tolkien both understood that God's image would shine through the excellence of their life and work, and each was dedicated to do everything for the glory of God.

Lewis pursued God in the company of friends, notably among the Inklings, a biweekly, ecumenical, convivial gathering of intelligent, imaginative Christians who met on campus and in a local pub to read and critique each other's work; to join in spirited debate about the art, literature, and ideas of the day; and to enjoy the benefits and duties of friendship. Members included C. S. Lewis, J.R.R.

Tolkien, Charles Williams, Dorothy Sayers, and Owen Barfield. They produced literary works that are still influential today and practiced a faith that blended spiritual devotion, intellectual vitality, and artistic creativity with practical, daily, loving service.

Lewis: Fulfilling Three Roles in Culture

We have seen that culturally savvy Christians are called to be a loving, transforming presence in culture and to play three roles in culture: to communicate like ambassadors, to counter culture like aliens, and to create culture like artists. C. S. Lewis was the embodiment of the culturally savvy Christian.

Communicating in Culture like an Ambassador. We often think of C. S. Lewis as a leading intellectual, yet Lewis understood his own calling as an explainer of faith to the everyday person. Indeed, people who read Lewis today appreciate him because he is intelligent, approachable, and comprehensible. Lewis described his role as ambassador in this way: "When I began, Christianity came before the great mass of my unbelieving fellow countrymen either in the highly emotional form offered by revivalists or in the unintelligible language of the highly cultured clergymen. Most men were reached by neither. My task was therefore simply that of a translator—one turning Christian doctrine, or what he believed to be such, into the vernacular, into language that unscholarly people would attend to and could understand. . . . One thing is sure. If the real theologians had tackled this laborious work of translation about a hundred years ago, when they began to lose touch with the people (for whom Christ died), there would have been no place for me."[11]

Countering Culture like an Alien. C. S. Lewis and J.R.R Tolkien were outsiders to the mainstream of faith and culture and, unlike today's evangelicals, were not preoccupied with relevance. Lewis and Tolkien operated like aliens in an ideologically inhospitable environment within both culture and the academy. Lewis was denied his due at Oxford largely because of his "ambassadorial" religious writing, in which he interpreted his beliefs for mere mortals instead of writing exclusively to scholars. Tolkien was ridiculed for his fanatical devotion to his art, which included an extraordinary depth of vision and expansive back-story for his beloved *Lord of the Rings*. Both men knew what it meant to be pilgrims in a barren land; both learned to relate faith and culture with a savvy that Jesus described as being "wise like a serpent, and innocent like a dove" (Matthew 10:16).

Creating Culture like an Artist.   Not every Christian is an artist in a literal sense, but each of us has the skills to perform some useful work for society. Whatever our work, it should be notable for its craftsmanship and artistry. Lewis's and Tolkien's writing has stood the test of time because of their relentless pursuit of excellence in their craft.

Lewis was a gifted, hard-working writer, personifying poet Dylan Thomas's description of a writer as one who will "treat words as a craftsman does his wood or stone, to hew, carve, mold, coil, polish, and plane them into patterns, sequences, sculptures, figures of sound."[12] Lewis was also an imaginative and creative writer. Believing that imagination is the "organ of meaning," he used metaphors to illuminate his reader's comprehension of the truth he was conveying. In virtually every paragraph, when Lewis introduces an important idea, we also find an illustrative metaphor, a word picture to help us grasp the abstract idea or concept.

Lewis understood his work to be an act of worship, a way to glorify God, and so he did it to the best of his ability. Swedish filmmaker Ingmar Bergman was raised in a Lutheran pastor's home, and his films often explored his personal dissonances with the Christian faith. Nevertheless, in his old age, he commented, "Art lost its basic creative drive the moment it was separated from worship. It severed an umbilical cord and now lives its own sterile life, generating and degenerating itself. In former days, the artist remained unknown and his work was to the glory of God. He lived and died without being more or less important than other artisans: eternal values, immortality and masterpiece were terms not applicable in his case. The ability to create was a gift. In such a world flourished vulnerable and natural humility."[13] When Walter Hooper arrived to work as Lewis's personal assistant in the summer of 1963, he began organizing Lewis's papers. A bemused Lewis was slightly embarrassed by all the fuss and commented, "Five years after I've died, nobody will remember C. S. Lewis!"[14] Lewis wrote not for fame or finance, and in his humility, he questioned his own long-term influence. He understood his life and work to be an act of obedience, worship, and praise for God, his audience of one.

C. S. Lewis: Embodying God's Love

I always knew that Lewis represented a dynamic synergy of spirit, mind, and creativity, but only over the last few years have I realized that it was powered by love. Lewis himself said, "Every Christian would agree that a man's spiritual health is exactly proportional to his love for God,"[15] and every aspect of Lewis's life was devoted to expressing his love for God through loving the people in his everyday life. Holocaust survivor Elie Wiesel reminds us, "The opposite of love is not hate, it's indifference. The opposite of art is not ugliness, it's indifference. The opposite of faith is not heresy, it's indifference. And the opposite of life is not death, it's indifference."[16] C. S. Lewis's life is a tribute to the opposite of indifference, because the opposite of indifference is love.

Lewis's personal life reflected his love. When his friend Paddy Moore was killed in World War I, Lewis (called Jack by his closest friends) took on responsibility for Moore's widowed mother and sister, who moved into the Kilns with Lewis and his brother Warnie. As her health declined, Mrs. Moore became irrational and demanding, and according to Doug Gresham, "barely fifteen minutes at a time would pass without her making some foolish demand interrupting Jack's work."[17] Yet Lewis cheerfully served her without complaint until the day she died. His dedication to weekly gatherings with the Inklings at a pub affectionately nicknamed "The Bird and the Baby" was testimony of his loyalty to friends. It was at Lewis's urging that Tolkien relented and reluctantly published *The Lord of the Rings* through contacts in the publishing world introduced by Lewis. Tolkien personally saw to it that Lewis secured the academic chair he deserved at Cambridge when it was not forthcoming at Oxford. Lewis's marriage to the American Joy Davidman began as a civil ceremony he agreed to so that she could stay in the United Kingdom but blossomed into a true marriage that resulted in his daily care for Joy as she died of cancer. Her son, Douglas Gresham, remembers, "I began to see the enormous wealth of compassion in him." After learning of his mother's death, Douglas returned home from school to the Kilns asking, "Jack, what are we going to do?" The man whose certainty and eloquence had helped so many others summoned compassion through his grief and answered the young boy, "Just carry on somehow, I suppose, Doug."[18] And for the next years, Lewis and young Douglas carried on, Lewis by writing *A Grief Observed* while Douglas witnessed "the finest man [he'd] ever known"[19] working out how to rekindle God's love when it felt cold and distant.

Lewis's public life reflected his love. Lewis's student Harry Blamires recalls that Lewis "was personally interested in his pupils and permanently concerned about those who became his friends. . . . No one knew better how to nourish a pupil with encouragement and how to press just criticism when it was needed, without causing resentment."[20] Lewis took his call to help everyday people understand the Christian faith very seriously and, while writing *The Four Loves*, asked a correspondent to "pray for me that God grant me to say things helpful to salvation, or at least not harmful."[21] Each sentence was crafted with a desire to illuminate the path of those he loved but had never met. He believed that God wanted him to personally answer all his correspondence, despite the time it consumed, and more than twelve thousand of his letters have now been collected from readers of all ages. He treated each correspondent with equal importance, once saying in his sermon *The Weight of Glory,* "There are no ordinary people. You have never talked to a mere mortal."[22] He regularly prayed for people with whom he corresponded, asking for updates in follow-up letters. His readers would trek out to the Kilns unannounced, and Lewis would cheerfully ask them in for tea, which he would make himself. His friend, scholar and theologian Austin Farrar, reports, Lewis's "characteristic attitude to people in general was one of consideration and respect. He did his best for them, and he appreciated them."[23] Lewis secretly funded the education of scores of promising students who couldn't afford a good education, stipulating that none should know about his contribution until his death. He opened the Kilns to children during World War II and provided temporary shelter to others who were down on their luck from time to time. One teenager who stayed with him was severely mentally disabled and had never learned to read. Lewis made flash cards, and during the boy's three-month stay, would arrive home from his teaching duties with the brightest and best at Oxford, roll up his sleeves, and work on the boy's reading skills.

I share all this because I have come to believe that the real legacy of C. S. Lewis and the measure of his character is his love. He exemplifies what happens when, within the bounds of human capacities, we allow our love for God and people to propel us to a surpassing excellence and service in everything we do. Aristotle said that persuasion requires logos (the logic and reason of our case), pathos (the passion with which we hold and advance our case), and ethos (the integrity that comes when our lives are consistent with our beliefs and values). Because he himself was living it, Lewis could write to Italian correspondent Don Giovanni Calabria in all sincerity, saying, "In the poor man who knocks at my door, in my ailing mother, in the young man who seeks my advice, the Lord

Himself is present. Therefore let us wash His feet."[24] Lewis was persuasive not just because he possessed a brilliant, well-educated mind and passionate spirit but because his daily, observable life was the embodiment and ultimate evidence of his ideas and beliefs. Lewis was fully human.

When we nurture the deep presence of God, pursuing God in the company of friends; allowing God to transform us toward becoming fully human; developing our spiritual, intellectual, creative, relational, and moral capacities to their fullest potential; and allowing our lives to be infused with and fueled by God's agape love, then we are prepared to enrich culture as a loving, transforming presence. This is the example of Jesus Christ, of the apostles, and, in our own age, of C. S. Lewis. This is our calling, and as we will see next, it involves being for our culture today what Lewis and Tolkien were for theirs: aliens, ambassadors, and artists.

SKILLED

The culturally savvy Christian is

serious about faith,

savvy about faith and culture,

and skilled in relating the two.

7

COUNTERING CULTURE
LIKE ALIENS

Now is the hour come. . . . Foes and fires are before you,
and your homes far behind. Yet, though you fight upon
an alien field, the glory that you reap there shall be
your own forever. Oaths ye have taken: now fulfill
them all, to lord and land and league of friendship![1]

J.R.R. TOLKIEN, *THE LORD OF THE RINGS*

With the renewal of deepening faith, we culturally savvy Christians are transformed into people who think and behave differently and are therefore set apart by our spiritual, intellectual, creative, relational, and moral sensibilities. As a result, we become countercultural, called both to citizenship in the kingdom of God and to citizenship on earth, experiencing an inevitable conflict between the two. Like aliens and exiles, we live in one country while also belonging in another.

As thoughtful, culturally engaged Christians, we resonate with this world but at the same time experience dissonance when exposed to its mindlessness, soullessness, and spiritual delusions. Our role is to be discerning, discovering points of disagreement between our faith and culture by listening to both, then choosing a path that pleases God. We will pray and work for the enrichment of culture, careful to avoid the threats and seize the opportunities it offers.

Chapter Nine will address the issue of creating culture like artists; but it is doubtful that we will influence culture without knowing firsthand the unavoidable dissonance that comes from our experience as countercultural aliens. This is a particularly important and corrective message for today's Christian subculture, which aims for relevance, and for artists of deep faith who wish to enrich culture through their art. We've already seen the outsider role played by both Tolkien and C. S. Lewis in the United Kingdom, and thoughtful, believing creatives had much the same experience in the United States. In his study of four influential twentieth-century Catholic writers, Paul Elie observes that Dorothy Day, Walker Percy, Flannery O'Connor, and Thomas Merton all wrote from the margins of both their faith community and the literary establishment: "Walker Percy saw writing, for example, as a message in a bottle, put in by one person to be urgently sent forth and read by another. That said, they situated themselves to some degree at the margins. And I think their Christian faith had to do with that. They didn't expect to be at the center of things."[2] If cocooning is the curse of fundamentalism, conformity and the abandonment of our alien status has been a tendency among today's evangelicals.

Given my background as a kid who exchanged the cocooned Christianity of my youth for immersion in culture intellectually and professionally, it seems odd that I am urging followers of Jesus to embrace their status as exiles. As a child, I was raised with a distorted view of what it meant to be an alien to culture, and later, I overcompensated by enthusiastically embracing culture. Having been warned away from popular culture, I ran headlong toward it. I'm glad I made the journey from cloistered faith into culture, because I learned important lessons in the process, but here, my tale takes a cautionary turn.

Having been raised in a cocoon and then immersed in popular culture, I now see that the extreme approaches taken toward culture by most Christians—cultural anorexia and cultural gluttony—are both spiritually unhealthy.[3] Today, though my deepening faith at times makes me feel like an alien, I am learning the balancing act of pursuing deep faith that is also culturally enriching. The fear of culture that I saw in the church of my youth made me want to understand more clearly what it means to be "in the world, but not of it" and what the Apostle Peter meant when he said to Jesus' disciples, "You are aliens and exiles."

"If you've had a freakish education, use it," said J. D. Salinger,[4] and so I will.

My Alien Childhood

I don't remember when I first heard a sermon about God's "peculiar people." It is a curious biblical phrase, applied to the Israelites three days into their flight from Egypt. In that text, God reminds the Israelites of their unhappy past in Egypt and how He carried them "on eagle's wings" and brought them to Himself. Then he promises them a bright future: If they obey Him, they will be a priestly kingdom, a holy nation, *a peculiar people* (Exodus 19:6; italics added). In the New Testament, Peter, quoting the Old Testament, expands on this idea, referring to Christians as God's "peculiar people, aliens and exiles" (1 Peter 2:9–11). I learned later that in both the Old and New Testaments, the Hebrew and Greek word translated as "peculiar" did not mean "quirky" or "weird" but rather was a wonderfully rich description of God's people as special, treasured, or set apart for a special purpose.

Like I said, I don't remember when I first heard a sermon about "God's peculiar people." All I know is that I attended a church full of them—and they didn't know the originally intended meaning of *peculiar* as translated from Hebrew or Greek. To be quirky and weird was just fine with them; they embraced it as their calling and executed it to near perfection.

The worship service in my church was surreal—mostly simple folks singing on or off key with the kind of unruly zeal you'd expect at an NFL playoff game or some sort of rave dance. They read the King James Bible and sang those hymns with Elizabethan lyrics and clumsy melodies. These people were characters. Old Zoe Parker was blind but always wanted to "see" me, which she did by cupping my face in her hands and tracing the contours of my mug, like it was some book in Braille. During one sermon, just as the pastor loudly quoted the verse, "Arise from the dead, oh thou who sleep," she jumped to her feet, agitated and confused, having just been awakened from her slumbers. Francis Hittle regaled us with an occasional solo on the saw, which he positioned between his legs (blade up and toward his vital organs), bending the blade with one hand and stroking it with a violin bow with the other, producing a sound vaguely reminiscent of the bizarre accompaniment in an episode of "The Twilight Zone." As the church choir sang John Stainer's "Crucifixion," their exuberant, untrained voices made sounds the composer could not have imagined in his wildest dreams or nightmares, recklessly wandering off the score into places no one had ever gone before. Bill Siewert once introduced Ray Brown by saying he would play a solo on his "constipated" trumpet. Immediately, a red-faced Ray intimated that he believed Bill meant to say "consecrated trumpet," but it was too late; the damage was done, and Ray played to an audience unsuccessfully struggling to suppress their laughter. One older, balding woman who taught children's Sunday School was endowed with a belly so ample that she could sit in a chair and rest the open Bible on her stomach, leaving both hands free to gesture.

I remember potlucks where people talked past mouths stuffed with food and old people with bad breath kissed me with scrambled eggs still stuck in their teeth. Way back in the 1950s, these wacky people performed the town's first living nativity scene at Christmas, only to see the escaped donkey straggle down the busiest street in Fullerton, California, with a few young, bathrobed faux shepherds and Mary Jane Sellers in hot pursuit. The Christmas pageants were like every hilarious montage of mishaps you've ever seen or heard about, with missed cues and lines delivered by frightened kids, who would cry out "Fear not!" to an ill-at-ease audience that was indeed terrified to see what might happen next. In its most bizarre moments as colored by my fertile imagination, my childhood church seemed like Lake Wobegon, *Northern Exposure*, *Hee Haw*, and *The Rocky Horror Picture Show* rolled into one, entertaining in retrospect, but at the time just weird and embarrassing to a young man trying to forge his identity in this world.

Everybody has to start somewhere, and my start was in this odd place where the world was considered evil and to be holy meant to separate yourself from the world. Churches like ours believed it was important to be behaviorally distinct, so they identified and made lists of illicit, "worldly" activities to be rejected by God's "peculiar people." At various times, the quantity of items on the list ranged from the filthy five or the sinful seven to the nasty nine or the dirty dozen. In addition to things like cursing, drinking, smoking, and gambling, the list might include dancing, smoking, card playing, attending the movies, watching television, or desecrating the Lord's day. In this cocoon, to please God, you gave up these sinful pleasures. For some of you, these recollections of legalistic holiness will seem painfully and personally familiar, and for others, they may sound more like a *National Geographic* special about some near-extinct primitive tribe.

Early in my life, it became clear to me that the peculiar tribe of my church was a subculture for which I was not well suited, for since birth, I had clearly been a "color outside the lines" kid. Blessed by God with a natural curiosity, I yearned to explore the ways of the world more fully, so in the second grade, I participated in an unspeakably wicked activity: dancing the bunny hop at Melvin Chambers's birthday party. Expecting to experience God's wrath, I was relieved that no divine retribution followed. However, illicit behavior seldom remains secret, and soon I stood before the judgment seat of God in the form of my privately amused but publicly stern parents.

My parents didn't totally agree with these lists, but because Dad was a pastor, his job was to make sure I set a good example. Being a good example was very big in fundamentalist circles, because it was believed that the weak among us might, in a fit of wild passion, be seduced into some nefarious, soul-compromising behavior simply because they saw others engaged in some enticing tomfoolery. Applied specifically to a second grader dancing the bunny hop, the message would go something like this: "Listen carefully, young man.

What if all the second graders in our church were to rebel against their parents, defiantly dancing the bunny hop? Can't you see where your behavior might lead?" So I was urged to do the right thing, to rein in my deviant streak, to set a good example. Privately, I wondered, What kind of bizarre, hoofer-averse God had these whacked-out adults been duped into revering?

By the fifth grade, having survived a multitude of behavioral and attitudinal lapses, I was tempted with yet another sin when a friend invited me to the Walt Disney film *White Wilderness*. I remember trying to mount a reasonable defense for attending this film to my parents. What could possibly go wrong in a film about polar bears in the wilderness? Did not God in all His glory create these animals and the pristine environment in which they frolic? The counter-argument went as follows: While I might be entering the theater to see *White Wilderness*, impressionable young Christians driving past the theater might think I was actually going to see a racy flick like Doris Day's *Pillow Talk* or something truly egregious like *Ben Hur* and, seeing me, a Christian they admired (huh?) engaged in such a questionable activity, might be tempted to lower their own high moral standards. I must not cause others to stumble in their spiritual walk. I must "avoid all appearance of evil" (1 Thessalonians 5:22 KJV). (Later, of course, I learned that the Apostle Paul's admonition against "avoiding every appearance" of evil was actually more accurately translated as a warning to avoid "every kind of evil," but who needs accurate translations when inerrant lists and wayward youth are concerned?) That same year, I "desecrated the Lord's day" by playing football on Sunday, an unconscionable act confirmed by church members who witnessed me returning home in my mud-splattered clothes. Of course, the same people eager to cast stones at me for playing football on Sunday eventually had absolutely no hesitation about watching Sunday football. (Somehow, over time, the viewing of television and movies, along with a few other items, was dropped from the list of forbidden activities.)

By age twelve, I had concluded that many of these "holy, sepa-rated people" in my church weren't holy; they were just various combinations of sincerely misguided and nuts! I also realized that the world was not a cesspool of immorality but rather was intermittently resplendent with God's creativity and presence. So my fellow rebels and I became cultural chameleons, conforming to our religious subculture's standards at church while mocking those rules when out "in the world." Some kids, lacking true conviction, worked the system, like my friend Leron, who, when assigned a square dancing partner in the seventh grade, tried to get excused from the class for "religious reasons," inquiring of the gym teacher, "What, know ye not that my body is the temple of the Holy Spirit? What fellowship has light with darkness?" (We were living proof of the famous "Doonesbury" comic strip aphorism: "Hypocrisy is the essence of fundamentalism!")

If you were raised outside fundamentalism, the religious rules of my childhood probably sound crazy and may confirm your worst fears about what it means for Christians to be aliens and exiles in the world. Ironically, the same fundamentalist tradition that tried to keep me from the world was devoted to world missions and to evangelization of lost, unbelieving souls living around us. As a result, my mandate as a Christian kid was to reach out to irreligious kids in order to attract them to something I thought was strange and irrelevant in my own life!

Deep Faith: Aliens and Exiles

It may seem odd, but despite my bizarre "alien" experience as a youth, today I embrace my calling as an alien and an exile and urge other Christians to do the same. This is because I now understand why following Jesus inevitably results in becoming aliens and a resistance force in culture. Here is what I have learned:

We are aliens and exiles because we are members of God's kingdom. Anyone who has traveled or lived abroad knows the feeling of disorientation and angst that accompanies geographic and cultural displacement. We experience something very similar when fully pursuing God's kingdom. As we learn to think and behave as God intends, we become less conformed to this world. Fully human, we experience both resonance and dissonance with culture because we are dual citizens, residents of this world and citizens in God's kingdom at the same time.

Throughout history, God's people have experienced physical relocation when following God's lead, but far more significant and universal has been the *spiritual* displacement of God's people that is caused by their countercultural outlook on life, which affects everything—their allegiances, purposes, beliefs, values, and behaviors. Followers of God are on a different path than those in the world around them. "Noah walked with God and found favor in the eyes of the Lord" when he was surrounded by people who continually pursued evil (Genesis 6). Abraham's family left Ur for Haran, and later, Abraham finished the sojourn to Canaan, where God promised to bless him and make of him a great nation. "He stayed a long time, as in a foreign land, living in tents, as did Isaac and Jacob" (Hebrews 11:8–9). Joseph was thrown into a pit by his jealous brothers and was rescued by traders who took him to Egypt, where he adjusted to foreign traditions and a language he did not know. Raised in the pharaoh's palace, Moses "chose rather to share ill treatment with the people of God than to enjoy the fleeting pleasures of sin (Hebrews 11:23–25). He led his people out of Egypt, and they wandered for forty years as strangers, pilgrims, and exiles.

Israel became a great nation, intentionally forged as a spiritual community with God as their king. Not content with a spiritual kingdom and with God as their king, they sought an earthly king, and after warning them of their misplaced hopes, God gave them kings and judges. Solomon built a great temple as the centerpiece of Israel's national identity. Forgetting that this world was not home and abandoning their spiritual identity for an earthly one, the rebellious Israelites were carried to captivity in Babylon, where they mourned, crying, "By the rivers of Babylon we sat down and wept when we remembered Zion. . . . How could we sing the Lord's song in a foreign land?" (Psalm 137). "All of these confessed that they were strangers and foreigners on earth, for they were seeking a homeland" (Hebrews 11:13–14).

God experienced exile from heaven when Jesus became flesh and dwelt among us, "though God had made the world with his Word He came into his own world but his own nation did not welcome him" (John 1:10–11). Jesus announced that God's kingdom is at hand and that the Lord God is its king and that while the fullest manifestation of God's kingdom is in the future, when every knee will bow and every tongue confess that Jesus is Lord, glimpses and tastes of God's kingdom are available now to those who seek, trust, and obey. Even now, "our food is to do the will of the Father" (John 4:34) and we may "drink from the springs of living water" (John 4:10). The psalmist said, "Lord, you have been our dwelling place in all generations. Before the mountains were brought forth, or ever you had formed the earth and the world, from everlasting to everlasting you are God" (Psalm 91:9). The metaphor of God as a dwelling place captures our dilemma. The more we experience God's presence, the more it feels like home, yet we also dwell on earth. For the culturally savvy Christian, dual citizenship means we are like the person with one foot on the dock and one foot on the departing boat. The deeper we go in God, the more we feel at home in God's kingdom and the less we feel at home in this fallen world.

Aliens are different by virtue of whom we serve, what we believe, and our values and behavior. As followers of Jesus, our citizenship in heaven is our highest calling. We are being transformed, so our beliefs, values, and behavior are reflections of our membership in God's kingdom. Such a transformation inevitably differentiates us from the general population. Citizens of the earthly kingdom are characterized by the "works of the flesh"; citizens of God's kingdom seek the "works of the spirit." Jesus categorized people in two groups—those who are members of the kingdom of God and those who are not. The Apostle John divided the world into two groups—those who walk in the light and those who walk in darkness. Jesus regularly challenged seekers to decide which group had their allegiance, asking, "Who do you serve, God or man?" Any self-described Christian who does not experience the tension of this dual citizenship has probably forsaken participation in one kingdom or the other.

Those who understand what it means to be a spiritual alien can learn strategic lessons from today's immigrants. At the turn of the twentieth century, as an influx of immigrants entered America, they abandoned their ethnic identity and embraced their new identity as Americans. The goal was to assimilate, to fit in, and become part of what was referred to as the "melting pot." Each ethnic group contributed to the mix, adding its own spicy, exotic flavor, resulting in an America that was envisioned as a wondrous, tasty stew achieved by mixing various flavors, each losing its distinctiveness in favor of a new and complex blend of tastes and textures that incorporated all the old ones.

Today, many ethnic groups resist total assimilation, choosing instead to retain aspects of their home culture that they prefer to Western ideas, values, and behaviors that they consider detrimental to their family life. In her fascinating book *The Middle of Everywhere*, psychologist Mary Pipher describes the range of refugee responses to their new culture: "In general there are four reactions refugees' families have to the new culture—*fight* it because it is threatening; *avoid* it because it is overwhelming; *assimilate* as fast as possible by making all American choices; or *tolerate discomfort and confusion* while slowly making intentional choices about what to accept and reject."[5]

Christians also choose one of these reactions in relationship to culture—fighting it (combating), avoiding it (cocooning), or assimilating into it (conforming). While for years, immigrants have been urged to assimilate into the melting pot, Pipher reports that a long-term study titled *Legacies* concludes that assimilation is not the healthiest path for the immigrant. A fourth option, "selective acculturation," is seen as the best, most sustainable option. In selective acculturation, immigrants retain their own identity while making intentional choices about what in the general culture they will accept or reject.

Selective acculturation is also the best path for the culturally savvy Christian. Because today's Christians are so assimilated into American culture, there is often little visible differentiation between self-identified Christians and the general population. Christians' absorption of the negative aspects of our fallen culture reflects our failure to resist the assimilative effects of enculturation. We cannot allow ourselves to be cocooned in a religiously defined gated community, for we are called into the world like Jesus, who lived and worked among the people in a local community. As we follow Jesus' example and engage with the world around us, we should not conform but should retain the distinctive beliefs, values, and behaviors that are consistent with God's kingdom. The only healthy way to live in the tension between the two worlds is selective acculturation; you often hear this described as being in the world but not of the world.

Aliens are not alone, but form a community. We pursue God in a unique company of friends described in two Greek words, *ekklesia,* which means "to be called out," and *koinania,* which means "a fellowship." Jesus' followers were formed into a church—an *ekklesia*—and a community fellowship—a *koinania.* We are called into the world to be a loving, transforming presence, and we are called out of the world to enjoy a community of fellowship with other followers of Jesus.

Christians are strangers, pilgrims, exiles, and sojourners whose lives are guided by the indwelling Holy Spirit. We are equipped, encouraged, and strengthened by our fellow Christians in the church. Surrounded by acquaintances and friends in the world who do not share their allegiance to God, the alien hungers for community with people who seek the kingdom of God above all else. This is precisely the spirit captured in Tolkien's *The Fellowship of the Ring,* in which Frodo's league of friendship sustained him as he sought to meet his challenges. Culturally savvy Christians yearn for a place they can call home, where they can have fellowship with other aliens and exiles, their kindred spirits in Christ. The church should be this home, where our own fellowship enables us to fulfill, in

Tolkien's language, our "oath to lord and land," God's kingdom and this world.

Only later in life have I come to realize that I inherited the richest of families in the people I once mocked as "peculiar" and "strange." In the alien community of my childhood, the songs were mostly sentimental, with archaic lyrics and clumsy melodies, but they gave voice to people who wanted God to be central in their lives. The ancient hymns that once made me cringe eventually drew me back to the faith: "When peace, like a river, attendeth my way, when sorrows like sea billows roll; whatever my lot, thou hast taught me to say, It is well, it is well with my soul."[6] "Great is thy Faithfulness, Oh God my Father, there is no shadow of turning with thee. You change not, your compassions they fail not."[7]

The people I knew as a child were characters, but they also *had* character. Though many of these folks were odd, there was never a shadow of doubt in my mind that they loved God and loved me. They were real, and their faith stood the test of time. The grey-haired, elderly saints whom I see today in a local retirement home remind me of them. In the twilight of their lives, I see them meditating on the word, reading their large-print Bibles, faithfully trusting God to the end. I would love to reintroduce into church life today the positive benefits and fellowship I experienced in my youth, a time when people spent a lot of time with each other— singing, praying, worshiping, eating, laughing, crying, and regularly going on retreats together. Building community takes time, but it is worth the effort.

Although as a child, I grew weary of spending so much time with people in our church, oddly, what I experienced then is what culturally savvy Christians need today, when our busy, isolated, disconnected lives prevent us from breaking bread together. In our media-saturated, virtual world, we need relationships that go deep and a place where we can pursue God in the company of friends. We need fellowship that is intergenerational, incarnational, and multi-ethnic. We need to create a place where God can draw people together across demographic lines: rich and poor; blue-collar and professional; country, hip-hop, and classical. We need churches that are multidimensional, not because those kinds of churches are hip or trendy or will make the church grow but because the nature of God's kingdom is multidimensional. We are supposed to be robust examples of God's kingdom on earth now. Based on our real-life experience, we jokingly chant, "To dwell above with saints we love, oh that will be glory, but to dwell below with saints we know, now that's a different story!" We somehow know that just such a motley fellowship of sojourners is our foretaste of heaven. Eugene Peterson once said, "Assemble in your imagination all the friends that you enjoy being with most. The companions that evoke the deepest joy, your most stimulating relationships, the most delightful of shared experiences, the people with whom you feel completely alive—that is a hint of heaven."[8]

Aliens influence culture by exhibiting a winsome alternative way of life. Culturally savvy Christians don't set out to be countercultural; such cultural distinctness happens as a natural by-product of faithfulness to the spirit and rule of God's kingdom. Jesus was so radically different from other teachers that observers described him as one who spoke with authority. He was persuasive because he taught with reason and passion, he lived what he taught, and there was a seamlessness between his private and public life. He embodied poise, self-control, and a confident presence in every situation. Whether drawn to him by his signs and wonders or by his teaching, his disciples stayed because of who Jesus was and how he lived. He was the real deal.

Today, we search for authenticity in our world and seldom find it. Society suffers from the ravages of divorce, family dysfunction, environmental degradation, war, consumerism, the trivialization of the sacred, the loss of innocence, gender confusion, ageism, lust, drunkenness, substance abuse, fiscal irresponsibility, sloth, obesity, vulgarity, incessant quarreling, violence, anger, disrespect for parents, rebellion, ruthlessness, gossip, pride, triviality, coarseness, covetousness, and more. Do followers of Jesus live in contrast to these societal corruptions?

Theologians Stanley Hauerwas and William Willimon refer to Christians as "resident aliens" whose life together offers a healthy, attractive alternative to today's unwell, fallen culture.[9] This was certainly the case in Jerusalem, where the first disciples' communal life was obviously winsomely countercultural. "They devoted themselves to the apostles' teaching and fellowship, to the breaking of bread and the prayers. Awe came upon everyone, because the Apostles were doing many wonders and signs. All who believed were together and had all things in common; they would sell their possessions and goods and distribute the proceeds to all, as any had need. Day by day, as they spent much time together in the temple, they broke bread at home and ate their food with glad and generous hearts and praising God" (Acts 2:42–47). The text adds two other comments. First, this dynamic community attracted "the goodwill of "all the people." Second, "the Lord added to their number day by day those who were being saved" (Acts 2:47). Similarly, the Apostle Peter urged the disciples "as sojourners and exiles to abstain from the passions of the flesh . . . to keep your conduct among the Gentiles honorable . . . so they may see your good deeds and glorify God in the day of visitation" (1 Peter 2:11–12). A healthy church should inevitably offer a winsome contrast to the substandard life of fallen culture, and as such, it should pose an irresistible invitation to people weary of this age to consider the alternative of the fully human life found in relationship with God.

The *ekklesia* of *koinania* (being called out for fellowship) should serve as evidence that people who drink from a deeper well can become deeply well, that broken human spirits can be healed and shattered souls made healthy, that deeply well people can form communities to pursue God in the company of friends. Christians living this embodied vision of God's kingdom offer hope. Our marriages can be healed, and our homes can become joyful places of love, acceptance, and forgiveness. Deeply well people will pursue wellness for all the earth, becoming advocates for justice and champions for the environment. Deeply well people will be known as self-disciplined people, able to control their tempers, lusts, and pocketbooks.

If culturally savvy Christians discern the appropriate reaction to and relationship with technology, money, marketing, and popular culture, and if the culture they create adheres to a higher standard, it seems logical that Christians, though dwelling on the edges of culture, will draw the attention of hungry souls seeking deep wellness. Would society not take notice of a fellowship pursuing lofty aims, bound together by the desire for radical transformation by God, humbly and honestly committed to confessing their failures, and united by a desire to love, accept, and forgive one another?

Aliens practice discernment and selective acculturation in regard to popular culture. And what of the culturally savvy Christian's relationship with popular culture? Culturally savvy Christians follow the path of neither the cultural glutton nor the cultural anorexic. Instead, they are marked by their discretion and thoughtful discernment.

To discern means to see something that is not very clear or obvious. The Apostle Paul taught that only renewed minds are able to discern God's will. Because popular culture is powerful, pervasive, and persuasive, each day we will be called upon to practice discernment, but what does it mean to show discernment? How do we do it?

Fortunately, the Apostle Paul used a concrete cultural example facing believers in Corinth to provide a set of timeless guidelines on how we should be discerning as we evaluate our involvement in culture. In first-century Corinth, pagan temples were common, and as part of their temple rites, pagans offered meat to the gods enthroned there. Not wanting to waste good meat, the priests gathered it up, ate what they needed, and sold the rest to the markets, where it would be resold to the Corinthians.

Wanting to be culturally savvy, some devout Corinthian Christians wondered whether buying and eating meat that had been offered to pagan gods was spiritually unwise. Because this meat wasn't specially marked, they were concerned that they would be spiritually polluted, even if they bought it unintentionally. Christians took different positions on the matter, some of them deeply held, and bitter disagreements began to divide the Corinthian believers. Paul was asked to rule on the matter, and he concluded that believers were free to eat the meat but should exercise their liberty responsibly.

Paul's guidelines can be summarized as follows:[10]

- *All things are lawful.* "The earth is the Lord's, and the fullness thereof." Paul began by establishing each individual's personal responsibility for making these decisions. Believers are not bound by some legalistic set of rules but are responsible before God for making prudent decisions. He reminds us that everything on earth is the Lord's, including meat offered to idols. Jesus taught similarly, that it is not what goes into us that defiles, but what comes out of us.

- *All things are not beneficial.* "Not all things build up." Paul asks what individual and community benefits will result from our decision. Having concluded that we are free to make our own decisions, Paul reminds believers that not everything is equally good for us. Applying Jesus' rule, you can eat anything, but not everything has equal nutritional value. Paul constantly pushes believers to ask what is the highest and best behavior, not just what we are allowed to do.

- *Do not be dominated by anything.* "I will not be enslaved by anything." Paul recognizes that regardless of how believers choose to exercise their liberty, under no circumstances should they allow any behavior or practice to master or control them.

- *Do not cause another to fall.* "Let no one seek his own good, but the good of his neighbor. Therefore, if what I eat causes my brother to fall into sin, I will never eat meat again, so that I will not cause him to fall." Paul recognizes that although we are free to make personal choices, believers should not use their freedom in a way that causes other believers to lose their faith. In legalistic circles, Paul's command to "not cause your brother to stumble" is used as a way to control and restrict other people's behavior, but Paul makes it clear that even in this matter, we exercise individual freedom and personal discretion. "As for the one who is weak in faith, welcome him, but not to quarrel over opinions. One person believes he may eat anything, while the weak person eats only vegetables. Let not the one who eats despise the one who abstains, and let not the one who abstains pass judgment on the one who eats, for God has welcomed him. Who are you to pass judgment on the servant of another?" (Romans 14:1–4).

- *Whatever you do, do it for the glory of God.* "So whether you eat or drink or whatever you do, do it all for the glory of God." Paul reminds believers of their ultimate calling to glorify God in everything they do, which is consistent with Abraham Heschel's classic teaching: "God is of no importance unless He is of supreme importance."[11]

Applying Paul's guidelines to our relationship with popular culture starts with acknowledging our liberty and then asking four specific questions about our choices: (1) Is it helpful? (2) Does it bring us under its power or have a controlling influence in our life? (3) Does it pose a serious risk to the faith of other believers? (4) Does it glorify God?

Discerning whether a specific movie or song or game belongs in your life starts prior to its consumption. Just as we might evaluate the ingredients in a box of cereal prior to eating it, there are plenty of resources available to help us gauge whether an element of popular culture is appropriate or not. Once we've decided to listen to a new CD, play a new game, or watch a movie, for instance, the discernment process continues. Paul advises believers to "take every thought captive," and this means monitoring the content we take in by asking, Is it helpful? Addictive? Harmful to others? Glorifying to God?

Paul stated these principles differently to the church at Philippi, saying, "Whatever is true, whatever is honorable, whatever is just, whatever is pure, whatever is pleasing, whatever is commendable, if there is any excellence and if there is anything worthy of praise, think about these things" (Philippians 4:8). Some people use this verse to argue against consuming any media item that includes violence, promiscuity, nudity, adultery, swearing, or other questionable behaviors. However, the Bible itself is packed with descriptions of these very behaviors because they are true aspects of human life.

The issue, therefore, is more nuanced. Because evil is part of the human experience, good art will take evil seriously. Rather than eliminating all popular culture that includes evil, culturally savvy Christians will want to discern how a piece of art handles evil. Does it simply *depict* evil in ways that maintain the integrity and truthfulness of the story? Does it *discourage* evil, elevating the good by revealing the nature and consequences of evil? Does it *endorse* evil, portraying it as normative and without consequence? Does it *incite* us to evil acts, as pornography might? Is the evil *gratuitous*, unconnected to the story, unnecessary except to appeal to our baser instincts?

Today, the toughest test we can apply is to ask whether the media items we consume represent the highest and best spiritually, intellectually, and aesthetically. As our faith grows deeper, our concern for nurturing our soul will affect our media consumption. Today, many Christians think discernment refers only to the content of art, but discernment extends to artistic quality as well. Our appetite for media products that excel in every way will motivate us to encourage thoughtful, talented artists of deep faith to create more and better art. Once, as I addressed a group of artists, one of them, a very accomplished craftsman, expressed his frustration with Christians' criticizing his work for its vivid portrayals of evil while readily accepting artistically inferior, romanticized art. I quickly shot back, "Bad art *is* evil." I was not trying to minimize the problem of content that pollutes our spirits by virtue of its superficiality or immorality but rather to articulate a holistic approach to the matter of discernment. So what can we conclude about practicing discernment in today's media culture?

Discernment means being serious about our faith commitment. If our allegiance is to God, we will want to please God in every area of our life, including our media consumption. Our greatest protection against the pollutants in culture is to love God with all our heart, mind, strength, and soul, and to live each day with a sense of God's indwelling presence.

Discernment means practicing a healthy respect for the dark side. The first challenge faced by Daniel, a Jewish believer exiled in Babylon, was an attack on his allegiance to God. An edict was signed that made it illegal to pray to anyone but the king. Daniel refused to yield, dropping to his knees and praying three times to God. In exile Joseph was tested with lust when Potiphar's wife offered herself to him. Joseph fled. Today, temptations tailored to our vulnerabilities are presented via the sights and sounds of entertainment media. Only a fool would think that the enemy of their soul has not mastered a devious competence in using these to his advantage in the fight for our souls. *Time* magazine's cultural critic Lance Morrow described one Oscar-winning movie as "sneaky in its philosophical emanations; gases may enter undetected and start to affect the brain before we realize what is happening. I begin to think we should each carry a canary into darkened movie theaters. If the canary starts to gasp and keel over, we should run for our lives."[12]

Discernment means evaluating the nuances of art, not just evaluating it based on a superficial checklist of unacceptable elements. Good art deals with truth, and we are required to think on things that are true along with things that are honorable, just, and pure. Some Christian media critics warned people not to watch *Schindler's List,* a film that depicted the horrors of the Holocaust, because of a brief scene depicting Jewish women being stripped of their clothes. Obviously, the truly horrifying depiction of evil in the film was the portrayal of ashes of incinerated Jews rising from the smokestacks. Similarly, the violence in *Training Day* is relentless and horrific, yet germane to the story. After first reading the script of this movie, for which he received a Best Actor Academy Award, Denzel Washington wrote across the title page, "The wages of sin is death." Evil is depicted in this movie but not endorsed.

As culturally savvy Christians, we will practice selective acculturation, allowing ourselves to experience resonance with art that connects us with the joy, pain, and realities of our fellow humans while also identifying and guarding against dissonant values, ideas, beliefs, and behavior. We can be both connoisseurs and critics of culture. At home and in church, our responsibility is to teach an appreciation for the arts, along with the skills of discovery and discernment that will allow us to enjoy, evaluate, and engage culture in ways that enrich both it and us.

The Church as Moveable Feast

Novelist Ernest Hemingway once described Paris as a "moveable feast," saying that once you've experienced it, wherever you go for the rest of your life, it goes with you.[13] I like to think of our communal gathering of the "called out" everywhere in the world as our "moveable feast." We bring the richness of our fellowship to all our endeavors, enhancing and transforming our daily experience and finding a home wherever we find other followers of Christ gathered.

The culturally savvy Christian's winsome countercultural life, even when coupled with active participation in building and enriching culture, will not guarantee our acceptance in the broader culture. The very decision to pursue the kingdom of God as your first priority will stand in stark contrast to a life ruled by the self.

Peter urges humility, gentleness, and reverence in our relationships with unbelievers, because even when we seek to live peaceably with fallen culture, the servant is not higher than the master, and we serve one who was nailed to a cross because of his radically countercultural life and beliefs. Nevertheless, on occasion, even in the most hostile environment, someone will step forth and ask the reason for our hope. The culturally savvy Christian resists culture, but also understands the gospel's relevance for culture. In the next chapter, we will address our ambassadorial role as people of deep, culturally enriching faith who are always ready to offer a reason for the hopefulness of our lives.

8

COMMUNICATING IN CULTURE LIKE AMBASSADORS

The world speaks of the holy in the only language
it knows, which is a worldly language.[1]
FREDERICK BUECHNER

We are becoming culturally savvy Christians. We are *savvy* about story we are in, and we are aware of the possibilities and pitfalls posed by our powerful but superficial popular culture and Christianity-Lite. We are *serious* about our pursuit of God, and we are experiencing God's loving, transforming presence in our lives, enabling us to become a loving, transforming presence in the world. We are countercultural like aliens, practicing our *skills* of discernment and selective acculturation in the world and enjoying the pursuit of God in the company of friends.

Because we are increasingly discovering what it means to be fully human, we have something exciting to share with people around us, but we agree with St. Francis, who, according to legend, said, "Preach, and if you must, use words."[2] Because we hold dual citizenship, we are like ambassadors who stand at the intersection between two countries, using their knowledge of both cultures to interpret each to the other in order to build a bridge of understanding between the two.

We are in good company. In the first century, the Apostle Paul described himself as an ambassador for Christ, and the situation he faced in Athens was surprisingly similar to the one we face today. First-century Athens was an irreligious place that, under the influence of the Stoics, had enthroned individuals as god and nature as the object of their worship. According to one historian, it was the most "sacred shrine of the fair humanities of paganism."[3] Highly individualistic Athenians could say with British poet William Henley, "I thank whatever gods may be / For my unconquerable soul. . . . I am the master of my fate; / I am the captain of my soul"[4]

People who will worship anything in fact worship nothing, and as in every spiritually delusional society, the enthronement of humans leads not to their elevation but to their debasement. Athens, which four hundred years earlier had been the birthplace of democracy and home of the world's leading thinkers (Plato, Socrates, and Aristotle), by Paul's day, had degenerated into a promiscuous pleasure palace, Asia Minor's center of prostitution and debauchery. The Epicureans embraced a philosophy of pleasure, reveling in Athens's "eat, drink, and be merry" spirit.

Self-enthronement produces hungry souls, and the Athenians and the foreigners visiting there were seekers, "spending their time in nothing except telling or hearing something new" (Acts 17:21). To the Athenians, unfamiliar with Hebrew Scriptures and stories of Jesus' life, death, and resurrection, Paul's ideas were novel and different. The news of Jesus, which was spreading like wildfire throughout the Roman Empire, struck them as strange, and they wanted to hear more about it. They gathered for spirited discussions at the Areopagus, the tribunal located on the Hill of Ares at the northwest corner of the Acropolis, gathering news and information, exploring the meaning of Paul's provocative words.

A brilliant communicator, Paul was faced with the ultimate cross-cultural assignment. How could he communicate the deep wellness available through reunion with God to cosmopolitan, highly educated, promiscuous, earth-worshiping, biblically illiterate, spiritually seeking, self-enthroning, highly individualistic people?

The ambassadorial challenge faced by Paul is nearly identical to the one we Christians face today. A few years ago, Cathy Grossman, religion writer for *USA Today*, asked me to comment on "godless Washington"; she was referring not to Washington, D.C., but to Washington State. Recent research had revealed that Washington was the most "unchurched" state in the country.[5] It has been called the "none zone" because while 14 percent of Americans considered themselves irreligious in 2002, in Seattle, those declaring their religion as "none" constituted 24 percent. Grossman used Seattleite Ralph Leitner as an anecdotal example, who, when asked what he did on Easter, replied, "Well, we [he and his children] like to go out in the woods. When you're in the great outdoors, you can't help but be spiritual out there."

By virtually every measurement, America is quickly becoming biblically illiterate; one survey revealed that the majority of church-going Christians believe that Noah was married to Joan of Arc and cannot name the four Gospels. Eighty percent of all Americans said that the most famous quote in the Bible is "God helps those who help themselves." This would be news to Thomas Jefferson, who, though he was known to edit the Bible, did not write it and who was the first to utter that phrase.

As I mentioned earlier, despite Americans' irreligiosity, 82 percent say they are spiritual seekers and 52 percent say they have talked about spiritual issues in the preceding twenty-four hours, according to George Gallup.[6] Like the Athenians, today's seekers spend their time on nothing except telling or hearing something new. Look at any cosmopolitan center in today's world, and you'll find an educated, promiscuous, earth-worshiping, biblically illiterate, spiritually seeking, self-enthroning, highly individualistic populace. Even though we who have found the deeper well will often feel like aliens or exiles in such a place, we should also, like Paul, seek to be effective ambassadors. By observing Paul's behavior in Athens, we learn three essential characteristics of an ambassador.

An Ambassador Cares Deeply About People

Paul was deeply distressed by what he saw in Athens. The Greek word translated "deep distress" is *paroxysm*, an intense attack or spasm. As he strolled around the city, Paul was profoundly distraught because of the abundance of idols that were kept and displayed in Athenian homes and temples. Like Jesus, who was moved to compassion when he saw the spiritually confused crowds, Paul saw spiritually hungry people seeking the restoration of their souls in places where it could never be found.

Our first response to the culture around us should be a mixture of distress and compassion. My friend the late Dwight Ozard once wrote in *Prism* magazine, "The greatest mission field we face is not in some faraway land. The strange and foreign culture most Americans fear is not across the ocean, it's barely across the street. The culture most lost to the gospel is our own, our children and our neighbors. It's a culture that can't say two sentences without referring to a TV show or a pop song. It's a culture more likely to have a body part pierced than to know why Sarah laughed. It's a culture that we stopped loving and declared a culture war on."[7]

In the early 1990s, when my family and I moved from Seattle to Naperville, a suburb of Chicago, Washington's "emerald city" had just been named by Rand McNally as the nation's most livable city. Eight years later, when we moved back to Seattle from Chicago, things had changed. The first time I went down to Pike Place Market (a favorite tourist spot on the waterfront), the sweet little park overlooking Elliott Bay was overrun with drunks, hookers, homeless people, and panhandlers. My first thought was "Man, if Mayor Daly was here, these guys would be busted. They'd be off the streets. No way would he allow Chicago's Michigan Avenue [a great tourist site like Pike Place Market] to be taken over by derelicts and the dregs of society." Then I visited Pioneer Square and saw all the nose rings, tattoos, and pink hair. I drove through Capitol Hill, not knowing that it was the day of the annual gay pride parade, and witnessed things I hadn't seen since I lived in San Francisco in the 1970s. My first reaction on returning to Seattle was to think like the chamber of commerce: "We need to clean this place up a bit for the visitors!" I was focused on how Rand McNally rated Seattle instead of seeing Seattle through God's loving eyes.

A few weeks later, I met a young guy named Lenny who was the lead singer for a Seattle-based rock group that had performed together for a decade, singing music that was stylistically like KoRn's. Four years earlier, he had become a Christian. About six feet, five inches tall and sporting hair dyed bright blonde and two giant earrings, he was wearing tight leather pants with laces down the sides from his hips to his ankles. I asked him, "What's happened to the Seattle music scene? For a while there, it was so hot." Without skipping a beat, Lenny said, "What happened to the Seattle music scene is the groups all got big, did heroin, and died."

I thought of Dave Williams, lead singer of Drowning Pool, who had died a few years earlier of natural causes resulting from a heart problem. In an interview, he had said, "I was always told when I was growing up that religious people shouldn't judge others by their appearance, by their attitude or by anything else, but it seems like they're among the first to judge you, even before they really know what they're judging. I had someone look at my sinner tattoo and tell me I was going to hell. Well, I guess that's okay. I never said I wasn't a sinner. I think just about everyone is in one way or another. Nobody's perfect, but I believe I'm a good person. I love my friends and family. I think we're bringing a lot of pleasure to people through music. If religious people have trouble with that, I'm sorry."[8] If we are not moved by what Williams said, I think *we* are the ones with a heart problem.

Since the 1960s, I had prided myself on my ability to see the image of God in each person. Eight years of comfortable midwestern suburban living (and probably middle age and growing protective instincts associated with parenting teenage daughters) had blurred my vision. I was reminded of a conversation with a young man who had decided to find creative ways to communicate God's love to his generation. He told me that it had all started with a serious mistake. What was his mistake? "Two years ago, I prayed to see my generation through God's eyes, and I've been weeping ever since."

Ambassadors care deeply about the people they encounter in daily life, seeing in each the faded image of God, knowing that God's loving, transforming presence could restore the glow.

An Ambassador Is Culturally Aware

Ambassadors listen carefully to culture because through it, we see and hear the hopes, fears, pains, and passions of the spiritual seeker. Upon arriving in Athens, Paul observed the cultural landscape very carefully, examining the idols, witnessing the promiscuity, and hearing the lively animated conversations. He saw the Athenians' religious devotion to irreligiosity. To increase his cultural awareness, Paul became educated in the popular culture of the day and even read pagan poetry carefully enough to quote it. Culture reveals a lot about people; by studying their culture, Paul knew quite a bit about the Athenians before ever talking to them.

In today's diversionary, mindless, and spiritually impoverished culture, the Christian ambassador remains familiar with culture in order to gain a fresh understanding of how to know and hear today's seekers and communicate more effectively with them. The skilled ambassador knows that every week, among the new movies, books, and songs released, there are revelatory messages that provide opportunities for understanding and communication. Identifying those messages requires the development of the ambassador's discovery skills.

If we wish to be culturally savvy Christians, we must hone our discovery skills to enable us to truly hear, see, and read the essence of our culture (for instance, in the art it produces). While we are trained to take every thought captive and we strive for deep literacy in our faith, we should not allow this prior knowledge to interfere with our willingness or ability to receive new perspectives and insights in unexpected places. The person of deep faith should be a fearless adventurer and explorer, a relentless pursuer of truth wherever he or she might find it. Explorers approach unknown territories with all senses on high alert; only by entering will they know whether exciting possibilities, life-threatening dangers, or a mixture of both await them there. The skilled ambassador approaches popular culture in the same way, whether watching a movie, listening to music, reading a newspaper, or playing a game.

Discovery skills enable us to get the most out of a cultural piece of work, so that we can understand and enjoy it more fully. *Discovery* is the process of approaching a piece of work with the aim of observing and documenting. This is different from just encountering something, reacting to it, and then forming a personal opinion. During the discovery phase, we compare and contrast without judgment, like anthropologists who take field notes (mental or recorded) and then evaluate them later.

Cultural discovery is an objective process, like that of a bird watcher, who, while experiencing the sheer excitement and joy of encountering a new bird, concurrently employs keen powers of observation: watching for markings in some detail, listening for sounds, observing flight patterns, noting body size and wingspan, calculating the placement of color, gauging the geographic setting, pondering the bird's usual range and habitat, and, when possible, examining a nest and eggs, scraping a fecal sample to see whether diet can be determined, or grabbing a stray feather to inspect more closely later. The bird watcher does all this in a few seconds! How much data, then, might we accumulate during a two-hour movie, a 700-page book, a four-minute song, or a full CD with fifty minutes of music?

To be effective as cultural ambassadors, we must be familiar with the components or building blocks of each type of art and use them to analyze and document our experience of media. Any work of art—whether in film, music, visual art, or architecture—can be broken into smaller constituent units. For example, a book is composed of chapters, chapters of paragraphs, paragraphs of sentences, sentences of words, and words of letters. Each word encompasses a definition that is derived from its placement and context in the sentence, and so forth. We can only understand any piece of art, as we would a book, by breaking it down into its bits and pieces. Art evokes at a macro level, but it is built at the micro level; discovery skills allow us to observe and investigate both.

The most useful assessment of any piece of art comes through a genuine encounter in which we make candid and even random observations about the work, without forcing it into any preconceived categories. A sample of questions useful for "discovering" a book, movie, song, or interactive media experience might include the following: What type of medium are you evaluating? What is the genre? What stylistic conventions are employed? What is the title? Who is the artist, creator, or author? What is the central theme, summarized succinctly in one sentence? What is the basic story? What beliefs are advanced? What provocative questions and issues are raised? What are the artistic merits (spiritual, intellectual, and aesthetic)? What are the points of resonance (that is, what elements common to human experience do you discover or connect with)? What are the points of dissonance (that is, what elements do you find jarring or discordant, and why)? What does this piece of art reveal about God? About humans? What are some key words or themes, and how do they relate to the work as a whole? Have you discovered any information about the artist's background or life situation that provides insight or that may illuminate the origin or their intention for this piece of work? What provocative words, phrases, symbols, or images appear in the work? What do you think the artist is saying? What do you think the artist means? What applicability and connectivity does this piece of art offer you personally?

Paul exercised his discovery skills in Athens, where he had a few days to kill while awaiting the arrival of Timothy and Silas. Before Paul communicated with Athenian seekers, he spent some time getting acquainted with them by strolling around their city. Picture him wandering the streets, taking in the architecture and sidewalk culture, overhearing the conversations. Later, when he did speak, his presentation was peppered with the language of an ambassador who has mastered discovery skills: he saw, he perceived, he passed through the city, he observed, he conversed, he listened to their questions, he went with them to the Areopagus, he found an idol and read the inscription "To an unknown god," and he quoted their favorite pagan poets.

Like Paul, our aim in the discovery process is to observe and investigate our popular culture so that we can understand and interpret what it means on its own merits. In this process, it is useful to examine the constituent elements of the art, to research the artist, and to be attentive to our reaction to the art.

An Ambassador Builds Bridges from Culture to Faith

Ambassador Paul cared deeply enough to become culturally aware. He was literate in his faith and had invested himself in the process of discovery, having studied Athens in some detail. Now Paul was ready to build the bridge connecting the Athenians' obvious spiritual needs and the good news of Jesus the Christ.

Once he had absorbed Athenian culture through listening and observing, Paul compared and contrasted Christian beliefs with those of the Athenians. I call this skill *dual listening,* which is like holding a Bible in one hand and a screenplay, script, lyric sheet, book, magazine article, or newspaper in the other. Holding the two side by side, the culturally savvy Christian engages in dual listening by assessing, comparing, contrasting, correlating, analyzing, evaluating, understanding, synthesizing, and conceptualizing in order to interpret faith in light of cultural insights and to interpret culture in light of insights from our faith.

Dual listening requires both biblical and cultural literacy. Over time, culturally savvy Christians should acquire a fairly comprehensive grasp of the essential themes, stories, and characters, as well as key verses in the Bible. Some Christians groan when I push for biblical literacy, arguing that we should focus on orthopraxy (right practice), not orthodoxy (right belief). While I agree that our faith is more than the mastery of a body of factual knowledge and I value orthopraxy, this is not an either-or situation. Today's Christians tend to be exceedingly literate in popular culture but lack a comparable biblical knowledge. When this is the case, they are doomed to display naïveté, ignorance, and an utter inability to discern the essential and the peripheral in both popular culture and faith. Biblical illiteracy cuts us off from revealed truth and makes us vulnerable to every new faddish idea.

While every culturally savvy Christian should possess a comprehensive literacy in faith, the cultural literacy of savvy Christians should be targeted more specifically. Our aim in cultural literacy should be personal usefulness and applicability, not encyclopedic knowledge. We should be literate in the cultural genre we personally appreciate (for example, film, music, TV, fine art, or opera), and we should also maintain a basic literacy in aspects of culture that are important for fulfilling our general calling. For instance, anyone wanting to enrich culture will stay abreast of the news, and periodicals and online resources are available to keep us up to speed in other areas of media and entertainment. There are also situations in which our cultural literacy will draw us into media awareness outside our personal tastes and interests. Parents, youth pastors, and anyone else in regular contact with young people will want to become literate in what kids are attracted to; the people with whom we work will talk about the movies they plan to see or the latest book they've read, and these conversations can be a guide to our own media consumption.

Through the process of dual listening, Paul identified points of agreement and disagreement between his Christian worldview and that of the Athenians. Armed with that knowledge, he then decided how to communicate in a language the Athenians could understand. An ambassador may not be fluent in the local language, but is able to speak enough of it to make the connection that is essential for effective communication. This is the nature of our bilingualism as ambassadors. We become fluent enough to understand the nuances of both faith and popular culture, and we use appropriate language to interpret each to the other. Once Paul selected his issues and identified some concepts that would be useful in connecting Christian faith with Athenian beliefs, he began to speak. By studying Paul's communication in Athens we learn some very important lessons:

Ambassadors build bridges by tailoring the style and content of their communication to fit the specific audience and place. Read Acts 17, and you will notice that Paul was *conciliatory* when speaking to the crowd in the Areopagus, that he *reasoned* with Jews and the devout in the synagogue, and that he *debated* the Epicurean and Stoic philosophers in the marketplace. Before saying a word, Paul considered his context and his audience—*where* he would be speaking and *whom* he would be speaking to. Both Jesus and Paul were contextual in their application of the good news, and we should be too; the idea of a cookie-cutter, one size-fits-all approach to sharing God's love would have been foreign to them. To effectively share God's intention to restore all that unraveled in the aftermath of humankind's foul revolt, the culturally savvy ambassador must discover the most effective point of entry for each person or group they encounter. Jesus never shared the story of God's love the same way twice, and neither did Paul. To underscore the importance of understanding the audience's unique identity and needs before communicating, Paul once said, "I have become all things to all people, that I might by all means save some" (1 Corinthians 9:22).

Jesus was also aware of his audience. In public, Jesus usually told parables that raised provocative questions and invited people into the process of exploring the answers. Some people just didn't get it; others were curious and came back for more. In private, Jesus explained things more fully, especially to his disciples. After telling a large group the parable of the sower and the seed (Mark 4), Jesus took his most serious followers aside and explained in detail what the parable meant. These disciples were apparently chosen, not because they got it, but because they *wanted* to get it. Their desire to go deeper was demonstrated when they left their nets to follow him. The Gospel of Mark explains Jesus' communication pattern very clearly: "He did not speak to them without a parable, but privately to his own disciples he explained everything" (Mark 4:34).

Jesus entrusted the task of communicating his teachings to every follower. When Jesus radically transformed people, they often wanted to travel with him, but Jesus usually told them to stay in their own community and to spread the word among their friends. This happened in Jesus' dramatic encounter with a man filled with demons. "As Jesus was getting into the boat, the man who had been possessed with demons begged him that he might be with him. And he did not permit him but said to him, 'Go home to your friends and tell them how much the Lord has done for you, and how he has had mercy on you.' And he went away and began to proclaim in the Decapolis how much Jesus had done for him, and everyone marveled" (Mark 5:18–20).

What we observe in Jesus is a diverse approach to communicating about the spiritual. Publicly and in groups, Jesus provoked interest and piqued curiosity, like an author who entices the reader to read another chapter. Privately, for those who were truly and demonstrably interested, Jesus went deeper and explained more. Personally, he encouraged his followers to talk with their friends about their personal journey. Jesus did this so that "by all means" he "might save some."

Ambassadors build bridges by starting with what their audience already believes and showing how it relates to the truth they need to know. The culturally savvy Christian learns that communication is most effective if it starts with the stories and experiences that people know and bridges to those that they need to know but don't. This requires *bilingualism*, the ability to relate the language, symbols, and stories of faith to the language, symbols, and stories of culture. Generally, this approach is more effective when the ambassador starts with culture and bridges to faith, rather than vice versa. Westminster Chapel's Bible expositor G. Campbell Morgan once said, "In every system of false religion there is an open door for the true!"[9] Culturally savvy Christians find the open door so that truth can enter it.

Paul started by acknowledging the Athenians' objects of worship, one of which was inscribed "To an unknown god." Provocatively, Paul announced that he knew something about this unknown god, starting with the god's identity as creator. Rather than quoting Scripture to a biblically illiterate audience for whom the Jewish Scriptures had no credence or authority, Paul quoted what two of their popular poets said about the creator: "For we indeed are his offspring" and "In him we live and move and have our being." By using what the Athenians already accepted as a provocative exploration of the deity and creation, Paul was able to attract interest and to build a bridge to the news of a coming day of judgment and to a "righteous man" "appointed by God" and "raised from the dead" for our salvation (Acts 17:31).

Culturally savvy Christians start productive conversations about the spiritual by entering the conversations provoked by today's art. I watched the Oscar-winning film *American Beauty* with Lou Carlozo, an entertainment writer with the *Chicago Tribune*. As we were leaving the theater, we overheard one teenage girl say to another, "I think it was saying life is meaningless, so we should party until we die." Her friend replied, "I think it was saying life is meaningless, so you might as well just kill yourself." Like a parable, movies and music are great conversation starters; they provide provocative questions, but seldom answers.

Each year, I teach a class at Seattle Pacific University that is designed to help college students learn how to relate faith and culture. At the heart of the class is an assignment in which individual students choose the movie that has touched them most personally and deeply and then prepare a nine-minute presentation in which they creatively communicate how and why the movie resonated with them. I'm always amazed at the range of movies the students select and the depth of emotion in the presentations. A young woman who attempted suicide chose *Girl Interrupted*, with its exploration of troubled young women who "hate themselves"; another woman whose father is an alcoholic chose *Father of the Bride*, saying, "This movie touched me, because I'll never have a deeply involved father like the one played by Steve Martin." A young guy chose *Braveheart* because he aspires to become a man of character; another student chose *Garden State* because he could relate to the feelings and experience of the central character, who had been in counseling and medicated since the age of nine and didn't know who he was or how he felt about anything. Over pizza on the last night of class, I watch as student after student explores his or her vulnerabilities by sharing how his or her personal story connects to the story in a movie. Good ambassadors know how to listen and connect today's stories to the story of Jesus and can then creatively show how God sent Jesus to restore all that unraveled in the fall of Adam and Eve because He cares about the issues raised by today's specific stories.

People respond in a variety of ways. When Paul finished his presentation, some of the crowd made fun of him, others said they wanted to hear more, and a third group believed. "Now when they heard of the resurrection of the dead, some mocked. But others said, 'We will hear you again about this.' . . . Some men joined him and believed, among whom also were Dionysius the Areopagite and a woman named Damaris and others with them" (Acts 17:32–34).

No matter how diligently the culturally savvy Christian works to share truth in ways that seekers can hear it, not everyone will accept it. Effective communication involves tailoring your style and content to a specific conversation. Shared cultural events, experiences, and art provide a wealth of conversation starters. Yet even when you care deeply and provide a clear, well-crafted explanation of the good news, people will react individually and differently. Our job is to be clear communicators of truth; ultimately, individuals will make their own decisions. We are called to faithfulness, not coercive persuasion.

Sometimes, just changing our style can tap into spiritual responsiveness. I interviewed Robert Duvall just before the film *The Apostle* was released and then challenged my radio audience to attend the movie with a seeker and engage in conversation afterward. A week later, a twenty-seven-year-old man called the show and shared that he had seen the movie with a childhood friend who had never been interested in talking about spiritual issues. The movie provoked a spirited conversation over coffee, during which, for the first time, our caller told his story about deciding to follow Jesus. Three hours and a lot of questions later, this young man's friend reacted the way some did to Paul in Athens. First, he wanted to hear more. Then he decided to believe Jesus and follow him.

The ambassador trusts God to do the rest. Popular culture is an unavoidably important place for humanity's creative endeavors. It teaches, preaches, tells stories, and shapes our identities. Communication through popular culture offers potential for the exchange of ideas that matter. For spiritual seekers and those trying to communicate with them, popular culture represents an opportunity because it is the storyteller and the common language of our culture, which, once learned, allows access to a spiritual conversation that is already taking place in culture. Jesus delivered deeply spiritual, highly intelligent but very simple messages to common people by calibrating his style to their level of understanding, and he did it without sacrificing the essence, content, or meaning of his communication. Like Jesus, we should be ambassadors who care deeply, are culturally aware, and build bridges from culture to the truth. Jesus and Paul communicated the gospel better than anybody, and yet not everyone they encountered became a follower of Jesus. This teaches us the most important lesson of all—our job is to faithfully present the good news as effectively as we can, but our most effective communication does not assure the outcome—that is between God and the people we communicate with. Paul compared the process to planting a garden: "I planted, Apollos watered, but God gave the growth. So neither he who plants nor he who waters is anything, but only God who gives the growth" (1 Corinthians 3:6–7).

The culturally savvy Christian counters culture like an alien and communicates in culture like an ambassador, but if we truly want to make a lasting contribution to culture, we will create culture like artists, and it is to this high calling that we turn next.

9

CREATING CULTURE
LIKE ARTISTS

No culture has appeared or developed except together
with a religion: according to the point of view of the
observer, the culture will appear to be the product of
the religion, or the religion the product of the culture.[1]

T. S. ELIOT

As culturally savvy Christians enter the world, aglow with the presence of God, cultural transformation is a by-product of their loving presence. The culture we create is the ultimate proof of who we are, because the proof of God's presence and transforming work in our life is imprinted on what we make.

Culturally savvy Christians evaluate our personal spiritual maturity by asking whether the culture we are creating fully bears the marks of God's image: Is it spiritual, intelligent, and creative? Does it encourage healthy relationships, morally appropriate behavior, and a just society? Measured by these standards, most of what we see in both popular culture and contemporary Christianity is substandard, mired as it is in diversion, mindlessness, and celebrity, and dependent as it is on money, marketing, and technology to prop it up. Can an entire civilization drown in the shallow end of the pool?

In the broader culture, thoughtful creatives labor in obscurity while those with minimal talent who are merely "known for being known" crank out insipid stuff meant to entertain the masses without engaging their brains. Eager for acceptance by the broader culture and wallowing in a separatist inferiority complex, so-called Christian artists too often imitate the fallen culture's art and are gleeful when they are even noticed by the mainstream. What comes to mind is Hank Hill's comment when his son Bobby joins a Christian rock band on the TV series "King of the Hill": "Can't you see, you're not making Christianity better, you're just making rock 'n' roll worse?"[2]

We are trapped in an age of unrestricted self-expression in which untalented people seize the platform, epitomizing the self-effacing joke told by renowned historian Edward Gibbon, who, after writing his classic *The Decline and Fall of the Roman Empire*, quipped, "Unprovided with original learning, uninformed in the habits of thinking, unskilled in the arts of composition, I resolved to write a book!"[3] We face the equally distressing situation of writers with talent who have nothing to say, as nineteenth-century British economist and intellectual gadfly Walter Bagehot observed: "The reason so few good books are written is that so few people who can write know anything!"[4] Or we are faced with works that deserve the comment attributed to Samuel Johnson: "Your manuscript is both good and original, but the part that is good is not original and the part that is original is not good!"[5] We're reaping the rewards of a popular culture that has lost the connection between art and glorifying God and a Christian subculture that has lost the connection between glorifying God and making good art. In the aftermath of the film *The Passion of the Christ*, we see the movers and shakers of popular culture trying to understand the spirituality craze so that they can exploit it for money while the movers and shakers of contemporary Christianity try to understand popular culture so that they can exploit it for evangelistic or economic purposes; the result is the same: artlessness, mindlessness, soullessness, and spiritual delusion.

A Renaissance of Faith and Culture

The way out of our predicament is to produce better art that reflects God's image—art that is well crafted, thoughtful, spiritual, original, and imaginative. In the 1960s, art historian Hans Rookmaaker was concerned about the decline of art in culture and the failure of Christians to develop a theology of art. He issued a prophetic call to Christian artists, craftspeople, and musicians to "weep, pray, think and work" before it was too late.[6] Forty years later, we are still awaiting a renaissance of both faith and culture. We know that it is up to us to make it happen; everything I have said so far calls for culturally savvy Christians to take the lead because as people serious about faith, savvy about faith and culture, and skilled in relating the two, we recognize that

- The renaissance requires men and women for whom God is of central importance, who are serious about pursuing God's loving, transforming presence in their life and are serious about glorifying God by becoming a loving, transforming, presence in the world.

- The renaissance requires individuals who are fully human, which means that they are deeply well, reflecting God's image holistically in a full and balanced expression of their spiritual, intellectual, creative, moral, and relational capacities. The restoration of God's image is ours as a gift provided through Jesus Christ, the reflection of God's glory and the exact imprint of God's very being.

- The renaissance requires fully human individuals who are countercultural in that they reject the mindlessness, soullessness, and spiritual delusions of today's popular culture and also reject any expressions of Christianity that are cocooned from, combative with, or conformed to the world, which are manifestations of the reductionist Christianity-Lite.

- The renaissance requires fully human women and men who are communicators, who care deeply, who are culturally aware, and who build bridges from culture to faith.

- The renaissance requires fully human individuals whose genius, the extraordinary talent God gives each human, has been identified, nurtured, fully developed, and then invested in purposeful mental or physical activity that creates a rich, dazzling, majestic culture for the glory of God.

Every individual is endowed with talents, which should be stewarded toward their highest and best use. Having identified our unique blend of gifts and talents, we should invest them in work that provides for our needs and advances God's purposes on earth, all the while reflecting the image of God in its spiritual, intellectual, creative, moral, and relational sensibilities. The work we produce should meet these standards, and as much as possible, the work we consume should do the same.

The Role of Artists and Creators

I think there is a special place in God's heart for artists and thoughtful creatives, for if all we knew about God was Genesis 1, all we would know is that God is creative.[7] God is the Great Artist. Created in the image of a creative God, each of us is imprinted with a creative dimension. Some have been specifically gifted with talents in making art—the music we listen to; the poems we recite; the novels we read; the plays, movies, and operas that engage us; the architectural wonders we behold; the fashion we wear; the dance, the visual arts, the paintings, the photography that delight both our eyes and our minds. The artists among us possess an extraordinary potential to fully engage us—body, soul, mind, and spirit—and to draw us into revelatory encounters with God, our selves, and each other. "An Artist is like God, but small. He can't see out of God's creation, for it includes him," said artist and writer M. B. Goffstein.[8] Thoughtful, creative artists are the prophets among us. Like the wild-eyed, half-crazed Old Testament oracles, a true artist will be faithful to truth, regardless of the consequences. Thoughtful artists are rare and valued treasures, as writer Anne Lamott observes: "I always loved books where people tell the truth. When people tell the truth, it's like finding an English language station in Morocco."[9]

The Great Artist saw to it that artists were there from the beginning. Every human activity, profession, and avocation is important in building culture, so occupations described in the earliest pages of the Bible include agriculture (Jabal) and industry (Tubalcain). But there in the list is an artist, Jubal, the father of those who play the lyre and the pipe (Genesis: 4:21). Although each of us creates culture through his or her own talents and in a variety of industries, in the final pages of this book, I want to narrow my focus to the arts, in part because I believe that cultural enrichers from the arts are the best hope for transforming today's popular culture. How might a deeper faith and a better understanding of the artist's calling enable thoughtful, creative artists of deep faith to enrich culture?

Few subjects are more important. The failure of twentieth-century Christians to develop and advance a contemporary theology of art is producing tragic results for both faith and culture. Fundamentalist Christians have emphasized their role as aliens for whom art is to be avoided or romanticized à la Thomas Kinkade; evangelical Christians have emphasized their ambassadorial role in culture, seeing art as something to be exploited for evangelistic purposes. Those caught up in the spirit of the age have exalted the self, seeing art as nothing more than self-expression. The spiritual, intellectual, and aesthetic impoverishment of the broader culture can be attributed to the exaltation of humans over God, and the boring, unimaginative, and imitative Christian subculture can be attributed to Christians' failure to take art seriously.

Any theology of art recognizes, as theologian Abraham Kuyper proclaims, that "there is not a single inch of the whole terrain of our human existence over which Christ does not proclaim, Mine, Mine, Mine."[10] Art belongs to God.

A theology of art takes creation as seriously as redemption. Reducing our human purpose to preparation for heaven and diminishing—or, worse yet, eliminating—our original mandate to create a better world now may be popular, but each is a dismal, diminishing distortion of God's fullest purpose for human existence. Thoughtful cultural critic Ken Myers reminds us, "Being human is the most profound aspect of the creation for which we ought to give thanks. If we can enjoy the beauty of all else in creation, how foolish to resent or ignore the image of the Creator, the pinnacle of creation. It is being human, not being saved—it is the image of God in us, not regeneration—that establishes the capacity to recognize the distinctions between the beautiful and the ugly, between order and chaos, between the creative and the stultifying. We were created beings before we were redeemed beings."[11] The restoration of the artistic endeavor is as close to God's heart as redemption, because it is evidence of that redemption.

A theology of art will take the artist seriously, because artists fulfill the image of God through their gifts, which are in turn a gift from God and an essential part of their calling. A theology of art ultimately recognizes the Creator's process.

The Creative Process

In the first chapter of Genesis, we learn something about God's creative process (and our own):

> The creator, God, knows the vacuum and silence in which the process starts. As the artist knows the blank canvas; the writer, the blank page; the musician, the blank score; and the scientist, the theory waiting to be tested, God knows a universe void and without form.
>
> The Great Artist created out of silence, making something out of nothing: "The earth was a formless void and darkness covered the face of the deep."
>
> The Great Artist communicated, speaking the heavens and earth into existence: "Then God said, 'Let there be light' and there was light."
>
> The Great Artist was a seer: "And God saw the light."
>
> The Great Artist brought order out of chaos: "Let there be a dome in the midst of the waters, and let it separate the waters from the waters."

The Great Artist was a craftsman: "And God saw that the
light was good."

The Great Artist named the work: "God called the light Day,
and the darkness he called Night."

Before brush, pen, or quill is lifted and touched to page, there
lives within the artist an idea. Ingenious people cannot explain how
their ideas are born any more than pre-scientific humans could
explain the conception of a child. We know only that our creations
begin as shadowy images or hunches, which eventually will be seen,
heard, touched, or tasted by others. Our work is the intimate expression of one self sent forth to be received by another. It is a message in a bottle, dropped in the expansive sea of humanity with the
hope that someone will find, understand, and respond to it. This
process is familiar to us because it is primal. Imagining something
where there is nothing, shaping it into existence until we can see
that the finished product is good, and then naming it—these are
basis of all creativity, and humans inherit these qualities from God,
who created us in His image.

The Creative Purpose

The planet Earth, our solar system, and the entire created order are
outward manifestations of God's essential artistic nature. Creation
is the inevitable activity of a creator, yet creation is more than the
expression of a creative nature or the inevitable consequence of a
creative process. God, like every artist, desires for His work to be
seen, heard, touched, and tasted. The Artist's work is on display so
that others may see it:

The heavens are telling the glory of God (Psalm 19:1). Human fas-
cination with the skies and stars can be traced to our earliest consciousness. In the first century, Romans gazed skyward while bathing
in the hot springs of what is now Bath, England, and the birthplace
of Jesus was marked for mystics from the East by an astronomical
phenomenon. Who has not gazed upward in awe at a dark night sky

punctuated with millions of stars and distant planets? Who is not thrilled with images captured in deep space by the Hubble telescope, providing us with rudimentary glimpses of the magnitude and mysteries of the heavens, seen through a glass darkly?

The firmament proclaims his handiwork (Psalm 19:1). Early explorers ventured forth on land and sea, from the known into the unknown; they reported back that the earth was not flat and that bountiful treasures awaited in undiscovered lands. Climbers scale peaks, botanists hack through jungles, ornithologists study unfamiliar feathers, entomologists trap bugs in jars, divers plunge beneath the sea; everywhere we hear reports of strange new things, fearfully and wonderfully made. The Great Artist's intention was that these created wonders in the heavens and on earth, beyond providing enjoyment, would be a means of connecting the Artist and the receiver of the art.

Today, I sense that I am the recipient of such a connection. It is early. My day started at 5 A.M. I am writing in a cabin located in the low mountain ranges just outside Cle Elum, Washington. In the distance, beyond the scruffy Scotch pines surrounding the cabin, a ribbon of fog snakes its way along the valley. Thick, white puffs of cotton separate the lowland from the jagged, snow-covered peaks of the Stuart mountain range, and here, far from any ocean, I am receiving a message floated in a bottle billions of years ago by God. Ever since the creation of the world, His eternal power and divine nature, invisible though they are, have been understood and seen through the things He has made. The Great Artist is saying, "I am here. I have made something for you and sent it out. I want to be known."

In Genesis 1, we learn that God is creative, imaginative, and even playful. The Great Artist has an eye for beauty and delight, making things that are pleasant to the sight and food that is delicious as well as nourishing. God's creation is not just utilitarian. Created in God's image, the artist reflects the spiritual, intelligent, and creative capacities of God as one who is free to create. And so every human is irrepressibly drawn to creative acts and their appreciation, because this instinct is woven into us at creation. The culturally savvy Christian should possess a heightened appreciation for the creative process, because we see in it traces of God and because we see in today's artist the same process and purposes that are seen in God's creativity.

And it is so.

Artists Speak: On the Image of God

The best way to explore the purpose of art and the image of God as expressed in art is by listening to the voices of artists themselves.

The Artist as Creator

Writers, filmmakers, painters, and songwriters are often conscious of the spiritual nature of their creative work. Novelist John Updike said, "I feel closest to God when writing. You're singing praises; you're describing the world as it is."[12] One of only two authors to win two Edgar Awards from the Mystery Writers of America, James Lee Burke describes the artist as a co-creator with God: "God might choose fools and people who glow with neurosis for his partners in creation, but he doesn't make mistakes."[13] Mystic Hildegard of Bingen describes art as a human response to the image of God: "And so the Spirit sweeps through the universe with resounding inspiring, and igniting power, evoking the response of renewed vitality until the last day. This is the purpose and action of God, who has no beginning and no end. He created humanity as the wonderful work of his hand, by equipping people with an impulse and inclination to higher things by enabling them to make their own responses. God did this because he loved people. After all, he is Love itself."[14] French author and winner of the Nobel Prize in literature André Gide is reputed to have said, "Art is a collaboration between God and the artist, and the less the artist does the better."[15]

The Artist as Orderer of Chaos

Creative people originate new ways of seeing and hearing, often developing structure where none previously existed. "To shoot a film is to organize an entire universe," said Swedish filmmaker and director Ingmar Bergman.[16] Operatic composer Giacomo Puccini said, "Music is noise submitted to order by wisdom."[17] The late playwright Arthur Miller said, "I'm a writer, so I write. That is my job. But it is more than a job. I just have a terrifically pleasant feeling if I create a form that completes itself and you can walk around it. It is a whole object."[18]

The Artist as Seer and Revealer

Artists see things before the rest of us, and they have an irresistible urge to express their vision. Writer Brennan Manning once told me, "I believe the real difference in America is not between conservatives and liberals, fundamentalists, charismatics, republicans and democrats; the real difference is between the aware and the unaware."[19] The artist is aware, sometimes painfully so. The painter Edgar Degas famously quipped, "Art is not what you see, but what you make others see."[20]

The similarities between artist and prophet are striking. The prophet sees unpleasant truth and cannot resist saying it. This is what journalist Malcolm Muggeridge meant when he said, "Only mystics, clowns and artists, in my experience, speak the truth, which, as Blake keeps insisting, is perceptive to the imagination rather than the mind. Our knowledge of Jesus Christ is far too serious a business to be left to theologians alone. From the Middle Ages these have monotonously neglected art and the imagination as guides to religious truth. I find myself in complete agreement with those who wish to reinstate the mystics, the clowns and artists alongside the scholars. To modify Wittgenstein; what we cannot imagine, we must confine to silence and unbelief."[21]

The Artist's Passion for Excellence

I first interviewed Pulitzer Prize–winning novelist Michael Chabon just after he had won critical acclaim for *Pittsburgh Stories* and *A Model World*. Then he disappeared for five years. I learned what had happened when I interviewed him later, in Chicago. He described how his early success had led to high expectations and a big book deal and how suddenly he had lost his way creatively. He had spent five years working on a book that he eventually threw in the trash, deciding to start all over. He described the calamitous situation this way:

> Five years and some 1,500 pages later, I was still trawling the murky waters of the innermost sea in search of that fabled wreck which by then I was calling *Fountain City*. In that time I had found fantastic shattered hulks and ruins down there, helmets and rimy flatware, chests of moldering silk, astrolabe, the skeletons of men and horses, but nothing that I felt could honestly be considered treasure. Five years, I've got a bunch of interesting artifacts, but I've got no treasure here. And I'm a writer. I've already missed five deadlines, and I've already spent the money they advanced me. And then at the end of 1992, with the help of my editor, Doug Stumpf, I tried one last time to hoist the whole rotten caravel to the surface and it all just fell apart. At the beginning of 1993, after 62 months of more or less steady work and four drafts, each longer than the previous one, I dumped it. I didn't tell anyone, not even my wife.[22]

This story has a happy ending. Within sixty days, Chabon wrote a complete draft of *The Wonder Boys*, which was well-received by critics and consumers, was made into a movie, and got him back on track. What fascinates me is Chabon's willingness to jettison his book project after working on it for five years. What is it about a thoughtful artist that drives him to keep pushing? I think it is the image of God. It is the true artist's need to say at the end of each day and upon completing a project, "It is good."

The Artist as Communicator

The great Irish writer Maeve Binchy talks about writing's honorable tradition as a connector of people through storytelling:

> In Ireland we used to have a class of people in the old days before books and printing. . . . They would walk around the country, going from house to house, just telling stories. All they had to do was to entertain with words and people gave them room and board. People just loved them and vied with one another to be their hosts. Nobody ever said, Oh heavens, here come those loud-mouth storytellers. Hide quickly and pretend we're not at home so they'll go and bother somebody else. I grew up believing that telling stories was good, and sitting there like a stone listening was dull and bad.[23]

Conceiving and crafting in private, often driven to satisfy only their personal urge to create, eventually artists display their work where other people can see it.

Artists Speak: On Art's Purpose

J.R.R. Tolkien described God as creator and humans as subcreators. Art's single, unifying purpose is to glorify the creator, God. Beyond this overriding purpose, artists' works will be as diverse as God's own creation, with each specific work of art serving one or more subsidiary purposes.

Exaltation

The Westminster Assembly's Shorter Catechism begins with the familiar words "Man's chief end is to glorify God, and to enjoy him forever." This is our life's ultimate purpose, and it takes on particular meaning in expressing the unique talents God has bestowed on us. The highest and best motivation for art is the artist's desire to enjoy and glorify God. Artist Edward Knippers tells the story of a journalist who asked both Matisse and Rouault whether they would continue to paint if they never had an audience again. "The pagan Matisse said, 'Of course not'; the Christian Rouault said, 'Of course.'" Knippers concludes that there is such a thing as an "audience of One."[24]

Enjoyment and Pleasure

The ultimate aim of art is to bring pleasure to God, and the artist also experiences pleasure by creating art that pleases God. Novelist Madeleine L'Engle describes her writing as a joyful affirmation of life: "To talk about art and about Christianity is for me one and the same thing, and it means attempting to share the meaning of my life. . . . It is what makes me respond to the death of an apple tree, the birth of a puppy, northern lights shaking the sky, by writing stories."[25] Each creative person feels God's pleasure in the exercise of their gift. But art also brings pleasure and enjoyment for those who experience it: "The woman saw that the tree was good for food and that it was a delight to the eyes" (Genesis 1:9).

Expression

Philosopher Jacques Maritain reminds us that "the first responsibility of the artist is to the work."[26] God gave certain individuals a profoundly refined ability to imagine what might be, an irrepressible desire to express what they feel and see, and a set of talents and skills enabling them to express themselves effectively through a particular art form. The craftsperson is apprenticed and hones his skills over many years, knowing expression alone is insufficient in art. Since the Middle Ages, we've seen the devolution of art from a craft to the unbridled, often decadent and undisciplined expressiveness of today. Art critic Brian Sewell bluntly derided the avant-garde gallery scene of the twentieth century's last decade: "If this is art, I know no word that fits the work of Michelangelo and Titian."[27]

Talent facilitates the artist's ability to express something; spiritual richness gives the artist something to say. Together, they produce rich artistic expressions. In an unguarded moment, filmmaker Sidney Pollack confessed, "Are American films bad? A lot of them surely are, and so are a lot of everybody else's, the way most anything produced is bad—breakfast cereals, music, most chairs, architecture, mail-order shirts. There probably hasn't been a really beautiful rake since the Shakers stopped making farm implements!"[28]

Transcendence

Having been made for God, humans are designed for a spiritual experience and long for the transcendent, for a reality beyond the limits of their pedestrian daily lives. Art provides a path for such an experience. Madeleine L'Engle concurs: "We don't want to feel less when we have finished a book; we want to feel that new possibilities have been opened to us. We don't want to close a book with a sense that life is totally unfair and that there is no light in the darkness; we want to feel that we have been given illumination."[29] The poet W. H. Auden put it this way: "Even the most commonplace things are tinged with glory."[30] In a 1935 book review, R. P. Blackmur said, "The art of poetry is amply distinguished from the manufacture of verse by the animating presence in the poetry of a fresh idiom; language so twisted and posed in a form that it not only expresses the matter in hand but adds to the stock of available reality."[31]

Revelation

We know that God speaks to us through special revelation, Jesus and the Bible being two examples of supernatural means through which to discover the knowledge of God. But God also speaks to us through general revelation, discovered through natural means such as observation of nature; philosophy and reasoning; and the human conscience. Artists can be the conduit of general revelation by speaking to us on behalf of God indirectly, under the radar. Art has a way of making us feel and reaches us initially at the intuitive level instead of the intellectual or propositional level. Art's indirect references, hints, and covertness can lead us to a deeper understanding of God without mentioning God. At the beginning of U2's song "Grace," we think Bono is singing about a woman named Grace, but then he adds, "Grace, it's a name for a girl; it's also a thought that changed the world."[32] From that point on, phrases take on a new meaning, with grace covering stains and shame.

Theologian John Calvin reminded us that insight might come from even the unbelieving artist: "In reading profane authors the admirable light of truth displayed in them should remind us that the human mind, however much fallen and perverted from its original integrity, is still adorned and invested with admirable gifts from its Creator. If we reflect that the Spirit of God is the only fountain of truth, we will be careful as we would avoid offering insults to Him, not to reject or condemn truth wherever it appears. In despising the gifts we insult the giver."[33] Similarly, filmmaker and professor Craig Detweiler and his coauthor Barry Taylor observe in their book *Matrix of Meanings*, "Common grace explains why the most spiritual movies are often made by people outside the formal borders of the church. . . . We will search for today's burning bushes, talking donkeys, pillaging Chaldeans, dishonest tax collectors and seemingly voiceless stones. We will look in surprising and humorous places to discover God's unlikeliest saints."[34]

Exploring Evil

In the great Messianic passage Isaiah 53, we read of "a man of sorrows" who was despised and lacking in any glory or allure that would draw people to him, yet this passage foretells the crucified Jesus, the Savior of the world.

Good art tells the story of evil so truthfully that you want to turn your eyes from it. Novelist Ron Hansen observes that a weakness of "Christian fiction" is not that it fails to deal with evil but that it misses the truth about it: "I guess maybe evil is just too stark in Christian fiction, whereas I think there is a more nuanced view of evil, which is that the devil doesn't propose temptations that are easy to resist. The devil proposes temptations that seem to be good. And you find yourself going down the wrong path for all kinds of good reasons. I think that Christian fiction often makes it kind of Manichaean where you have good versus evil, black versus white, and it's all very easily solved."[35] Prolific writer Orson Scott Card agrees: "Evil is more entertaining than unrelenting goodness because any depiction of life without evil is a lie."[36] Today's art often knows and tells only the worst truth, relentlessly exposing the dark side and leaving us with only hell. This is just as distorted as romanticized or Pollyanna-ish art.

Exploring Mystery

Art engages spiritual themes in myriad ways: chronicling our sense of loss, describing and depicting our search for meaning, offering explanations about truth, and regularly revealing something about mystery. Niall Williams's *As It Is in Heaven* is an Irish novel about a man who loses his wife and child in an automobile accident. Williams writes, "There are only three great puzzles in the world. The puzzle of love, the puzzle of death, and between each of these and part of both of them, the puzzle of God. God is the greatest puzzle of all. When a car drives off the road and crashes into your life, you feel the puzzle of God."[37] The day after I read this book, a disheveled guy wandered into the lobby of our church, looking very distressed. I introduced myself and asked if he needed help. He said, "I want to know what is going to happen to Marie." I asked him to elaborate, and he explained: "A year ago today, a drunk driver named Marie was responsible for a head-on collision with my wife of twenty-eight years; my wife was killed instantly. I'm here today because I need to know what is going to happen to Marie." The synchronicity of having thought about those questions while reading Niall Williams's book, then encountering a troubled soul the next day was eerily illustrative of art's effectiveness in provoking and illuminating visceral thinking about situations we have never personally encountered.

Empathy

Jesus saw God's image in individuals and empathized with them and their situation: a woman caught in adultery, a demoniac, a leper, a despised tax collector, a busy hostess, an impulsive disciple, a doubter, a rich man who could not part with his wealth, a widow who gave all she had, a man paralyzed since childhood, a commander of troops, a son who rebelled against his father, an older brother who resented the father's forgiving the rebellious son. Jesus was able to get inside the hearts and minds of the people he encountered, resonating with them and, through his parables, transforming their stories into lessons for others.

Poet Jose Marti said, "The knowledge of different literature frees oneself from the tyranny of the few."[38] Art provides us with the knowledge of others' lives and frees us from the limitations of our own. Whenever we encounter art, whether in print, on a screen, or in music, we are invited into a sacred place, another human's story. Art helps us understand poet William Blake's assertion that "Everything that lives is holy."[39]

Evoking

When humans encounter art, we do so as emotional, mental, spiritual, physical, and sensory beings. Our response to art emanates from any or all of these aspects of our humanness. The image of God within us resonates with the image of God reflected in art.

Art can evoke

Praise for God. Art needs no justification, but, according to Hans Rookmaaker, it demands "a response, like that of the twenty-four elders in Revelation who worship God for the very act of creation itself."[40]

Community. Art facilitates our fellowship with humans. Artists can tell us the story of a generation. They are the caged canaries gasping in the coal mines to warn us of danger. Princeton theologian Max Stackhouse reminds us, "The bard, the artist, the creator of theater, the poet, the teller of tales have all been seen as the creators of culture, refiners of social life, the conscience of humanity that exposes its foibles, clarifies its virtues and celebrates its approximation to them."[41]

A hunger for new life. In *Jesus Rediscovered,* Malcolm Muggeridge reports, "Books like *Resurrection* and *The Brothers Karamazov* give me an almost overpowering sense of how uniquely marvelous a Christian way of looking at life is, and a passionate desire to share it."[42] Tolstoy was compelled to write of life's complexities with an eye toward emboldening his reader to love life: "If I were told that what I wrote would be read twenty years from now by people who are children today and that they would read my book and love life more because of it, then I should devote all of my life and strength to such a work."[43]

Advice for Artists

Culturally savvy Christians are called to create a richer culture—a task in which all of us partake in our daily lives—but when it comes to popular culture, the task falls to the thoughtful creatives and artists among us. Here is some closing advice for artists and those with artistic aspirations:

Be an artist who is deeply Christian, not a Christian artist. C. S. Lewis quipped that we don't need Christian writers, we need great writers who are Christian.[44] Culturally savvy Christians are serious about God, and their deep faith gives them something to say. Likewise, culturally savvy artists have developed their talents, techniques, and skills to the highest level, and their art reflects it, yet they are humble because they know, as did George MacDonald, "We make, but Thou art the creating core."[45] Culturally savvy artists do not expect their work to be accepted because they are Christian, but because their art is good.

Produce art, not just religious art. Christian artists are not bound to create "religious art," but they understand that their exploration of everyday human occurrences is gilded by their walk in faith. Nick Park, creator of the popular Wallace and Gromit films, wrestled with this issue and concluded, "I felt guilty for a long time that I was getting excited about ideas that had nothing to do with God, but I never got any ideas about God that were any good. I feel I've just got to do things which mean something to me and which come from the heart. I have to listen to myself. But I do regard my films as Christian."[46] Catholic novelist Flannery O'Connor explained, "Your beliefs will be the light by which you see, but they will not be what you see and they will not be a substitute for seeing. I have found from reading my own writing that my subject in fiction is the action of grace in territory held by the devil."[47]

Strive for the spiritual, intelligent, and inventive. Rather than rehash old debates about what is good art, let us agree that art from a gifted artist of deep faith should reflect the spiritual, intelligent, creative image of God manifest in work that resonates with the truth of human experience and aspirations. Writer Murray Watts recounts a possibly apocryphal story of self-described poet and hack Sir John Betjeman, who was once handed a poem by a Christian writer with the words, "The Lord has given me this poem." Scanning the appalling doggerel, Sir John threw it in the [trash] bin with the reply, "The Lord has given and the Lord has taken away; blessed be the name of the Lord!"[48] Ned Bustard reminds us that "it is not the believer's goal to integrate their art with their faith; rather, the art of God's chosen people must spring from faith."[49] Your art is born out of the confluence of your knowledge of the one true myth; the narrative of creation, fall, and redemption; your understanding of God and humanity; your own unique experiences and life journey; your vision for what could be; your skill and training in your craft;

and much more. Your ability to convey this mix honestly and well is required if your work is to ring true and authentic.

The depth of your personal relationship with God should deepen your work and broaden your range of content and vision. Artist Makato Fujimura once said, "I believe that true, Christ-filled expression results in more diversity than what Christ-suppressing expression would allow. The more we center ourselves in Christ, the freer we are to explore new arenas of expression."[50] James Romaine reports on the essential role that faith played in Michelangelo's work, observing that, according to Robert Clements in *Michelangelo's Theory of Art,* "Michelangelo was one of the most devout men of the Renaissance, lay or cleric." His faith was central to his life and art; for him "religion was not a set of opinions about reality. . . . It was reality itself." In his biography of Michelangelo, George Bull states, "Religious faith was second nature to Michelangelo in every unguarded utterance. . . . He had absorbed Catholic piety and belief almost through his pores."[51] Far from limiting our artistic boundaries, deep faith should enrich and expand our possibilities, moving us beyond imitation to originality, beyond mediocre to excellence.

The deeper our faith, the more profoundly our art should convey a qualitatively different perception of the world. This means Christian artists should also be true to the countercultural nature of who we are and not be afraid to be alien. Novelist Chaim Potok built an entire career out of the dissonance he experienced within his own Hasidic tradition and concluded, "While this tension is exhausting, it is fuel for me. Without it, I would have nothing to say."[52] Dana Gioia, chair of the National Endowment for the Arts, says, "the basic donnée of the Catholic writer is to examine the consequences of living in a fallen world."[53]

Lead, don't follow. Most "Christian art" produced today is fueled by an insipid desire to measure up to the so-called standard of the wider culture's art, yet this measurement is insufficient if excellence and quality are what we're striving for. If today's art is spiritually, intellectually, and creatively bankrupt, why would we aspire to meet its standard? To lead artistically takes guts. Your truest art will be both authentic and original and will flow from the combination of your deep faith and your artistic vision. To lead in the arts means to contribute to new directions in your medium, to expand the parameters, to innovate in form and style.

Remember the Apple ad about the crazy ones and misfits who change the world? Culturally savvy Christians should aspire to meet the Apple creed and that created by Pat Hanlon, my friend, author, and founder of Thinktopia, Inc., whose mantra is "Success is for the people at the precipice. The entrepreneurs, innovators, risk takers, and dreamers. We remind you to never stop thinking. Proactively seek out fresh answers. Find partners. Remember that you are only as smart as the people you surround yourself with. Seek out people who are smarter than you are. Nurture them. Reward them. Because they are the future. Become cosmonauts of change. Motivate forward. Find your buzz. Remember that life is a continual uncovering. Most of all, discover the things that thrill you and do them. In the end, they are the only reason to get up in the morning."[54]

Play "real good," for free, if need be. Find the line between fiscal responsibility and selling out, and don't cross it. To be an artist of integrity in a dumbed-down, superficial, commercially driven pop faith, pop culture age is risky and is not the obvious or easy path to financial or even critical success. The liner notes of *Acquiring the Taste*, a 1971 recording by the avant-garde band Gentle Giant, explained, "It is our goal to expand the frontiers of contemporary popular music at the risk of being very unpopular. We have recorded each composition with the one thought—that it should be unique, adventurous and fascinating. It has taken every shred of our combined musical and technical knowledge to achieve this."[55] Their work was astounding, but they never became a popular or commercial success. The old Joni Mitchell song "For Free" tells of a well-known celebrity who, while staying in a nice hotel, admires an unknown musician performing on a street corner, playing "real good for free."[56] True artists push ahead, find a way to make their best art, and, if unable to pay the bills with their art, find a way to earn sufficient daily bread in other ways. But none of us, artists or their admirers, should ever march to the beat of a lesser drummer, because we hear the drumbeat, faint or loud, of the Lord of the Dance.

Make art, don't just appropriate art. In its quest for relevance, the religious community has seized on the opportunity to use movie and song clips to build bridges of communication to the broader culture. While this is strategically expedient, it is vastly inferior to making brilliant original art. Rather than skim the surface and exploit the art of others, people of deep faith need to identify, encourage, and support the work of artists in their midst whose work flows from deep faith.

Demand better art. Too many people who profess to know the living God are lemming-like consumers of the impoverished offerings of today's bankrupt culture. If we eat a steady diet of drivel, the culture will keep making and serving it. This junk food diet, lacking in nutrients, will soon emaciate us as it has those who produce it, and we'll soon be a planet of wasted Gollums. Huge chunks of contemporary film music and art are like the emperor who wears no clothes. Until someone has the courage to declare that the emperor is naked, the deception will continue. Commit to consuming only good art.

The path to a deeper, richer culture is through the deeper, spiritually enriched lives of individuals. The creative enterprise awaits artists of deep faith, possessed of a spiritual, intellectual, imaginative vision. What higher calling exists than to be an artist whose work flows from the image of God and to the glory of God? In the words of songwriter Nick Cave's chorus, "There is a kingdom. There is a king. . . . And He is everything."[57]

Artists, remember the words of British poet Arthur O' Shaughnessy:

> We are the music makers.
> We are the dreamers of dreams.
> We are the movers and shakers.
> Wandering by lone sea-breakers,
> And sitting by desolate streams;
> World-losers and world-forsakers,
> On whom the pale moon gleams:
> Yet we are the movers and shakers
> Of the world for ever, it seems.[58]

Go into all the world and create a richer culture.

EPILOGUE

My course is set for an uncharted sea.[1]
DANTE, *PARADISO*

I started out to write a simple book, and along the way, I was told it was a manifesto. Conferring such weight upon my modest efforts resulted in severe personal consternation and manifold rewrites. Along the way, a dear friend and fellow writer's witty wife told me, in reference to her husband, "Everything he says is either obvious or wrong." Knowing that such a telling observation could easily be made more forcefully and credibly by those who travel life's road with me was sobering. Nevertheless, I proceeded with this book because I believe the ideas are right, even if—to me, anyway—they seem obvious.

There was a certain pain in writing this book, because my critique cuts across both culture and faith, which means I risk the alienation of dear friends in both arenas. But after forty years of observing and operating in both popular culture and the Christian community, what I see so distresses and saddens me that I have no choice but to report it and hope it serves a constructive purpose. My proximity to San Francisco's cultural quakes of the 1960s started my wild ride with popular culture, transporting me from the high hopes of unbridled creatives to the dashed dreams of today's insipid entertainment culture. My personal roots in evangelicalism provided a disturbing vantage point from which to observe its rise and subsequent descent into superficiality, triumphalism, and a reductionist, tame, and toothless gospel.

At its heart, this book originates in our common ground. All humans are created in God's image, with a universal need for God and a rich capacity to love God and neighbor, to become fully human, and to embody and express our highest and best reflection of God's image in our individual lives and in the culture we collectively make. Both today's popular culture and Christianity-Lite are producing a spiritual superficiality that cannot satisfy our deep, universal spiritual human longings. Today's intellectual and political climate is polluted by hostile talk that is polarizing, demonizing, and dehumanizing. But as John Adams wrote to Thomas Jefferson, I say to you, "You and I ought not to die before we have explained ourselves to each other!"[2]

Together, we need a fresh start, a renewed pursuit of God, the digging of a deeper well, which will allow God's transforming presence to make us deeply well. As God's spiritual, intellectual, creative, relational, and moral qualities begin to dwell in us, we will be restored to our full humanity and God's imprint on us will be seen in the culture we make.

And so I ask you, the brave, bold dreamers of dreams, to join me in the affirmations of a culturally savvy Christian:

I will make God of central importance, digging a deeper well through nurturing God's loving, transforming presence in my life, denying self, no longer conforming to culture, and renewing my mind through the daily practice of the spiritual disciplines, fully committed to discovering and doing God's will in daily life.

I will pursue a deep mystical union with God, whose loving, transforming presence is to me what the metamorphosis from a caterpillar is to a butterfly; I am changed and being changed into a full human, again aglow with God's spiritual, intellectual, creative, relational, and moral presence, reflecting God's image for God's glory.

I will go into the world as a loving, transforming presence, holistically fulfilling my calling to counter culture like an alien, to communicate in culture like an ambassador, and to create culture like an artist, honing my skills of discernment, discovery, and dual listening.

I will be vigilant in my consumption of popular media culture, recognizing that it is often characterized by superficiality, soullessness, and spiritual delusion; yet because I recognize its importance and potential, I will actively take my place as a cultural participant healthily, not as a cultural glutton or a cultural anorexic.

I will be vigilant in my association with the church, recognizing that it often falls into the unhealthy patterns of cocooning from, combating, or conforming to culture and that today's Christianity-Lite too often mirrors popular culture; yet because I recognize the church's importance and potential, I will take my place as an active participant in it.

I will affirm that the story I am in starts with an original good creation—humans made in the image of God with spiritual, intellectual, creative, relational, and moral capacities—and that our story is tainted by a foul human revolt against the creator; yet it continues as a love story in which God initiates a reunion with humans through Jesus Christ, whose death halts the unraveling of the fallen human race and whose resurrection signals that all things can become new; and I will embrace God's grand finale, the restoration of God's image in humans, starting now and perfected in eternity.

I will pursue these aims in the company of friends, enjoying the moveable feast together with followers of Christ committed to the pursuit of God and the nurturing of meaningful relationships. Together, our restless souls will find their rest in God and our creative souls will find their outlet in our co-creation of a renewed faith community and culture for the glory of God.

Finally, for the rest of my days, I will aspire to be a culturally savvy Christian who is serious about faith, savvy about faith and culture, and skilled in relating the two, and I will urge others to do the same.

NOTES

Introduction

1. J.R.R. Tolkien, quoted in a letter to his friend Father Robert Murray, written in 1953, just before *The Fellowship of the Rings* was published.
2. Chuck Palahniuk, author of *Fight Club,* from the movie script based on the book.
3. Michael Stipe, quoted in *Rolling Stone*, Jan. 6, 2000.
4. I first heard the Walker Percy quote on Garrison Keillor's "The Writers Almanac," National Public Radio, May 28, 2004.
5. John Adams, letter to Thomas Jefferson, quoted in Patricia Nelson Limerick, "Dining with Jeff," *New York Times*, June 25, 2005.
6. British Broadcasting Corporation News, "'Extinct' Woodpecker Found Alive." [http://news.bbc.co.uk/1/hi/sci/tech/4493825.stm]. Apr. 28, 2005.
7. Hans Rookmaaker, as reported by Nigel Goodwin and other of Rookmaaker's students at L'Abri in Huemoz, Switzerland.
8. Jon Johnstone, *Will Evangelicalism Survive Its Own Popularity?* (Grand Rapids, Mich.: Zondervan, 1980).

Chapter One

1. Joni Mitchell, "Woodstock," from the album *Ladies of the Canyon*, 1970.
2. Norman Greenbaum, "Spirit in the Sky" (single recording), 1970.

3. "Aquarius," lyrics by Gerome Ragni and James Rado, music by Galt MacDermot, from the musical *Hair*, 1968.

4. John Lennon, quoted in "Jesus Affair Press Conference, Chicago 08/11/66," on the CD *Rare Photos and Interviews*, Vol. 1 (Master Tone Multimedia, 1995).

5. Michael Wolfe, *The New Yorker*, Dec. 2000.

6. Andrew Greeley, *God in Popular Culture* (Chicago: Thomas More Press, 1988).

7. Robert Johnston, *Reel Spirituality* (Grand Rapids, Mich.: Baker Academic, 2000).

8. George Gallup, *The Next American Spirituality* (Colorado Springs, Colo.: Cook, 2000).

9. Simon Frith, *Performing Rites* (Cambridge, Mass.: Harvard University Press, 1996).

10. *Seattle Times*, Mar. 8, 2004.

11. Sydney Pollack, quoted in Michael Petracca and Madeleine Sorapure (eds.), *Common Culture* (Upper Saddle River, N.J.: Prentice Hall, 2004).

12. Neil Gabler, *Life the Movie* (New York: Knopf, 1998).

13. George Clooney, quoted in Reuters, Feb. 11, 2003.

14. Pitirim Sorokin, *Social and Cultural Dynamics* (New York: American Book Company, 1941).

15. Flannery O' Connor, *Mystery and Manners* (New York: Farrar, Straus & Giroux, 1961).

16. E. B. White, quoted in Herbert Mitgang, *Words Still Count with Me: A Chronicle of Literary Conversations* (New York: Norton, 1995).

17. Neil Postman, *Amusing Ourselves to Death* (New York: Viking Penguin, 1985).

18. Bob Pittman, quoted in Quentin Schultze and Roy Anker, *Dancing in the Dark* (Grand Rapids, Mich.: Eerdmans, 1991).

19. David Harvey, *The Condition of Postmodernity: An Enquiry into the Origins of Cultural Change* (Cambridge, Mass.: Blackwell, 1990).

20. Orson Welles, *New York Herald Tribune*, Oct. 12, 1956.

21. Richard Schickel, *Intimate Strangers: The Culture of Celebrity in America* (Chicago: Ivan Dee, 2000).
22. Peter Jennings, quoted in David Shaw, *Los Angeles Times*, Sept. 25, 2001.
23. *Vanity Fair*, Dec. 13, 2004.
24. *Christianity Today*, Apr. 1, 2002.
25. The young woman was quoted in Paul Krassner, "Celebrities. Aren't They Something?" *Los Angeles Times Magazine*, June 13, 1999.
26. Daniel Boorstein, *The Image* (New York: HarperCollins, 1961).
27. Andy Warhol, *The Philosophy of Andy Warhol* (New York: Harcourt Brace Jovanovich, 1975).
28. Milton Friedman, quoted in Brian Walsh, *Subversive Christianity* (Seattle: Alta Vista College Press, 1994).
29. *Wall Street* (motion picture) (20th Century Fox, 1987).
30. Robert Bateman, "Homo Sapiens Teenager Consumerensis." [http://www.batemanideas.com/teenager.html].
31. Douglas Rushkoff, quoted in "The Merchants of Cool" (DVD produced by WGBH Educational Foundation and the Public Broadcasting System, 2002).
32. Robert McChesney, quoted in "The Merchants of Cool" (DVD produced by WGBH Educational Foundation and the Public Broadcasting System, 2002).
33. John de Graaf, David Wann, and Thomas H. Naylor, *Affluenza* (San Francisco: Berrett-Koehler, 2001).
34. Wikipedia comments on this oft-quoted Watson statement as follows: "Although Watson is well known for his alleged 1943 statement: 'I think there is a world market for maybe five computers,' there is no evidence he ever made it. The author Kevin Maney tried to find the origin of the quote, but has been unable to locate any speeches or documents of Watson's that contain this, nor are the words present in any contemporary articles about IBM. The earliest known citation is from 1986 on Usenet in the signature of a poster from Convex Computer Corporation."

35. Marshall McLuhan, *The Medium Is the Message* (San Francisco: Hardwired, 1967).

36. Neil Postman, *Technopoly: The Surrender of Culture to Technology* (New York: Knopf, 1992).

37. Carl Sandburg, quoted in Robert Konzelman, *Marquee Ministry* (New York: HarperCollins, 1971).

38. Phyllis Tickle, *God Talk in America* (New York: Crossroad, 1997).

39. Adin Steinsaltz, *Simple Words* (New York: Touchstone, 1999).

40. Bruce Springsteen, quoted in *Rolling Stone*, Aug. 22, 2002.

41. Bruce Springsteen, quoted in *Time*, Aug. 5, 2002.

42. Frederick Buechner, *Beyond Words* (San Francisco: HarperSanFrancisco, 2004).

43. Todd Gitlin, "Pop Goes the Culture." *U.S. News & World Report*, June 1, 1998.

44. Arthur Kroker, *The Will to Technology and the Culture of Nihilism* (Toronto: University of Toronto Press, 2004).

45. Edward Hallowell, *Connect* (New York: Pocket Books, 2001).

46. Kenneth Gergen, "The Self: Death by Technology," *Hedgehog Review*, Fall 1999.

47. Zero 7, "In the Waiting Line," from the album *Simple Things* (Palm Pictures, 2001).

48. Christian Smith, *Soul Searching: The Religious and Spiritual Lives of American Teenagers* (New York: Oxford University Press, 2005).

49. Tom Cruise, quoted in *Parade*, Apr. 9, 2006.

50. Roma Downey, quoted in an Associated Press article, Apr. 23, 2003.

51. Mark Pinsky, *The Gospel According to Homer Simpson* (Louisville, Ky.: Westminster John Knox Press, 2001).

52. Bjork, quoted in John Mulvey, *The Twilight World of Bjork*, cited by Ed Winkle on the radio program "The Dick Staub Show," Aug. 11, 2001.

53. David Kinnaman, in a Barna report. [http://www.biola.edu/admin/connections/articles/03fall/truth.cfm]. Oct. 2003.

54. Stephen Simon, *The Force Is with You* (Charlottesville, Va.: Hampton Roads, 2002), p. 87, quoted in radio interview on "The Dick Staub Show," Oct. 10, 2002.
55. Craig Detweiler and Barry Taylor, *A Matrix of Meanings* (Grand Rapids, Mich.: Baker Academic, 2003).
56. Andrei Tarkovsky, quoted in *Time*, Mar. 25, 2004.

Chapter Two

1. James Bryan Smith and Rich Mullins, *An Arrow Pointing to Heaven* (Nashville, Tenn.: B&H Publishing Group, 2002).
2. Charles Finney, quoted in Os Guinness, *Fit Bodies, Fat Minds* (Grand Rapids, Mich.: Baker Books, 1994).
3. *Christian Century*, Aug. 13, 1930.
4. Michael Medved, *Hollywood vs. America* (New York: Harper-Collins, 1992).
5. Francis Schaeffer, *The Complete Works of Francis Schaeffer: A Christian Worldview*, Vol. 1: *A Christian View of Philosophy and Culture* (Wheaton, Ill.: Crossway Books, 1968).
6. Harry Blamires, *The Christian Mind* (Ann Arbor, Mich.: Servant Books, 1978).
7. James Davison Hunter, *Culture Wars: The Struggle to Define America* (New York: Basic Books, 1991).
8. Alan Nierob, quoted in Laurie Goodstein, "Some Christians See 'Passion' as Evangelism Tool," *New York Times*, Feb. 5, 2004.
9. Rick Warren, quoted in Marc Gunther, "Will Success Spoil Rick Warren?" *Fortune*, Oct. 18, 2005.
10. Dietrich Bonhoeffer, *The Cost of Discipleship* (New York: Macmillan, 1963).
11. Alan Bloom, quoted in Jay Tolson, "The New Old-Time Religion," *U.S. News & World Report*, Dec. 8, 2003.
12. Lesslie Newbigin, *The Gospel in a Pluralist Society* (Grand Rapids, Mich.: Eerdmans, 1989).
13. Dallas Willard, *The Divine Conspiracy* (San Francisco: Harper-SanFrancisco, 1998).

14. Barna Research Report, Dec. 12, 2000.
15. Louis Dupré, "Seeking Christian Interiority," *Christian Century*, July 16–23, 1997.
16. Alan Wolfe, quoted in Tolson, "New Old-Time Religion."
17. Beth Spring and *Christianity Today* Staff, "Carl F. H. Henry, Theologian and First Editor of Christianity Today, Dies at 90," *Christianity Today*, Dec. 12, 2003.
18. Ted Baehr, *The Media Wise Family* (Colorado Springs, Colo.: Chariot Victor, 1998).
19. George Barna, "The Jesus Market," *The Weekly Standard*, Dec. 16, 2002.
20. Brian Godawa, *Hollywood Worldviews* (Downers Grove, Ill.: InterVarsity Press, 2002).
21. George Barna, "A Biblical Worldview Has a Radical Effect on a Person's Life," *Barna Update*, Dec. 1, 2003.
22. George Barna, "Practical Outcomes Replace Biblical Principles as the Moral Standard," *Barna Update*, Sept. 10, 2001.
23. Bud Paxson, quoted in Bill Romanowksi, *Eyes Wide Open* (Grand Rapids, Mich.: Brazos Press, 2001).
24. *Maxim Online*, "Life's Greatest Questions Answered." [http://www.maximonline.com/articles/index.aspx?a_id= 572]. Apr. 1999.
25. Ken Myers, *All God's Children and Blue Suede Shoes* (Wheaton, Ill.: Crossway Books, 1989).
26. Alan Wolfe, quoted in Jeffery L. Sheler, "Nearer My God to Thee," *U.S. News & World Report*, May 3, 2004.
27. Walter Kirn, "The Way We Live Now: God's Country," *New York Times*, May 2, 2004.
28. John Lennon and Paul McCartney, "Golden Slumbers," from the album *Abbey Road*, 1969.
29. Joni Mitchell, "Woodstock," from the album *Ladies of the Canyon*, 1970.

Chapter Three

1. Wendell Berry, quoted on the International Art Movement's Web site. [http://www.iamny.org].
2. Joni Mitchell, "Woodstock," from the album *Ladies of the Canyon,* 1970.
3. Jim Morrison, "Stoned Immaculate," from the Doors album *An American Prayer* (Elektra, 1978).
4. Augustine, *Confessions* (Oxford, U.K.: Oxford University Press, 1992).
5. Blaise Pascal, *Pensees* #425 (New York: Penguin Classics, 1995). More specifically, Pascal refers to an infinite abyss that can only be filled with the infinite.
6. Robert Graves, "To Juan at the Winter Solstice," in Robert Graves, *Complete Poems* (Beryl Graves and Dunstan Ward, eds.) (Manchester, U.K.: Carcanet, 1995, 1996, 1997). Used by permission.
7. W. H. Auden, "September 1, 1939," in *The English Auden* (London: Faber and Faber, 1977).
8. Mitchell, "Woodstock."
9. *Chariots of Fire* (motion picture) (Warner Brothers, 1981).
10. Dorothy Sayers, *The Mind of the Maker* (San Francisco: HarperSanFrancisco, 1987).
11. Igor Stravinsky, quoted in Joanna Laufer and Kenneth Lewis, *Inspired Lives* (Woodstock, Vt.: Skylight Paths, 2001).
12. Laufer and Lewis, *Inspired Lives*.
13. Laufer and Lewis, *Inspired Lives*.
14. John Tavener, *Belief* (Joan Bakewell, ed.) (London: Duckworth, 2005).
15. James Weldon Johnson, "The Creation," in James Weldon Johnson (ed.), *The Book of American Negro Poetry* (New York: Harcourt, Brace, 1922).
16. Flannery O'Connor, *Mystery and Manners* (New York: Farrar, Straus & Giroux, 1961).

17. Martin Buber, *I and Thou* (New York: Scribner's, 1958).
18. J.R.R. Tolkien, "On Fairy Stories," in *The Tolkien Reader* (New York: Del Ray, 1986).
19. Hildevert of Lavardin, quoted in Madeleine L'Engle, *Walking on Water* (New York: Bantam, 1982).
20. T. S. Eliot, *The Waste Land and Other Poems* (New York: Signet Classics, 1998).
21. Christopher Lasch, *The Culture of Narcissism: American Life in an Age of Diminishing Expectations* (rev. ed.) (New York: Norton, 1991).
22. John Milton, *Paradise Lost*, quoted in Dennis Danielson (ed.), *The Cambridge Companion to Milton* (2nd ed.) (Cambridge, U.K.: Cambridge University Press, 1999).
23. Nevada Barr, *Seeking Enlightenment—Hat by Hat* (New York: Berkley Books, 2003).
24. Morrison, "Stoned Immaculate.
25. Robert Stone, radio interview on "The Dick Staub Show," May 5, 1998.
26. Fyodor Dostoevsky, *Crime and Punishment* (New York: Knopf, 1993).
27. Milton, *Paradise Lost*.
28. Julian of Norwich, *The Revelation of Divine Love in Sixteen Showings Made to Dame Julian of Norwich* (M. L. Del Mastro, trans.) (Liguori, Mo.: Liguori Publications, 1994).

Chapter Four

1. Brennan Manning and Michael W. Smith, *Above All* (Franklin: Integrity, 2003).
2. Augustine, *Confessions* (Oxford, U.K.: Oxford University Press, 1992).
3. Blaise Pascal, *Pensees* #425 (New York: Penguin Classics, 1995). More specifically, Pascal refers to an infinite abyss that can only be filled with the infinite.

4. Peter Berger, quoted in Huston Smith, *The Soul of Christianity* (San Francisco: HarperSanFrancisco, 2005).

5. A. W. Tozer, *Worship: The Missing Jewel of Evangelism* (Harrisburg, Pa.: Christian Publications, 1996).

6. The statistics on young adults are from a longitudinal study of teens and religion conducted by the National Opinion Research Center at the University of Chicago.

7. George Barna, "Teenagers Embrace Religion But Are Not Excited About Christianity," *Barna Report*, Jan. 10, 2000.

8. Arnold Toynbee, *A Study of History* (Oxford, U.K.: Oxford University Press, 1987).

9. "Joy to the World," lyrics by Isaac Watts set to a melody by George Frideric Handel.

10. Robert Munger, *My Heart—Christ's Home* (2nd rev. ed.) (Downer's Grove, Ill.: InterVarsity Press, 1992).

11. Dallas Willard, *The Divine Conspiracy* (San Francisco: HarperSanFrancisco, 1998).

12. C. S. Lewis, *Mere Christianity* (New York: Macmillan, 1960).

13. H. Richard Niebuhr, quoted in Kenneth Woodward, *Newsweek*, Feb. 24, 2004.

14. Robert Stone, radio interview on "The Dick Staub Show," May 5, 1998.

15. *Jerry Maguire* (motion picture) (Sony/Columbia, 1996).

16. Isak Dinesen, *Out of Africa* (New York: Modern Library, 1992).

17. John Kirvan, *Let Nothing Disturb You: A Journey to the Center of the Soul with Teresa of Avila* (Notre Dame, Ind.: Ave Maria Press, 1996). When she died, the sisters found a bookmark in Teresa of Avila's breviary. These seven terse sentences were written in her own handwriting.

18. Karl Rahner, quoted in Brennan Manning, *Ruthless Trust* (San Francisco: HarperSanFrancisco, 2000).

19. Andy Crouch, Michael S. Horton, Frederica Mathewes-Green, Brian D. McLaren, and Erwin Raphael McManus, *The Church in Emerging Culture: Five Perspectives* (Leonard Sweet, gen. ed.) (Grand Rapids, Mich.: Zondervan, 2002).

20. Annie Dillard, *Pilgrim at Tinker Creek* (New York: Harper-Collins, 1974).

21. Lewis, *Mere Christianity*.

22. Rick Moody, radio interview on "The Dick Staub Show," Sept. 6, 2002.

23. Lewis, *Mere Christianity*.

24. Mircea Eliade, *No Souvenirs* (Paris: Gallimard, 1973).

Chapter Five

1. Jose Miguel Bonino, quoted in Alister McGrath, *Christian Theology: An Introduction* (3rd ed.) (Oxford, U.K.: Blackwell, 2001).

2. Abraham Maslow, *Toward a Psychology of Being* (3rd ed.) (New York: Wiley, 1998).

3. Hans Rookmaaker, as reported by Nigel Goodwin and other of Rookmaaker's students at L'Abri in Huemoz, Switzerland.

4. Irenaeus, *Against Heresies* (Whitefish, Mont.: Kessinger, 2004).

5. Abraham Heschel, *I Asked for Wonder: A Spiritual Anthology* (Samuel Dresner, ed.) (New York: Crossroad, 1998).

6. Søren Kierkegaard, *Purity of Heart Is to Will One Thing* (New York: Harper Perennial, 1956).

7. This widely circulated quote has been attributed to both Henry David Thoreau and Ralph Waldo Emerson.

8. Dick Staub, *Too Christian, Too Pagan* (Grand Rapids, Mich.: Zondervan, 2000).

9. Richard Foster, *Celebration of Discipline* (San Francisco: HarperSanFrancisco, 1978).

10. Thomas Merton, *Seeds of Contemplation* (New York: New Directions, 1987).

11. Harold Best, *Unceasing Worship* (Downers Grove, Ill.: InterVarsity Press, 2003).

12. A. W. Tozer, *Knowledge of the Holy* (San Francisco: HarperSanFrancisco, 1961).

13. C. S. Lewis, *The Weight of Glory* (Grand Rapids, Mich.: Eerdmans, 1975).

14. Blaise Pascal, *Pensees* #739 (reissue ed.) (New York: Penguin Classics, 1995).

15. Rodney Stark, *The Rise of Christianity* (San Francisco: HarperSanFrancisco, 1996).

16. Aleksandr Solzhenitsyn, speech at Harvard University, Jan. 1, 1978.

17. Oscar Wilde, *The Picture of Dorian Gray* (New York: Modern Library, 1998).

18. Stanley Kunitz, "The Layers," in *Passing Through* (New York: Norton, 1995).

Chapter Six

1. C. S. Lewis, *The Four Loves* (New York: Harcourt Brace Jovanovich, 1960).

2. Review of William Morris poem, quoted in Lewis, The *Four Loves*.

3. Lewis, The *Four Loves*.

4. C. S. Lewis, quoted in Jeffrey Schultz and John West Jr. (eds.), *The C. S. Lewis Reader's Encyclopedia* (Grand Rapids, Mich.: Zondervan, 1998) (italics in original).

5. Madeleine L'Engle, *Walking on Water* (New York: Bantam, 1982).

6. Lewis, *The Four Loves*.

7. William Blake, "The Lamb," in *Selected Poems* (London: CRW Publishing, 2004).

8. C. S. Lewis, *Mere Christianity* (New York: Macmillan, 1960).

9. David Van Biema, "Beyond the Wardrobe," *Time*, Nov. 7, 2005.

10. Paul Ford, speech at C. S. Lewis Foundation event, San Diego, Calif., June 2004.

11. C. S. Lewis, *God in the Dock* (Walter Hooper, ed.) (Grand Rapids, Mich.: Eerdmans, 1994).

12. Dylan Thomas, "Poetic Manifesto," in *The Poet's Work* (Reginald Gibbons, ed.) (Boston: Houghton Mifflin, 1979).

13. Ingmar Bergman, quoted by Barry Moser, *Image Journal*, Sept. 7, 2004.

14. Douglas Gresham, conversation with Dick Staub aboard the sailing vessel *The Sea Cloud*, summer 2004.

15. Lewis, *The Four Loves*.

16. Elie Wiesel, quoted in *U.S. News & World Report*, Oct. 17, 1986.

17. Douglas Gresham, conversation with Dick Staub aboard the sailing vessel *The Sea Cloud*, summer 2004.

18. Douglas Gresham, *Lenten Lands* (New York: Macmillan, 1988).

19. Douglas Gresham, conversation with Dick Staub aboard the sailing vessel *The Sea Cloud*, summer 2004.

20. Harry Blamires, quoted in Lyle Dorsett, *Seeking the Secret Place: The Spiritual Formation of C. S. Lewis* (Grand Rapids, Mich.: Brazos Press, 2004).

21. *The Latin Letters of C. S. Lewis* (Martin Moynihan, ed.) (South Bend, Ind.: St. Augustine's Press, 1998).

22. C. S. Lewis, *The Weight of Glory* (Grand Rapids, Mich.: Eerdmans, 1975).

23. Austin Farrar, quoted in James Como, *C. S. Lewis at the Breakfast Table* (New York: Macmillan, 1979).

24. *The Latin Letters of C. S. Lewis*.

Chapter Seven

1. J.R.R. Tolkien, *The Lord of the Rings* (New York: Houghton Mifflin, 1994).

2. Paul Elie, *The Life You Save May Be Your Own* (New York: Farrar, Straus & Giroux, 2003).

3. Thanks to Brian Godawa for his useful terminology ("anorexic, gluttony"), which is used in his book *Hollywood Worldviews* (Downers Grove, Ill.: InterVarsity Press, 2002).

4. J. D. Salinger, *Franny and Zooey* (New York: Little, Brown, 1961).

5. Mary Pipher, *The Middle of Everywhere* (New York: Harcourt, 2002), italics added.

6. "It Is Well with My Soul," lyrics by Horatio Spafford, music by Philip Bliss, in *Hymns of the Christian Life* (Harrisburg, Pa.: Christian Publications, 1962).

7. "Great Is Thy Faithfulness," lyrics by Thomas Chisholm, music by William Runyan, in *Hymns of the Christian Life* (Harrisburg, Pa.: Christian Publications, 1962).

8. Eugene Peterson, *Perseverance: A Long Obedience in the Same Direction* (Downers Grove, Ill.: InterVarsity Press, 1996).

9. Stanley Hauerwas and William Willimon, *Resident Aliens* (Nashville, Tenn.: Abingdon Press, 1989).

10. The sources of the principles in the list are 1 Corinthians 6:12–20, 1 Corinthians 10:23–32, and Romans 14.

11. Abraham Heschel, *I Asked for Wonder: A Spiritual Anthology* (Samuel Dresner, ed.) (New York: Crossroad, 1998).

12. Lance Morrow, "The Subtle Stink That Mars 'American Beauty,'" *Time*, Mar. 24, 2000.

13. Ernest Hemingway, *A Moveable Feast* (New York: Scribner, 1996).

Chapter Eight

1. Frederick Buechner, *A Room Called Remember: Uncollected Pieces* (reissue ed.) (San Francisco: HarperSanFrancisco, 1992).

2. John Michael Talbot and Steve Rabey, *The Lessons of Saint Francis* (New York: Plume, 1998).

3. G. Campbell Morgan, *The Acts of the Apostles* (Grand Rapids, Mich.: Revell, 1924).

4. William Ernest Henley, "Invictus," in *Poems by William Ernest Henley* (London: Kessinger, 2005).

5. Cathy Grossman, "Godless Washington," *USA Today*, Mar. 7, 2002.

6. George Gallup, *The Next American Spirituality* (Colorado Springs, Colo.: Cook, 2000).
7. Dwight Ozard, "The Last Great Missions Frontier," *Prism*, July–Aug. 1996.
8. Dave Williams, quoted in *Hit Parader*, Aug. 14, 2002.
9. Morgan, *Acts of the Apostles*.

Chapter Nine

1. T. S. Eliot, *Christianity and Culture* (New York: Harcourt, 1967).
2. "Reborn to be Wild," episode from the television series "King of the Hill," Nov. 8, 2003.
3. Edward Gibbon, *Memoirs of My Life and Writings* (London: Kessinger, 2004).
4. Walter Bagehot, *The Works of Walter Bagehot*, Vol. 1 (Forrest Morgan, ed.; with memoirs by R. H. Hutton) (Boston: Elibron Classics, 2001).
5. Samuel Johnson.com reports that this quote is often attributed to Johnson, but the source has not yet been found; it may be apocryphal.
6. Hans Rookmaaker, *Art Needs No Justification* (Downers Grove, Ill.: InterVarsity Press, 1978).
7. Dorothy Sayers, *The Mind of the Maker* (San Francisco: HarperSanFrancisco, 1987).
8. M. B. Goffstein, *An Artist* (New York: HarperCollins, 1980).
9. Anne Lamott, quoted in the *Los Angeles Times*, Sept. 16, 2002.
10. Abraham Kuyper, *Abraham Kuyper: A Centennial Reader* (James Bratt, ed.) (Grand Rapids, Mich.: Eerdmans, 1998).
11. Ken Myers, *All God's Children and Blue Suede Shoes: Christians and Popular Culture* (Wheaton, Ill.: Crossway Books, 1989).
12. John Updike, quoted in an interview by Marjorie Leet Ford, National Public Radio host and author of *The Diary of an American Au Pair: A Novel*, in Anchor Books press kit, Apr. 2003.

13. James Lee Burke, "Writers on Writing: Seeking a Vision of Truth, Guided by a Higher Power," *New York Times*, Dec. 2, 2002.

14. Hildegard of Bingen, *Scivias* (Mahwah, N.J.: Paulist Press, 1990).

15. Wikiquote, "André Gide" [http://en.wikiquote.org/wiki/Andre _Gide].

16. Ingmar Bergman, "What Is Making Films?" *Cahiers du Cinéma*, July 1956.

17. Giacomo Puccini, quoted in Mars Hill Graduate School catalogue, Bothell, Wash., 2005.

18. Arthur Miller, "What I've Learned," *Esquire*, July 2003, *140* (1).

19. Brennan Manning, radio interview on "The Dick Staub Show," Dec. 6, 2002.

20. Edgar Degas, quoted in Patty Crowe, *Quotes on Art and Artists* (Arlington, Va.: Richer Resources, 2006).

21. Malcolm Muggeridge, quoted in Gerald O'Collins, *What Are They Saying About Jesus?* (New York: Paulist Press, 1977).

22. Michael Chabon, radio interview on "The Dick Staub Show," Oct. 9, 2002, reading an adapted version of an article that appeared in *Swing* magazine in 1995.

23. Maeve Binchy, "Writers on Writing: For the Irish, Long-Windedness Serves as a Literary Virtue," *New York Times*, Nov. 3, 2002.

24. Edward Knippers, "Subject and Theme," in Ned Bustard (ed.), *It Was Good: Making Art for the Glory of God* (Baltimore, Md.: Square Halo Books, 2000).

25. Madeleine L'Engle, *Walking on Water* (New York: Bantam, 1982).

26. Jacques Maritain, *Art and Scholasticism with Other Essays* (J. F. Scanlan, trans.) (Whitefish, Mont.: Kessinger, 2003).

27. Brian Sewell, *An Alphabet of Villains* (London: Bloomsbury, 1995).

28. Sydney Pollack, quoted in Michael Petracca and Madeleine Sorapure (eds.), *Common Culture* (Upper Saddle River, N.J.: Prentice Hall, 1995).

29. Madeleine, L'Engle, *Walking on Water*.

30. W. H. Auden, *The English Auden*, edited by Edward Mendelson, (London: Faber and Faber, 1977).

31. R. P. Blackmur, quoted in a 1936 book review cited in Gregory Wolfe, *Intruding Upon the Timeless* (Baltimore, Md.: Square Halo Books, 2003).

32. "Grace," from U2's album *All That You Can't Leave Behind* (Interscope Records, 2000).

33. John Calvin, *Institutes of the Christian Religion* (Philadelphia: Westminster Press, 1960).

34. Craig Detweiler and Barry Taylor, *Matrix of Meanings* (Grand Rapids, Mich.: Baker Academic, 2003).

35. Ron Hansen, radio interview on "The Dick Staub Show," Feb. 7, 2003.

36. Orson Scott Card, "A Mormon Writer Looks at the Problem of Evil in Fiction." [http://www.nauvoo.com/library/card-talk.html].

37. Niall Williams, *As It Is in Heaven* (New York: Warner Books, 1999).

38. Jose Marti, quoted on bronze plaque on the sidewalk leading to the New York Public Library.

39. William Blake, *The Complete Poetry and Prose of William Blake* (rev. ed.) (David V. Erdman, commentator; Harold Bloom, ed.) (Berkeley: University of California Press, 1982).

40. Hans Rookmaaker, *Art Needs No Justification* (Downers Grove, Ill.: InterVarsity Press, 1978).

41. Max Stackhouse, quoted in Bill Romanowski, *Eyes Wide Open* (Grand Rapids, Mich.: Brazos Press, 2001).

42. Malcolm Muggeridge, *Jesus Rediscovered* (London: Hodder & Stoughton, 1995).

43. Henri Troyat, *Tolstoy* (Nancy Amphoux, trans.) (New York: Dell, 1969).

44. C. S. Lewis, *God in the Dock* (Walter Hooper, ed.) (Grand Rapids, Mich.: Eerdmans, 1994).

45. George MacDonald, *Diary of an Old Soul* (Minneapolis, Minn.: Augsburg Fortress, 1994).

46. Nick Park, quoted in Hilary Brand and Adrienne Chaplin, *Art and Soul* (Carlisle, U.K.: Piquant, 1999).

47. Flannery O'Connor, *Mystery and Manners* (New York: Farrar, Straus & Giroux, 1961).

48. Murray Watts, interviewed in *Art in Question* (David Porter and Tim Dean, eds.) (Basingstroke, U.K.: Marshall Pickering, 1987).

49. Ned Bustard (ed.), *It Was Good: Making Art for the Glory of God* (Baltimore, Md.: Square Halo Books, 2000).

50. Makato Fujimura, "Form and Content," in Ned Bustard (ed.), *It Was Good: Making Art for the Glory of God* (Baltimore, Md.: Square Halo Books, 2000).

51. James Romaine, "Creativity," in Ned Bustard (ed.), *It Was Good: Making Art for the Glory of God* (Baltimore, Md.: Square Halo Books, 2000).

52. Chaim Potok, from his *New York Times* obituary, July 24, 2002.

53. Dana Gioia, interview in *The Irish Review*, Nov. 18, 2002.

54. Pat Hanlon, "Thinktopia Creed for a company dedicated to building communities around brands." [www.thinktopia.com].

55. Gentle Giant, *Acquiring the Taste* (LP recording) (Repertoire, 1971).

56. Joni Mitchell, "For Free," from the album *Ladies of the Canyon*, 1970.

57. Nick Cave and the Bad Seeds, "There Is a Kingdom" from the album *The Boatman's Call* (Reprise Records, 1997).

58. Arthur O'Shaughnessy, "Ode," in Louis Untermeyer (ed.), *Modern British Poetry* (Whitefish, Mont.: Kessinger Publishing, 2003, p. 8; originally published 1920).

Epilogue

1. Dante Aligieri, *Paradiso* (Barry Moser, illus.; Allen Mandelbaum, trans.) (New York: Bantam Classics, 1986).
2. John Adams, letter to Thomas Jefferson, quoted in Patricia Nelson Limerick, "Dining with Jeff," *New York Times*, June 25, 2005.

THE AUTHOR

Dick Staub is an award-winning broadcaster, writer, and speaker whose work flows from observations at the intersection of faith and culture. He advocates a deep, fully human spirituality that enriches culture intellectually and creatively. His books include: *Too Christian, Too Pagan;* and *Christian Wisdom of the Jedi Masters.* Visit him at www.dickstaub.com.

INDEX

The Blogging Church
Sharing the Story of Your Church Through Blogs
Brian Bailey, Terry Storch

Paper
ISBN-10: 0–7879–8487–6; ISBN-13: 978–0–7879–8487–8

"I had a lot of questions about blogs and their value for my church. I'm thankful that Brian and Terry are sharing their experiences to answer those questions. Their insights are for everyone in ministry. Whether you are reading blogs, writing blogs, or just trying to figure out how to use the word in a sentence, this book is for you."

—Mark Beeson, senior pastor, Granger Community Church

"My talking head is limited to the pulpit proper. I thank God that there's a tool to reach outside the church, to those that are sadly, outside the church. Thank you Terry and Brian for *The Blogging Church*."

—Pastor Bob Coy, senior pastor, Calvary Chapel, Ft. Lauderdale

The Blogging Church offers church leaders a field manual for utilizing the social phenomenon of blogs to connect people and build communities in a whole new way. Inside you will find the why, what, and how of blogging in the local church. Filled with illustrative examples and practical advice, the authors answer key questions learned on the front lines of ministry: Is blogging a tool or a toy? What problems will blogging solve? How does it benefit ministry? And what motivates the user? You will be inspired to implement blogs in your church and equipped with the tools to make it happen.

Includes contributions from five of the most popular bloggers in the world—Robert Scoble, Dave Winer, Kathy Sierra, Guy Kawasaki, and Merlin Mann, as well as interviews with blogging pastors such as Mark Driscoll, Craig Groeschel, Tony Morgan, Perry Noble, Greg Surratt, Mark Batterson, and many more.

BRIAN BAILEY (Dallas/Ft. Worth, TX) is the web director at Fellowship Church, one of the five largest churches in America, with more than 20,000 members. Brian leads the design and development of the church's four websites. A staff member for five years, he has spent the last three championing weblogs in the church, leading to the launch of official Fellowship Church blogs, as well as numerous staff and internal blogs.

TERRY STORCH (Dallas/Ft. Worth, TX) is the chief operations and technology pastor for Fellowship Church. As a member of the executive team, he is responsible for the technology and business operations for the church. Terry has spoken at many different conferences across the country and is widely considered by the experts to be a true church technology visionary.

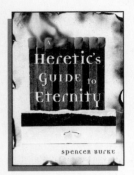

A Heretic's Guide to Eternity
Spencer Burke, Barry Taylor
Foreword by Brian D. McLaren

Cloth
ISBN-10: 0–7879–8359–4; ISBN-13: 978–0–7879–8359–8

"It's easy for inquisition-launchers to go on fault-finding missions; they have lots of practice and they're really good at it. What's more challenging, and regarding this book, much more worthwhile, is to instead go on a truth-finding mission. And yes, even in a book with 'heretic' in the title, I believe any honest reader can find much truth worth seeking."
—From the Foreword by Brian D. McLaren

"Some Christians have the ability to make you want to be a Christian just by being who they are. They make the gospel alive, real, healing, and utterly attractive. I think Spencer Burke is just one of those people. In his writings he shares himself and his vision,
—Fr. Richard Rohr, Center for Action and Contemplation,
Albuquerque, New Mexico

With its focus on the limitless grace of God, *A Heretic's Guide to Eternity* offers a new way of seeing an old faith, of practicing "mystical responsibility" and understanding that salvation is something that happens between God and people, not something regulated by institutions and gatekeepers. It is filled with surprising insights into and encouraging thoughts about how to live a spiritual and moral life in today's complex world. Burke and Taylor may be asking heretical questions, but they are deeply committed to the teachings of Jesus, guiding readers to see those teachings afresh and, as a result, live more passionately and thoughtfully.

SPENCER BURKE is the creator of The OOZE.com, which receives 200,000 unique visitors a month, and of ETREK.com, a website facilitating the formation and curriculum for alternative learning groups. He is the host of Soularize: A Learning Party, which is the original postmodern/emergent annual conference.

BARRY TAYLOR wears many hats—he is a teacher, musician, writer, and speaker. He lectures on a wide variety of subjects from advertising and consumer culture to art and postmodern spirituality. He has a master's degree in cross-cultural studies and a Ph.D. in intercultural studies, both focusing on the relationship between popular culture and issues of faith.

OTHER BOOKS OF INTEREST

A New Kind of Christian
A Tale of Two Friends on a Spiritual Journey
Cloth
ISBN-10: 0–7879–5599–X; ISBN-13: 978–0–7879–5599–1

Winner of the *Christianity Today* Award of Merit for Best Christian Living title, 2002

"This is a book that heightens the depths and deepens the peaks. Like all the best things in life, it is not to be entered into lightly, but reverently and in the fear of a God who is waiting for the church to stop asking WWJD, 'What would Jesus do?' and start asking WIJD, 'What is Jesus doing?'"—Dr. Leonard Sweet, E. Stanley Jones Chair of Evangelism at Drew University, founder and president of SpiritVenture Ministries, and best-selling author

The Story We Find Ourselves In
Further Adventures of a New Kind of Christian
Cloth
ISBN-10: 0–7879–6387–9; ISBN-13: 978–0–7879–6387–3

"As with *A New Kind of Christian*, once I started reading this book I could not possibly put it down. Be prepared once again to go on the adventure of having your heart and mind feeling both comforted and uncomfortable, stimulated and stirred, challenged and changed, agreeing and disagreeing. . . ."—Dan Kimball, author, *The Emerging Church: Vintage Christianity for New Generations*, and pastor, Graceland/Santa Cruz Bible Church

The Last Word and the Word After That
A Tale of Faith, Doubt, and a New Kind of Christianity
Cloth
ISBN-10: 0–7879–7592–3; ISBN-13: 978–0–7879–7592–0

"Brian McLaren has written a remarkable book on hell and the grace of God. And it is one hell of a book! . . . It evidences yet again why McLaren is an emerging voice to be taken seriously concerning new modes of church and new practices of faith."—Walter Brueggemann, minister, United Church of Christ; professor, Old Testament, Columbia Theological Seminary, Decatur, Georgia

BRIAN D. McLAREN, named a "Paradigm Shifter" and one of the twenty-five most influential evangelicals in America by *Time Magazine*, is the founding pastor of Cedar Ridge Community Church in the Washington-Baltimore area, and the author of several books on contemporary and postmodern Christianity.

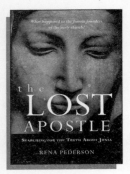

The Lost Apostle
Searching for the Truth About Junia
Rena Pederson

Cloth
ISBN: 0–7879–8443–4; ISBN-13: 978–07879–8443–4

"The apostle was one of the first victims of identity theft. Restoring her name is a service to women everywhere."
— Linda Ellerbee, award-winning television producer, journalist, and best-selling author of *Take Big Bites, Move On,* and *And So It Goes*

"Reading Pederson's work is like perusing a reporter's notebook. She invites anyone who turns these pages to help her think about which question to ask next in the search for truth. In the end, she rewards her readers for sharing this spiritual, intellectual, and journalistic pursuit by reminding us that the best human searches are satisfied with the discovery that the truth we seek is actually seeking us."
— William B. Lawrence, dean; professor of American church history, Perkins School of Theology, Southern Methodist University

"As a clergywoman, I am strengthened by Rena Pederson's work. She has done what should have been done years ago. Junia is the role model we've been searching for."
— Dr. Sheron Patterson, senior minister, Highland Hills United Methodist Church; newspaper columnist; and author, *Sisters: A Mile in Her Shoes, Lessons from the Lives of Old Testament Women*

In *The Lost Apostle* award-winning journalist Rena Pederson investigates a little-known subject in early Christian history—the life and times of the female apostle Junia. Junia was an early convert and leading missionary whose story was "lost" when her name was masculinized to Junias in later centuries. Based on extensive research, international travel, as well as discussions and correspondence with top historians and biblical experts, *The Lost Apostle* unfolds like a well-written detective story, presenting Pederson's lively search for insight and information about a woman some say was the first female apostle.

RENA PEDERSON is a speech writer in Washington, D.C., and served as an editor at the Dallas Morning News for sixteen years. She was a finalist for a Pulitzer Prize in editorial writing and served on the Pulitzer Prize board for nine years. She also has been featured on *The Oprah Winfrey Show* and was profiled by PBS for the *She Says* documentary about the top women in the news business.

Christian Wisdom of the Jedi Masters
Dick Staub

Cloth
ISBN-10: 0–7879–7894–9; ISBN-13: 978–0–7879–7894–5

"Dick Staub's tour through the spirituality of *Star Wars* is inspiring and fun. Anyone, like me, who grew up lionizing Luke Skywalker and Princess Leia should read this book. It will both carry you back to your childhood and support your spirit as you make your way through adulthood."

—Lauren Winner, author, *Girl Meets God* and
Real Sex: The Naked Truth About Chastity

"For years Dick Staub has been digging into popular culture to expose the threads of spiritual gold that run through it. *Star Wars* is his mother lode, and with eloquence he echoes Master Yoda announcing to young seekers, 'Already know you that which you need.'"

—Jeffrey Overstreet, film columnist/critic, *Christianity Today*
and *Paste Magazine*

"Like a Jedi master, Dick Staub delivers sharp, counter-intuitive insights that the next generation seeks. Prepare to discover a force far greater than any you ever imagined."

—Craig Detweiler, author, *A Matrix of Meanings:*
Finding God in Pop Culture

"Few public figures have as much experience brokering the conversation between media culture and Christianity as Dick Staub. Both pop culture artists and inquisitive Christians know that his reputation rests on his ability to speak to both audiences, to keep it real."

—Tom Beaudoin, author, *Virtual Faith: The Irreverent Spiritual*
Quest of Generation-X and *Consuming Faith*

Written by award-winning radio personality Dick Staub, this compelling book is filled with anecdotes from the *Star Wars* films that serve as a launching pad into rediscovering authentic Christianity. *Christian Wisdom of the Jedi Masters* also contains quotes from revered "Jedi Christians" such as Thomas Merton, Teresa of Avila, the Apostle Paul, G. K. Chesterton, and other theologians, mystics, writers, and philosophers. The author sheds new light on the struggles and challenges of living faithfully in postmodern life and offers a reintroduction to what C. S. Lewis and J.R.R. Tolkien called the "one true myth," Christianity.